A Chinese-English Book
中英文对照

The Traditional Chinese Festivals and Tales

中国传统节日及传说

靳海林 白雪飞 （英文）

靳海林 白雪飞 （中文）

CHONGQING PUBLISHING HOUSE

重庆出版社

前　言

　　中国有着5 000多年的历史。在这漫长的岁月中,中华民族吮吸着黄河和长江的甘甜乳汁,在广袤而富饶的祖国土地上繁衍生息,艰苦奋斗,创造了辉煌灿烂、丰富多彩的中华文化。传统节日便是中华文化中一颗璀璨的明珠。本书的编者和译者经过辛勤的努力,将此书奉献给广大读者,以求共同分享中国传统节日带来的幸福与欢乐。

　　本书介绍了中国传统节日中影响较大的45个节日。每个节日的介绍内容包括悠久的历史、相关的优美传说、丰富多彩的庆祝活动、绚丽夺目的节日服饰、特色鲜明的节日饮食和饶有趣味的风土人情。本书系汉英对照读物。中文力求通俗易懂、语言畅达,重视知识性、趣味性和可读性;译文力求达意流畅、语言准确。本书可供中外旅游者、旅游工作者、翻译爱好者、民俗研究者以及其他读者使用。

　　本书中文部分,第1篇由靳海林编写,第2、4、6、9、12、13、18、19、21、24、25、27、29、30、32、34、35、37、38、39、40、41、42、43、44、45等篇由何元智编写,其余各篇由白雪飞编写。本书英文部分,第1、2、4、6、9、12、13、18、19、21、24、25、27、29、30、32、34、35、37、38、39、40、41、42、43、44、45等篇由靳海林翻译,其余各篇由白雪飞翻译。限于水平,本书难免有缺点乃至错误,诚

望读者指正。

　　成书过程中，编者参考了《中国风俗大辞典》(申士*Yao* 傅美琳)、《中国的民间节日》(范玉梅)、《中国传统节日》(罗启荣　阳仁煊)等作品。在此,谨向有关作者表示诚挚的谢意!

编者

2000年7月

目 录

Contents

1. 春 节

　　春节在阴历正月初一,是我国汉族和许多少数民族的传统佳节。它起源于原始社会的"腊祭"。传说那时每逢旧岁新年交替之际,人们以农猎所获祭祀祖先和上天,一则感谢恩赐,再则祈求来年五谷丰登。这种祭祀称为"腊祭"。按照汉族风俗,人们实际上将旧年腊月初八到新年正月十五这段时间视为春节,在此期间举行丰富多彩的庆祝活动。至今仍然盛行的主要活动有扫尘、贴春联、贴年画、守岁、放鞭炮、拜年、舞龙、舞狮等。

　　扫尘古称"扫年",相传始于尧舜时代,源于古人为除病疫而举行的一种宗教仪式。扫尘在每年腊月二十四日至月底进行,届时家家户户都要洒扫庭院,清洗家具,拆洗被褥,以便干干净净迎接新年。

　　春联贴在门框或楹柱上,故又称"门帖"。它由上联、下联和横批组成。联语多表吉祥喜庆,是我国特有的一种文学形式。春联源于古代桃符。相传在上古时期,度溯山上有一株枝繁叶茂的大桃树,树旁石屋里住着神荼和郁磊两兄弟。他俩爱桃成癖,天旱浇水,雨淋排涝,整枝除虫。辛勤的汗水浇灌出春天似锦繁花,换来夏天累累硕果。那些桃子甜美多汁,食之可消灾除病,延年益寿,成仙变神,人称仙桃。住在度溯

· 1 ·

山野牛岭的野王子贪得无厌,横行乡里,鱼肉百姓。他得知神荼兄弟所育桃子的妙用之后,便亲率数百兵卒到度溯山夺取仙桃。仅战数个回合,野王子一伙便被打得落花流水,狼狈逃回野牛岭。强取不行,野王子心生邪计。一天夜里,他率几百名扮成鬼怪的兵卒来到神荼兄弟住地,企图吓唬他俩献出仙桃。两兄弟毫无惧色,勇敢迎敌。神荼手执桃枝在前,郁磊带着一卷棕绳随后,双双向鬼怪冲去。说来奇怪,那些鬼怪一触桃枝便浑身瘫软,束手被擒。神荼在前擒一个,郁磊在后绑一个。不一会儿,几百个鬼怪全数被缚。从此,人们认为桃木是仙木,有驱鬼避怪的威力。于是,每年除夕之夜,家家户户在桃木片上分别画上神荼和郁磊的像,挂在门的两旁,以驱鬼避邪。这样的桃木片古称桃符。来年除夕,人们以新桃符替代旧桃符,因此有北宋王安石的诗句:"千门万户曈曈日,总把新桃换旧符"。五代时候,人们开始在桃符上题写一些吉祥诗句来表达自己的美好心愿。据史料记载,最早的这个题辞是五代后蜀君主孟昶的"新年纳余庆,佳节是长春"。这也是有文字记载的最早的春联。宋代,贴春联成为民间习俗。明代,春联更为盛行,这与明太祖朱元璋重视有关。朱元璋出身农民,识字不多,但十分喜爱春联。据传,某年他微服巡游,见一屠户家未贴春联,很是纳闷。屠户解释说他不识字。于是朱元璋立即亲手为之书写一联:"两手劈开生死路,一刀割断是非根。"明代,春联获得它现在的名称,并被写在红纸上,以增加节日气氛。春联的内容或寄物言志,或针贬时弊,具有喜庆吉祥、珠玑精炼的特点,读后给人以启迪。例如,"喜见阳春花千树,笑饮丰年酒一杯"是农家春联,表现我国农村的兴旺景象和丰收农民的喜悦心情;"炉光上升冲霄汉,锤声远闻震乾坤"

是贴在铁匠铺门旁的春联，于打铁情景的生动描写中体现铁匠的豪迈情怀；"不教白发催人老，更喜春风满面生"是贴在理发店门旁的春联，读来妙趣横生。

春节时，人们在门上和墙壁上张贴一定题材的绘画，叫做贴年画，是春节习俗之一。相传，年画始于尧舜时代，其中的门画起源最早。时代不同，门画的题材各异。唐代以前，门画里画的是两员武将，一个名叫神荼，另一个名叫郁磊。据《山海经》记载，此二人善于捉鬼降妖，因此人们将其画在门画里以避邪。到了唐代，门画里画的是当朝大将秦叔宝和尉迟敬德。他俩上门画与一传说有关。据说，唐太宗李世民有段时间夜里常闻宫外鬼魅抛砖掷瓦、哀哭凄号，致使他夜里难以入眠、心烦意乱。秦叔宝提出和尉迟敬德一起为皇帝站岗。烦恼不堪的李世民同意试试。于是二人身着戎装，一人握剑，一人执鞭，把守宫门。打那以后，皇宫果然安宁无事。后人遂将二人戎装守宫的画像贴在门上，以求平安。从宋朝开始，门画多以王昭君、赵飞燕、班姬、绿珠等我国历史上四大美女，以及岳飞、郑成功等民族英雄为题材。 目前，门画的题材主要有五谷丰登、春牛、婴儿、风景、花鸟等。就整个年画而言，天津杨柳青、山东潍县、江苏苏州桃花坞等地的产品最为流行，它们多为木刻水印，线条单纯，色彩鲜明，画面热闹。

除夕之夜，家家户户鸿烛高照，彩灯长明，合家欢聚，通宵不眠，进行各种节日活动，以待天明，此谓守岁，有辞别旧岁、展望新年之意。节日活动丰富多彩。一是吃"团年饭"。顾名思义，吃"团年饭"即合家围桌就餐，即使因事在外的家庭成员也须返家，它是合家团圆的象征。"团年饭"极为丰盛。南方人一般要吃年糕，因为年糕与"年高"谐音；北方人一般要吃饺子,因饺子形如元宝。两种事物都象征吉祥。吃"团年饭"时要饮屠苏酒。这与一个古老传说有关。南朝梁人沈约在《俗说》中说,古代一座名叫屠苏的茅屋里住着一个隐士,每到除夕,他都给邻居们送去一剂草药,嘱他们投入井中,次日取水饮用。邻居们照嘱而为,结果家家健康长寿。邻居们认为此药可祛瘟除疫,便用它泡制药酒在吃"团年饭"时饮用。二是给压岁钱。除夕子夜时分,家中小孩向长辈作揖叩头,表示辞岁。受拜的长辈给予钱币。钱币用红线穿成吊,织成龙形,以示望子成龙。这种习俗称为给压岁钱。三是藏钩。这是一种游戏。游戏的一方将一钩或一枚戒指及其他类似环状东西藏起来,另一方竭力寻找隐藏之物,找到为止。其他的活动有打麻将、推牌九、小儿骑竹马、老鹰抓小鸡、玩陀螺等。现在,全家吃着点心,喝着饮料,观看中央电视台的春节联欢晚会节目是守岁时必不可少的活动。

放鞭炮是春节最盛行的习俗之一。除夕交子时刻一到,噼噼啪啪的鞭炮声顿时响彻夜空。春节拜年、祭祀等场合也要燃放鞭炮。鞭炮又称爆竹,得名于古代的"爆竹"。据东方朔在《神异经》中记载,古时西方深山里居住着一种异人,身高尺许,裸身捕捉虾蟹为食,常从普通人家盗盐佐食。常人若遇他们便会犯寒发烧。这种异人不惧常人,但怕竹子燃烧时发出的噼啪声,所以人们燃烧竹子驱赶他们。后来,人们以为"爆竹"有神奇作用,遂在除夕之夜燃烧竹子以驱赶一切邪恶。宋代,人们有火药制作鞭炮,代替以前的爆竹。现在,放鞭炮驱赶邪恶的用意逐渐淡化,更多的是为了增加节日的喜庆气氛。由于燃放鞭炮易伤人和引起火灾,近年来我国一些大城市做出规定,禁止在春节期间和其他场合燃放鞭炮。

春节期间,人们向长辈或亲友祝贺新年,称为拜年,是盛行的春节习俗之一。拜年的时间根据不同受拜对象而不同。一般情况是:正月初一拜本家近房,初二拜本家远房,初三、初四拜亲戚朋友。民族不同拜年赠礼各异。例如,藏族拜年献哈达,回族拜年赠香油,汉族拜年送酒、肉、糕点等。文人雅士和其他有些影响的人物拜年时还赠送贺年卡。贺卡上有绘画、贺语、赠送人和接受人的姓名等。贺卡的制作工艺十分精美。拜年的来历与一传说有关。据说,古代有一种名叫"年"的野兽,头长独角,口似血盆,牙若利刃,凶猛异常。每年除夕之夜,它都从深山老林出来,到农家寻食吃人。万分恐惧的村民们,家家户户在庭外大路上放些鸡、鸭或猪肉,然后禁闭大门躲避野兽。"年"饱餐一顿之后当夜归山。村民们正月初一早晨一开门便互相祝贺,庆幸免遭灾祸。后来便有了拜年的习俗。

　　龙是我国古代传说中一种能兴云作雨的神异动物,是吉祥的象征和汉民族远祖崇拜的图腾。这种传说中的动物谁也没有见过,人们想象的龙的形象是头如骆头、角如鹿角、身如蛇身、鳞如鱼鳞、爪如鹰爪和尾如鱼尾。在春节和其他喜庆场合,人们用多姿多彩的方式挥舞按想象制作的龙,以增加喜庆气氛,这便是舞龙。舞龙所用的龙身一般有9节、11节和13节,每节长约5尺,两节相交处有一灯笼;龙头、龙尾和各个灯笼以布相联,浑然一体,成为一条栩栩如生的巨龙;龙头、龙尾及各个灯笼各带有一握柄,以供挥舞。舞龙始于汉代,至今不衰。这表明中国文化光辉灿烂,具有强大的生命力。

　　舞狮也是庆贺春节的一项传统娱乐活动。据史料记载,汉朝已十分流行。舞狮分北方舞狮和南方舞狮两种。北方舞狮用的狮子状如真狮,分成年狮和幼年狮,前者双人舞,后者单人舞,一装扮武士手执绣球在前引导,狮子合着锣鼓声做着逐绣球、上下阶梯、过板桥、舔脚、搔耳、朝拜、翻滚等舞蹈动作。南方舞狮以广东舞狮为代表,故又称广东舞狮。广东舞狮用的狮子头大、额突;舞狮的两个人下穿灯笼裤;一装扮大头和尚手挥佛掸在前引导,狮子也合着锣鼓声做着追逐佛掸和其他与北方舞狮大致相同的各种舞蹈动作。两种舞狮的舞者配合默契,动作自然优美,可增加节日的喜庆气氛。

1. Spring Festival

The Spring Festival is a traditional festival joyously celebrated by the Hans and many of the minority nationalities of China on the first day of the first lunar month. It originated from laji, a Chinese term for a sacrificial ceremony held at the turn of a year in the primitive society. At the ceremony, it is said, people offered to their ancestors and Heaven sacrifices of gains from farming and hunting, a token of their gratitude for their bounty as well as a manifestation of their wish for an abundant grain harvest in the coming year. According to the actual Han custom, the festival lasts from the eighth of the twelfth lunar month of the old year up to the fifteenth of the first lunar month of the new year. During this period, not merely on the first day of the first lunar month, varied celebrations are held. The most popular ones are dusting, pasting Spring Festival couplets, pasting New Year pictures, waiting for New Year, setting off firecrackers, paying New Year calls, performing the Dragon Dance, performing the Lion Dance, etc. .

The dusting was anciently known as New Year cleaning. It is said to have originated from a religious rite supposed to eliminate epidemic diseases in the times of Yao and Shun, two legendary sage kings in ancient China. Following this custom, all households clean their courtyards, articles of furniture and bedclothes from the 24th to the end of the 12th lunar month to usher in the New Year.

The Spring Festival couplet is to be pasted on doorposts or hall pillars, hence also known as the doorpost scroll. It consists of two vertical lines and one horizontal line, and all the lines convey the idea of good luck or jubilation, constituting a unique form in the Chinese literature. The Spring Festival couplet was born of the peachwood charm. A legendary story has it that long long ago, two brothers named Shen Tu and Yu Lei lived in a stone house near a big lush peach tree in the Dushuo Mountains. They addicted themselves very much to the tree, watering it in dry spells, often pruning off its branches and eliminating insect pests for it. Thanks to the brothers' painstaking work, the tree was in full blossom in spring and laden with big peaches in summer. The peach, sweet and succulent, was reputed as the immortality peach and its eaters, some say, would be free from disasters and diseases, live to a ripe old age or even become immortals. A prince, known as Wild Prince, lived at the same time on the Wild Ox Ridge of the same mountains. He was insatiably avaricious and rode roughshod over the common locals by dint of his power. Having learned of the magical peach, he commanded several hundred soldiers to fight for it from Shen Tu and Yu Lei. Just through a couple of rounds, the prince and his gang were defeated and fled helter-skelter to the Wild Ox Ridge. Covetous of the peach, he devised an evil scheme. One night he led to the house of the brothers several hundred soldiers disguised as ghosts and monsters, intending to scare the brothers into presenting the magical fruit. Utterly undaunted, the brothers charged at the enemy, with Shen Tu ahead holding a peach tree branch and Yu Lei behind grasping a coil of coir rope. It was so strange that the masked soldiers collapsed, helplessly allowing themselves to be caught, the moment they touched the branch. Shen Tu did catching ahead while Yu Lei trussed the caught behind. Before long, they subdued all the soldiers. The incident made people think that peachwood was immortal and able to exorcise spirits and ward off evils. Hence later on New Year's Eve, every household hung on two doorposts two peachwood strips, one on each side, respectively bearing the pictures of Shen Tu and Yu Lei. Such strips were anciently referred to as peachwood charms. On the next New Year's Eve, the old strips were to be replaced with new ones. Hence the verses by the writer Wang Anshi (1021–1086) of the Northern Song Dynasty: "To every home the sun imparts its brighter rays, Old peachwood charms, renewed, against evil shall insure." In the Five-dynasty period (907 –960), people began to inscribe on peachwood strips some auspicious verses conveying their good wishes. Meng Chang, the King of the Kingdom of Later Shu of the Five-dynasty period, inscribed on two peachwood strips the verses, "New Year sees lingering jubilation, Joyous festival ushers in a long spring." Historical records show that the inscription is the first of its kind as well as the first recorded Spring Festival couplet. In the Song Dynasty (960 – 1279), pasting Spring Festival couplets grew into a popular folk custom. The Ming Dynasty (1384–1644) saw a greater popularity of the custom. This was partly owed to Zhu Yuanzhang (1328 – 1398), the Ming Dynasty Emperor Taizu who attached importance to the couplet. Born in a peasant's family and almost illiterate, Zhu loved the Spring Festival couplet very much. One year on an incognito inspection tour, he was puzzled about the absence of Spring Festival couplets on the doorposts of a butcher's house since the New Year was drawing near. It turned out that the butcher could not read and write. So the emperor immediately wrote for him a couplet, which read, "Open up a way out with two hands, Cut off the roots of trouble with a single blow." Also in the Ming Dynasty, the Spring Festival couplet got its present name and began to be written on red paper to heighten the joyous festive air. Some couplets of the kind give expression to the writer's aspirations, and others point out ills of the times and offer salutary advice. All, whatever contents, are marked by jubilation, auspiciousness, exquisiteness, succinctness and instructiveness. Take for instance. Often seen on the doorposts of a peasant's house is the couplet, "Joyful to see one thousand bushes of spring flowers, Beaming to drink one cup of wine of a good year," which describes well the countryside's prosperity and the peasant's joy; usually pasted on the doorposts of a blacksmith's shop is the couplet, "The stove fire radiates up into the sky, The hammer sound shakes afar the cosmos," which gives a vivid expression to the blacksmith's heroic spirit; on the doorposts of a barber's shop is usually the couplet, "A haircut renders one younger looks, A shave makes one radiant with happiness," which reads very witty and humorous.

To mark the Spring Festival, people like to put up pictures of certain favorite motifs on doors and walls. This is referred to as pasting New Year pictures, one of the Spring Festival customs. The birth of the custom is said to date back to the times of Yao and Shun. Of the different kinds of New Year pictures, the door picture is of the longest standing. It varies with times in the motif. Before the Tang Dynasty the two leafs of a door were respectively pasted with the pictures of two generals, one named Shen Tu and the other Yu Lei. The two, according to the Classic of the Geographical Features and Customs, were good at subduing ghosts and monsters, hence they were taken as motifs for the door pictures to ward off evil spirits. In the Tang Dynasty Qin Shubao and Yuchi Jingde, two famous generals of that dynasty, began to appear in the door pictures in place of Shen Tu and Yu Lei. The change is linked to a legend. Li Shimin, the emperor Taizong of the Tang Dynasty, once seemed to often hear ghosts and goblins throwing brick-tile debris and wailing at night. This put him on pins and needles so much that he could hardly fall asleep. Qin Shubao suggested that he himself and Yuchi Jingde keep guard for the emperor at the court gate. Extremely perturbed, Li Shimin agreed. So the two generals did as they suggested, both in martial attire, one holding a sword and the other having an iron lash in hand. It was so strange that the imperial court really became peaceful. Later people, therefore, began to paste the door pictures of the two generals for peace. From the Song Dynasty (960 –1279), door pictures began to bear the images of Wang Zhaojun, Zhao Feiyan, Ban Ji and Lu Zhu, and Yue Fei and Zheng Chenggong, the first four being great beauties and the last two being famous national heroes in ancient China. Today, the door pictures are mainly produced in Yangliuqing Town in west Tianjin, Weixian

County of Shangdong and Taohuawu of Suzhou in Jiangsu. They are products of watercolor block printing, characterized by simple lines, bright colors, and lively scenes.

Throughout New Year's Eve, all members of a family get together to enjoy themselves to their heart's content through varied entertainments while all rooms are illuminated by red candles and decorated by colorful lanterns. This custom is referred to as waiting for New Year, an expression of a strong attachment to the old year and looking for the coming year. The festive activities for the night are varied and colorful. Firstly, taking a family reunion feast. Such a feast, a symbol of a family reunion as the expression suggests, is to be taken by all members of a family. Even those out on business, if any, would have to hurry back for it. The feast is sumptuous. Two indispensable foods on the menu are the New Year cake for the southerners and jiaozi for the northerners, the former being made of glutinous rice flour and the latter being dumplings with meat and vegetable stuffing. Both of the foods symbolize auspiciousness, as the Chinese term for the New Year cake is niangao, which is homonymous with a Chinese expression meaning a venerable age while jiaozi looks like a shoe-shaped silver ingot. At the feast a kind of wine named tusu is usually drunk. The custom has a legend behind. According to About Customs by Shen Yue (441–513), a writer in the Liang period of the Southern Dynasties, a hermit lived in a thatched cottage named Tusu in ancient times. Whenever New Year's Eve approached, he gave his neighbors a dose of Chinese medicine, and told them to soak it in well water for a night and drink the water the following morning. The neighbors did as they had been told and, as a result, all lived a long life without any trouble. Thinking that the medicine had the effect to prevent pestilence and other diseases, the neighbors made medicinal liquor with the medicine to be drunk at the family reunion feast. Secondly, giving coins to children as New Year gifts. Children of a family are given such coins by their seniors at the midnight of New Year's Eve when the former make a bow with clasped hands and kowtow to the latter as a symbol of tribute on the festive occasion. The coins are strung into the shape of a dragon with red thread, suggesting seniors' wish to see juniors win success in their future careers. Thirdly, hiding a hook. It is a game, in which some players hide a hook or a finger ring or a ring-like object while others seek it, with the object of finding. Other merry-making items for the night are playing mahjong, playing Chinese dominoes, riding a bamboo pole imagined as a toy horse, playing a hawk-catching-chick game, whipping a top, etc. Now it is very popular that people across the country enjoy the evening party programs given by CCTV while they have light refreshments and drinks.

Setting off firecrackers is one of the most popular customs in the Spring Festival celebration. The crackles of firecrackers will burst reverberating across the heavens the moment the clock strikes twelve on New Year's Eve. Firecrackers are also set off when people pay New Year calls and offer New Year sacrifices to their ancestors. The firecracker is also known as the bamboo-cracker, which is linked with a tale. According to Shen Yi Jin (Classic of Rare Gods) by

Dongfang Shuo (154–93B.C.), a writer in the Western Han Dynasty, a group of odd people, a little more than a feet tall, lived in the high mountains of west China in ancient times. Naked, they lived on shrimps and crabs and often stole salt from villagers' houses to spice their food. These odd people would make villagers run a fever if the latter encountered them. They feared nothing but the crackles produced by burning bamboo tubes. Hence villagers resorted to burning bamboo tubes to threaten them away. Thinking the way magical, later people burned bamboo tubes on New Year's Eve, supposed to exorcise all evil spirits. In the Song Dynasty people began to set off firecrackers filled with gunpowder, instead of burning bamboo tubes, on New Year's Eve. Now, firecrackers are set off more for heightening the festive air than for the original purpose. In recent years, the governments of some big cities in China have laid down bans on setting off firecrackers in the Spring Festival and on some other occasions as it is liable to inflict injuries and cause fires.

Another custom popular in the Spring Festival is paying New Year calls on venerable seniors, relatives and friends to extend New Year greetings. The dates for the calls vary with different groups of callees. Usually, the first lunar month's first day is for calls on close members of the same clan, its second day for remote members of the same clan, and its third and fourth days for relatives or friends. The callers of different nationalities present different New Year gifts. Take for instance. The Tibetans present hadas; the Huis give sesame oil; the Hans offer liquor, pork, pastries, etc.. Men of letters, refined scholars and other influential figures present, beside other gifts, New Year cards bearing paintings, congratulatory words and names of both callers and callees, which are as fine as exquisite handicraft articles. The custom has a legend behind. It is said that in ancient times existed a species of wild beasts named nian (Chinese for New Year) . The beast, extremely ferocious, had a single horn, a basin-sized mouth and sword-like sharp teeth. Every New Year's Eve, they would come from forested mountains to villagers' houses for food and human beings to eat. Panic-stricken villagers would put for the beasts some chickens, ducks or pork on main roads outside their courtyards, and stay behind closed doors to hide from the beasts. The animals would eat their fill and then go back to the mountains on the same New Year's Eve. Early the next morning, villagers would congratulate each other on a lucky avoidance of disaster. Hence the custom later.

The dragon is described in legend as a miraculous animal able to create clouds and fogs. A symbol of auspiciousness, it was worshipped as a totem by the Han people's ancestors. However, the dragon has never been seen. Its imaginary image is something that has a camel-head-like head, two dearhorn-like horns, a snake-body-like body, some fish-scale-like scales, some hawk-claw-like claws, and a caudal-fin-like tail. In the Spring Festival or on other joyous occasions, people dance, playing in varied manners with an image of dragon made from imagination so as to make the air more jubilant. This is known as performing the Dragon Dance. The body of the dragon image may be made up of nine sections, eleven sections or thirteen sections, each a little bit shorter than two meters; at the juncture of every two sections is a lantern; these lanterns, the head and the tail are linked up with cloth, forming into an integrated imaginary dragon; each lantern, like the head and the tail, has a handle for the dancer to hold. The Dragon Dance, first seen in the Han Dynasty (206B. C –220A. D), is still popular to this day. This shows the great vitality of the splendid Chinese culture.

Performing the Lion Dance is also a traditional item on the Spring Festival celebration program. Historical records show that it was very popular as early as the Han Dynasty. The dance falls into the north China lion dance and the south China lion dance. The lion image played with in the north China lion dance, looking lifelike, falls into the grown-up lion image and the young lion image; the former is played with by two dancers and the latter by one dancer; to the accompaniment of the gong and drum and guided by a colored silk ball waved by a warrior-like dancer, the lion keeps chasing the ball, climbing up and down steps, crossing wooden board bridges, licking its feet, scratching its ears, bowing to audiences, rolling about, etc. The south China lion dance is most popular in Guangdong province, hence also known as the Guangdong lion dance. The lion image played with in the Guangdong lion dance has a bigger head with its forehead protruding; its two players are dressed in ankle-length sports trousers; also to the accompaniment of the gong and drum but guided by a Buddhist brush waved by a dancer with a mask looking like a smiling big-headed Buddhist figure, the lion keeps chasing the brush and doing other movements, which are almost the same as the north China lion. All dancers make elegant and natural movements in perfect unison, adding much to the joyous festive air.

2. 元宵节

农历正月十五日的元宵节是中国民间的传统节日。元宵节又叫做灯节,旧称上元节。据说元宵节起源于汉代,汉高祖刘邦死后吕后当权,吕后死后重臣周勃与陈平定计于农历正月十五日诛杀了企图夺取汉室政权的吕产、吕禄等人,拥文帝刘恒为主。其后每年一月十五日晚上文帝就微服出宫与民同乐,以示纪念。农历一月又称元月,古时候的"夜"同"宵",因此文帝就将一月十五日定为元宵节,这一天的晚上就是元宵。

在元宵节,人们要吃应节食品和开展一些娱乐活动。

元宵节已有两千多年的历史。不同历史时期的应节食品各不相同。据史籍所载,南北朝时期元宵节的应节食品是加入了肉或动物油脂煮成的豆粥或米粥;唐代是吃蚕豆状的面食和烤饼;北宋是吃绿豆粉做的蝌蚪羹;从南宋至今人们喜爱的应节食品是元宵。

元宵一般是用糯米粉做的,为圆形,里面包有糖馅。元宵粘软,味美可口,历来受到人们的喜爱。此外吃元宵还象征千家万户团圆。

元宵节的娱乐活动主要有放灯、猜灯谜等。虽然元宵节定在农历正月十五日,但开展娱乐活动的日子因时代不同而多少不等。

放灯是元宵节的一大观赏奇观。古时候人们把元宵节燃点花灯供人观看的这种活动称为放灯。元宵节放灯的活动始于西汉，时间为一个晚上，即从正月十五日的黄昏一直点到次日的天明。据说放灯是为了祭祀"太一"，它是传说中主宰一切的天神。东汉明帝刘庄提倡佛法，敕令正月十五日放灯，并亲自去寺院点灯祭祀神佛。南北朝时期元宵放灯已广泛流行。南朝梁简文帝曾著文描写元宵节放灯时的景况：有油灯，有漆灯，或燃香，或燃蜡。灯月交辉，倒映水中，人观为乐。唐代玄宗规定元宵节放灯为国定例假日，放灯三个晚上，即正月十五日加上前后各一日的晚上，元宵节之夜长安的大街小巷灯光通宵达旦，人们熙来攘往，竞相观灯。据诗文描述，当时长安供观赏的灯楼用丝绸装饰，大到20间房屋，高150丈，灯楼悬挂珠玉和金银穗坠，风吹金玉丁当作响，有声有色，蔚为壮观。有的地方用灯装饰的灯树高达80尺，竖在山顶上，光彩夺目，百里可见。在千姿百态的灯中，有人物、花草、山水、鱼虫，还有最为壮观的"龙宫"，"天宫"等。在灯市中，天上人间浑为一体，十分美丽。宋代元宵节放灯规定为五夜。元宵节的京都开封城内满城灯火，热闹非常。各式灯中有彩色玻璃灯，灯上绘有人物、花草、山水和翎毛等图案；有白玉灯，灯上绘有"嫦娥奔月"、"西施采莲"等人物故事；有丝绸灯，灯上绘有荷花、菊花、牡丹、瓜果等花果；有彩纸灯，灯上绘有龙、马、虎、鹤等动物；还有规模较大而又极富观赏价值的灯塔、灯山、灯牌坊等组灯。朝廷为了鼓励人们去御前街观灯，规定："凡来观灯者赐御酒一杯"。在御前街还有魔术、杂技、杂剧和讲史等演出活动。皇帝和嫔妃们坐在宣德楼上观赏，百姓在露天台下观看，人们通宵愉悦。明代将放灯期限规定为十天，从正月八日晚开始到十七日晚落灯。明成祖朱棣迁都北京后,在东华门外修建了二里灯市,元宵节时花灯、烟花通宵达旦。清代元宵节放灯的规模仍然很大,北京以琉璃厂为中心,把灯与市合为一体。宫廷内的灯十分考究,装饰得更加富丽堂皇。元宵节时还把蟋蟀放在灯里面,蟋蟀唧唧鸣叫,别具一格,最吸引游人观赏。

近百年来,中国北方的元宵节还有别具风情的冰灯,为元宵节放灯增添了新的内容。冰灯的制作方法有两种,其一是冷冻法,用于制做小型冰灯,是将清水注入模具中冷冻成冰,取出后装上光源即成冰灯;其二是冰雕,用天然大冰块砌成冰堆,然后用斧、锯、铲、锉等工具精雕细刻,制做成冰峰、冰塔、冰楼,或雕刻成各种动物和花卉等,安装上各色各样的电灯,在夜幕中明灯后光辉灿烂,灯场内一片灯的海洋,供游人尽情领略欣赏。

猜灯谜则是元宵节的一项文化娱乐活动。其做法是把谜语写在纸条上,再贴在灯上,放灯时一并展出,供游人猜谜。灯谜始于宋代,广泛流传于明清,保留至今,千百年来一些文人学者编写了不少谜语书,有力地促进了灯谜文化的发展。

在元宵节期间,还有舞龙、舞狮、拔河、扭秧歌等文化体育活动。

2. Lantern Festival

The Lantern Festival is a traditional festival celebrated by Chinese on the 15th of the 1st lunar month. It is also known as the Yuanxiao Festival and the Shangyuan Festival.

It is said that the festival dates back to the Han Dynasty (206B. C.–220A. C.). According to the story, after the death of the Han Emperor Liu Bang, his Empress Lu usurped the throne; after Lu's death Zhou Bo and Chen Ping (two important ministers in Lu's reign) killed Lu Chan and Lu Lu (two members of the Lu family and covetous of the throne) by a ruse on the 15th of the 1st lunar month, and helped Liu Hen (a member of the same family as Liu Bang) onto the throne, with Wen Di as the dynastic title; from then on, Emperor Liu Hen merged incognito with common people on the night of that day every year to mark the event. Later, the emperor made the day the Yuanxiao Festival, "as the first lunar month" is called "yuan yue" and "night" means "xiao" in classic Chinese.

The festival celebrators usually eat festive foods and enjoy entertainments.

The festive foods are different in the different periods of the festival's 2000-odd-year history. Historical records say: The foods popular in the period of the Northern and Southern dynasties (420–589) were bean gruel and rice gruel, both mixed with pork or lard; the foods popular in the Tang Dynasty (618–907) were broad-bean-like dough balls and roast cakes; the food popular in the Northern Song Dynasty (960–1127) was a thick soup with tadpoles made of mung bean flour; the food popular from the Southern Song Dynasty (1127–1279) to the present time has been yuanxiao, dumplings made of glutinous rice flour with sweet stuffing.

The yuanxiao, ball-like and sticky, has long been favored by festival celebrators, not only because it is delicious but because it symbolizes family reunion in the Chinese culture.

The Lantern Festival entertainments include, in the main, lantern displays, riddle guessing and so on. They last for various numbers of days in different times, though the festival was officially made on the 15th of the 1st lunar month.

The lantern display is a magnificent scene. It originated in the Western Han Dynasty (206B. C. –25A. C.), and usually lasted the whole night from the dusk of the 15th of the 1st lunar month to the dawn of the next day. This festivity, some say, was designed to memorize Taiyi, a god supposed to dominate all. In the Eastern Han Dynasty (25–220) Emperor Liu Zhuang, a Buddhism believer, issued an edict to hold lantern displays on the 15th of the 1st lunar month and personally lit lanterns in a temple to worship Buddha on that day. In the period of the Southern and Northern dynasties the lantern display got very popular. In the Liang period (502–557) of the Southern Dynasty, Emperor Wen Di made a vivid description of the lantern display in his writing: Of the lanterns, some gave light from burning oil lamps, some were painted, some had burning joss sticks inside, and some gave light from burning candles. All these and the moonlight added radiance and beauty to each other, and were reflected on water, making visitors joyous. In the Tang Dynasty, Emperor Xuan Zong made the festival a national one, which was marked by lantern displays of three nights beginning on the 14th night of the 1st lunar month. The lanterns usually illuminated all the streets in Chang'an (the then national capital) throughout the 15th night of the 1st lunar month, which drew bustling crowds of holiday-makers. According to descriptions in some poems and essays, some of Chang'an's buildings for lantern displays each consisted of up to 20 rooms and were high up to 150 zhang (a Chinese measure unit, 3-odd meters); they were decorated with silk cloth, lanterns, strings of pears, and gold or silver pendants; jingles came from them when wind blew, which made the buildings an even more wonderful view. Some trees, decorated with lanterns, stood atop the hills near Chang'an and were tall up to 80 chi (a Chinese measure unit, about a foot). Their dazzling brilliance could be seen even 50 kilometers away. The lanterns on display were made in the shapes of figures, flowers, plants, mountains, fish, insects and many other things. Of them, the lanterns in the shape of the Dragon King's Palace and the Heavenly Palace were most eye-catching. All the lanterns were found mingling with stars, presenting a very attractive view. In the Song Dynasty, the lantern display usually lasted five nights on end. Kaifeng (the then national capital) was a city of lanterns when the display was on. The lanterns were varied. Some were made of co-lored glaze and drawn with the patterns of figures, flowers, plants, mountains, rivers or plumes; some were made of white jade and drawn with pictures telling the stories of "Chang'e the goddess flying to the moon" or "Xi Shi the classic Chinese beauty plucking lotus seeds"; some were made of silk cloth and painted with the patterns of lotus flowers, chrysanthemum flowers, peony flowers, melons or fruit; some were made of colored paper and painted with the images of dragons, horses, deer, cranes or other animals; some were series of lanterns in the shapes of pagodas, hills or memorial archways, which were of much more ornamental value. To draw more visitors, the imperial government decided that every visitor would be rewarded with a cup of imperial wine. Magic, acrobatics, variety plays and lectures on history were offered in the Imperial Street of Kaifeng during the festival. The audiences included the emperor and his concubines, and common people; the former sat enjoying the scene in Xuande Tower while the latter on the open ground, all enjoying themselves all night long. In the Ming Dynasty, the lantern display usually lasted ten days beginning from the 8th night of the 1st lunar month. Emperor Zhu Di, also known as Chen Zu, allocated a one-kilometer-long section of Beijing's Donghuamenwai Street for lantern displays after he had had the national capital moved to the city. There, lantern displays and fireworks were offered all night long. In the Qing Dynasty (1616 –1911), the lantern display remained grand. Take Beijing's for instance. It was held at a market around the Colored Glaze Works in the city. The lanterns in the imperial court were even more handsome and splendid. Some lanterns had crickets chirping inside, which were a particular attraction to audiences.

The ice lantern display first appeared one hundred years ago to mark the Lantern Festival in the northern provinces of China. There are two ways to make ice lanterns. One is to fill water into different moulds and then to freeze the water; the taken-out fillings, when connected to electric sources, are lanterns in different shapes. This is a way preferable for making smaller ice lanterns. The other is to cut different figures from great masses of natural ice with tools like axes, saws, shovels, files and so on. The figures may be in the shapes of mountain peaks, pagodas, towers, flowers and animals. When connected to electric sources, they are illuminating lanterns. An ice lantern display is a sea of lights, a feast for any visitors' eyes.

The riddle guessing is another entertainment for the Lantern Festival. Varied riddles are written on slips of paper and the slips are pasted on lanterns for visitors to guess. The entertainment originated in the Song Dynasty, spread widely in the Ming and Qing dynasties, and remains now. Over the long years many books on riddles have been written, which contribute a lot to the entertainment.

The Lantern Festival is also marked by sports and other entertainments, such as the tug-of-war, the Dragon Dance, the Lion Dance and the Yanko Dance.

3. 清明节

四月五日这一天是清明节,即扫墓节,也称踏青节。

清明原是标志时序的二十四节气之一。时间的推移加上寒食节的并入使它成为重要节日。寒食节本在清明前几日,后因其延长而成为清明的一部分。寒食节要禁火。据说这是为了纪念春秋时期晋文公的忠臣介子推。

春秋时期,晋献公宠爱骊姬。为把王位传给宠妃生的儿子奚齐,他迫使太子申生自杀。申生的弟弟重耳流亡异国。

逃亡途中,有一次重耳几乎饿昏过去时,随从介子推竟悄悄从自己的大腿上割下一块肉来烤给主人吃。重耳后来夺得王位,称晋文公。他奖赏所有的功臣,惟独疏漏了介子推。待他发现时,子推已偕同母亲去绵山隐居。文公派人请子推前来受赏未果,遂令火烧绵山逼他出来。大火后,人们发现子推身背老母亲靠在柳树桩旁死了。为纪念他,文公下令,每年子推的忌日全国禁食烟火。那正是清明前一天,由于禁火,人们只能吃寒食。寒食禁火的习俗由此产生。

除了禁火,清明节还有扫墓、踏青、插柳、蹴鞠、荡秋千等活动。

扫墓即墓前祭祖。这项清明节的重要活动历时久远,可以追溯到秦朝。但选定寒食至清明祭祖却始于唐宋。唐朝诗人杜牧的《清明》在中国几乎家喻户晓:"清明时节雨纷纷,路上行人欲断魂。借问酒家何处有,牧童遥指杏花村。"到了宋代,清明节正式成为人们扫墓的时节。都城居民倾城而出,去市郊扫墓,四野如市。清明祭墓主要有两种方式:或是墓前为死者焚香烧纸;或是为坟墓铲墓培土。民间认为墓穴是死者的房屋,应该好生照料。

祭祖扫墓既是为了怀念祖先,也是为了维护家族的团结。这一习俗延续至今,只是在内容和形式上已有诸多变化。譬如,黄帝是中华民族的祖先,因而在清明节时人们去陕西桥山的黄帝陵前祭奠他。此外,人们还去烈士或祖先的墓前敬献花圈或花束,以表达崇敬、怀念之情。就在1976年清明节,百万群众曾自发组织到天安门广场沉痛追悼周恩来同志、愤怒声讨"四人帮"的罪行。

清明节适逢春季,所谓清明,按古书的说法,指万物萌生、清洁而明净。三月的清明,春回大地、草木萌发,处处生机盎然,一派清明景象,正是外出远足的大好时节,故有清明踏青的习俗。过去,人们常在踏青时往头上戴柳、给轿顶挂柳,用以避邪;有的地方还兴插柳。民间有"清明不戴柳,红颜成皓首"一说。插柳这一习俗现在已不多见,踏青的习俗却保留至今。为了消除清明寒食的不良影响,人们积极参加各类活动:或踢球、拔河;或荡秋千、放风筝等等。放风筝时,放飞者往往在风筝放高飞远后松开手中的线,让风筝带走全家的烦恼与不幸。

3. Pure Brightness Festival

Pure Brightness Festival, also known as Tomb-sweeping Day or Spring Outing Day, falls on April 5.

The Pure Brightness was originally the 5th of the 24 solar terms marking the sequence of time. With the incorporation of Cold Food Festival celebration, it developed into an important festival in the course of time. Cold Food Festival was originally observed days before Pure Brightness Festival, and it was later observed together with the latter. Fire was to be banned during Cold Food Festival. This is intended, some say, to commemorate Jie Zitui, who was a faithful minister of King Wengong of Jin State in the Spring and Autumn Period.

Legend has it that King Xiangong of Jin State intended to pass the throne to Prince Xi Qi, son of his favorite concubine Li Ji. As a result, Shen Sheng the Crown Prince was made to commit suicide and his brother Chong Er to go into exile.

In his exile, Chong Er once nearly got faint from hunger. Jie Zitui, also known as Zitui, who was then a follower of Chong Er, cut a piece of meat from his own thigh and roasted it as food for his master. When Chong Er became the King of Jin, he rewarded all his meritorious subjects except Zitui out of his carelessness. By the time the King was aware of the carelessness, Zitui had gone to Mt. Mian, where he led a secluded life with his mother. The King sent for him to be rewarded but was rejected. He then had a fire set on Mt. Mian to force Zitui out. After the fire was put out, Zitui was found dead, leaning against a burnt willow stump, with his mother on his back. To commemorate Zitui's virtues, King Wengong ordered that fire be banned on his anniversary of death, which happened to be a day previous to the Pure Brightness. Since fire was forbidden, all households could only eat cold food on that day, hence the custom of banning fire and eating cold food on the day of Cold Food Festival.

Apart from banning fire, people sweep their ancestors' tombs, go spring outing, transplant willow cuttings, kick balls and swing during the festival.

Tomb sweeping, which is an important activity of the festival, is to offer sacrifices to ancestors at their tombs. It traces back to the Qin Dynasty. But not until the dynasties of Tang and Song did people sweep their ancestors' tombs during the days from Cold Food Festival to Pure Brightness Festival. A widely known poem on the Pure Brightness Festival written by the Tang Dynasty poet Du Mu reads:

On the day of Pure Brightness Festival it's raining hard,
On his way to the graveyard the passerby's distressed.
"Where can I have a drink?" enquired he of a cowherd,
To a tavern far amid the Apricot Blossoms who pointed.

In the Song Dynasty the festival was designated as the occasion for tomb sweeping, and the capital's residents went to the outskirts for this purpose, which made the country as hilarious as the fairs. There are two ways of sweeping tombs: one is burning joss sticks and paper money for the dead, and the other rooting out weeds and earthing up tombs. The common people believe that graves are home of the dead and need taking good care of.

The practice of tomb sweeping serves to pay homage to the dead and to consolidate family ties as well. It has lasted to the present, and seen different contents and forms. For instance, Huang Di is supposed to be the forefather of the Chinese people, hence many Chinese pay homage to him at his mausoleum situated in Mount Qiao of Shaanxi Province during the festival. Meanwhile, people pay homage to the martyrs by laying flowers and wreaths at their tombs. The Pure Brightness Festival of 1976 saw a great mourning movement spontaneously formed by millions of people at Tian'anmen Square to mourn for Premier Zhou Enlai and denounce the crimes of the Gang of Four.

The festival comes just in spring. According to the ancient Chinese books, 'pure brightness' suggests that all things on earth come back to life in the season with clear weather. This season is a good time to make an excursion because it sees all plants sprouting in bright sunshine and a vast country full of life. So people like to make spring excursions. In old days, when people went spring outing, they either wore green willow wickers on their heads or hung them on the top of their sedan chairs to ward off evil spirits. In some regions, people liked to transplant willow cuttings around the festival. There even went the proverb of "He who wears no willow wickers around Pure Brightness Festival grows old fast". Today, this custom is rarely observed, yet the custom of spring outing remains. In addition, to alleviate the possible negative effect of the cold food, people go for varieties of sports. They play soccer and tug-of-war, have a swing and fly kites. While flying a kite, one usually sets the kite free when it is high in the air in the hope that the whole family's adversities would be gone with it.

4. 端午节

  农历五月五日的端午节是中国民间的传统节日。在中国的五十六个民族中,过端午节的有汉族、朝鲜族、蒙古族、回族、彝族、白族、苗族、壮族等二十七个民族。其主要习俗有赛龙舟、吃粽子、饮雄黄酒和悬挂白艾等。

  赛龙舟主要流行于我国水资源丰沛的南方。此习俗与一传说有关。世传楚国的爱国诗人屈原于公元前278年农历五月五日投汨罗江殉国之后,当地百姓驾舟顺江而下打捞他的尸体,最后来到洞庭湖。当时正在湖上打鱼的渔夫们听说缘由之后,也竞相划舟帮助打捞。从此,便有了端午节赛龙舟的习俗。

  现在赛龙舟的形式各地不尽相同。湖南省汨罗江畔的百姓在端午节进行龙舟比赛之前要举行隆重的仪式,首先身着新装的人们点着几十对蜡烛,绕舟三周祭鲁班;然后抬着龙头去屈子庙朝拜;最后挂红下水,开始比赛。只听一声炮响,舟如矢发,两岸人声鼎沸,鞭炮齐鸣,彩旗飞舞,热闹非常。四川泸州等地区的龙舟上除桡手外还有指挥者和擂鼓手,指挥者手持令旗站在船头喊号子,使桡手们统一动作,鼓手拼命擂鼓,让桡手们奋力划桨。厦门、漳州在赛场终点停一艘大木船作为标船,赛舟一到终点,标船上的人们就将鸭子抛入水中,让桡手们追捉，观众呐喊助威，场面十分热烈壮观。广西赛龙舟分为男队和女队，可用手划和脚划。

端午节吃粽子这一习俗的由来也与传说有关。相传，爱国诗人屈原深受百姓敬仰，因此，汨罗江上的渔人常常赠他以粽子和鸡蛋。屈原投江殉国后渔人们悲痛万分，就在当天，一位渔夫将带给屈原的粽子和鸡蛋投入江中，以期鱼虾饱食之后免去吞食屈原的尸体。此后，这种做法逐渐形成全国性的端午节习俗，以寄托人们对屈原的哀思。

饮雄黄酒也是端午节的习俗之一。据说在屈原殉难的当天，一名老医生把一坛雄黄酒倒进江里，想以药昏蛟龙水兽，不让它们吞食屈原的尸体。后来人们在过端午节祭奠屈原时也效仿，久而久之就形成为过端午节的活动内容之一，但形式不同了。人们在节日前将菖蒲根和雄黄泡酒，于阳光下晒，到端午节家人团聚时共饮，以防虫伤害。小孩不会喝雄黄酒，就擦点在他们的鼻子和耳朵上。也可把雄黄酒洒在地上消毒防虫。

端午节悬挂白艾，别具特色。农历五月五日日出之前，人们就到野外采集白艾，带回家与菖蒲一起悬挂在门框上。关于端午节悬挂白艾的由来，在民间也有一段有趣的传说。据说唐末黄巢带领一部分人马来到河南邓州城下察看地形，见一位妇女怀抱一个五六岁的大男孩，手拉着一个两三岁的小男孩，神色惊恐不安，黄巢觉得奇怪，下马询问，妇女说："县衙今天传令说，黄巢要来血洗邓州，要我们赶快逃命！"黄巢又问："你为何手拉小的，怀抱大的？"妇女悲切道："怀抱的孩子父母双亡，是个孤儿；手拉的是我亲生儿子，若黄巢追来，我就丢掉亲生儿子，抱走孤儿。"黄巢听后说："大嫂，你爱孤儿，我爱天下百姓。"说罢伸手拔了路旁两株白艾给妇女，说："有艾不杀，你快回城传话，让穷苦百姓在门上都插上白艾，有此记号者不受伤害。"次日正是端午节，黄巢军队攻下邓州，杀了县官，开仓分粮，百姓欢喜。此后端午节在门上悬挂白艾便逐渐演变成习俗，并沿袭至今。

有关端午节的种种传说毕竟是传说。其实据专家考证，端午节起源于四、五千年前的远古时代，比屈原生活的年代早得多。我们华夏民族的祖先，认为龙是最强大的神灵，遂以之为部族的标志。以后的华夏子孙们把伏羲、神农、女娲、颛顼和大禹等早期部族首领也尊为龙，并把每年农历五月五日定为祭龙节。为庆祝节日，人们要赛龙舟，吃粽子、饮雄黄酒和悬挂白艾。据信，这才是端午节的真正起源。

4. Dragon Boat Festival

It is a popular and traditional festival celebrated on the 5th of the 5th lunar month by the Hans, Koreans, Mongolians, Huis, Yis, Bais, Miaos, Zhuangs and others, altogether 27 of the 56 nationalities in China. The festival is marked by holding dragon boat races, eating zongzi (a pyramid-shaped dumpling made of glutinous rice wrapped in bamboo or reed leaves), drinking realgar wine and hanging mugwort plants on doors.

The dragon boat race is mainly popular in the south of China, where water in rivers and lakes is plentiful. The custom has a legend behind. The wide-spread legend says that when Qu Yuan, a great patriotic poet of the State of Chu (present Hubei Province) in the period of the Warring States (475 – 221 B.C.), drowned himself in the Miluo River of present Hubei for his motherland on the 5th day of the 5th lunar month in 278 B.C., the local people boated down the river retrieving his corpse. They were joined by fishermen who were fishing in boats on Dongting Lake in present Hubei when they came to the lake. Since then the dragon boat race has been held to celebrate the Dragon Boat Festival.

Today, people hold the race differently from place to place. Here are some instances. Along the Miluo River in Hubei Province, the festival celebrators hold a grand opening ceremony before the race starts. At the ceremony dozens of men in new clothes, with burning candles in hands, walk around boats three times to show worship of Lu Ban the master craftsman; then they carry, on their shoulders, an image of a dragon's head to the Temple of Qu Yuan, where they pay their respect to this saint; finally they tie red ribbons to the boats and pull them into the river for the race. At the crack of a signal gun, the boats race ahead like discharged arrows fitted to bowstrings while both banks are a hubbub of voices, a babel of firecracker explosions and a scene of fluttering colored banners. In Sichuan's Luzhou and its nearby regions, the racers in a dragon boat include a commander, a drummer and some rowers. The commander, standing on the bow, waves a pennant and sings a race song to synchronize rowing movements while the drummer beats a drum with all his might to cheer the rowers on. In the areas of Xiamen and Zhangzhou of Fujian Province, a big wooden boat is arranged lying at the finishing line. When race boats reach the line, a number of ducks are released from the big wooden boat into the river for all the racers to catch amid thunderous cheers of spectators on the banks. In Guangxi, racers may be either men or women, and they may row race boats either by hand or by foot.

The custom of eating zongzi is also linked to a legend of Qu Yuan. It is said that people revered Qu Yuan, when he was alive, so much that the fishermen on the Miluo River often presented him some zongzi and eggs. They were all overwhelmed with grief when they learned that Qu Yuan had drowned himself in the Miluo River for his country. On the day of Qu's death, one of the fishermen threw into the river the zongzi and eggs, which he had intended to give to Qu, in the hope that the fish and shrimps, after eating too much of these foods, would not eat Qu's corpse. This is said to be the origin of the present nation-wide custom, which is the common people's expression of grief over Qu's death.

The custom of drinking realgar wine likewise hangs a legend about Qu Yuan. It is said that, on the day of Qu's death, an old practitioner of Chinese medicine poured a jar of realgar wine into the Miluo River, supposedly to make drunk the dragon and other aquatic animals which might devour Qu's corpse. Later people followed suit to worship Qu Yuan at the Dragon Boat Festival, hence the present custom. Yet the present custom is a little different from what it used to be. Today, the festival celebrators soak calamus roots and realgar in wine and keep sunning the wine until the Dragon Boat Festival. At the festival, adults of a family drink it as a prevention against vermin and children, who are unfit to drink wine, have some of the wine applied to their noses and ears for the same purpose. People also like to sprinkle the wine over their floors for sterilization on that day.

It is unique to hang mugwort plants on doors on the festival day. Before the sunrise of the day people go to the mountains to collect mugwort plants and, after they come home, hang them and calamus plants together on doors. This custom hangs an interesting folk tale. Towards the end of the Tang Dynasty (618 – 907) a nation-wide peasant uprising took place. It is said that one day its leader Huang Chao, commanding his army, came to present Dengxian County city of Henan Province to survey the terrain for a battle. On the outskirts Huang came across a panic-stricken woman who held a child about six years old in one arm and took a child about three years old by the hand. Puzzled, Huang dismounted from his horse and asked why she behaved so. The woman replied, "An order from the county government office warns us all to flee as Huang Chao's soldiers are coming to massacre the inhabitants of Dengzhou city." Huang asked again, "Why do you hold the older child in one of your arms and take the younger one by the hand?" The woman replied in a plaintive voice, "The older is an orphan and the younger is my own son. In case we run into Huang Chao's soldiers, I would flee with the older alone at the sacrifice of my own son." Huang was moved by the reply and said, "Elder Sister, you love an orphan and I cherish all common people." Pulling up two mugwort plants at the roadside immediately and giving them to her, Huang added: "Tell the poor residents in Dengzhou city to hang this kind of mugworts plants on their doors. Seeing this sign, my soldiers will not kill them." The next day, Huang Chao's army captured Dengzhou city, killed the magistrate and distributed grain from the official granaries to the poor. And all the common people were overjoyed. That day happened to be the Dragon Boat Festival; hence the custom of hanging mugwort plants on doors.

The legends are probably untrue. According to surveys, the Dragon Boat Festival dates as far back as 5 000 years ago, much earlier before Qu Yuan's life. The Chinese nation's earliest ancestors thought the dragon a most powerful god; hence they revered it as the totem of the nation. The later Chinese worshipped their tribe chiefs, like Fu Xi, Nu Wa, Zhuan Yu and Yu the Great, as the incarnation of the dragon and made the 5th of the 5th lunar month a day to hold a sacrificial ceremony for the legendary animal. To mark the day, people also hold dragon boat races, eat zongzi, drink realgar wine, and hang mugwort plants on doors. This is believed to be the real origin of the Dragon Boat Festival.

5.中秋节

　　农历 8 月 15 日是中秋节。这是我国仅次于春节的一个重要节日。由于一年当中此夕的月亮最圆、最亮、最美,骚人墨客纷纷以此为题吟诗作赋。苏轼在 1076 年的中秋节思念阔别多年的兄弟所作的《水调歌头》就是咏中秋月的名篇。每逢佳节,人们就想起苏轼的"但愿人长久,千里共婵娟"。

　　一曲《水调歌头》之所以引起大家的共鸣,是因为中秋节与春节一样,是团圆的日子。民间认为,月儿圆了,一家人也该团圆了,故中秋节也称团圆节。甚至"其有妇归宁者,是日必返夫家,曰团圆节也"。不能与家人团聚的游子们,仰望天上的明月时,往往从心底深处流露出浓浓的乡愁。

　　中秋节的传统食品是月饼。圆圆的月饼既象征月圆,也象征团圆。但溯其源宗,月饼最初却是中秋赏月时的供品。后来为了强调宗族团结,才赋予它幸福团圆的意义。民间流传着另一种说法:元朝末年,统治者禁止老百姓使用铁器,规定十家合用一把菜刀,十家供养一个"鞑子"(元兵)。残酷的统治激起了人民的不满。农民起义军领袖——高邮的张士诚通过散发内夹"8 月 15 日杀元兵"纸条的月饼,成功地将群众组织起来反抗元朝统治者。推翻元朝统治后,为纪念这次群众斗争,人们开始了吃月饼的习俗。

民间传说月亮上有广寒宫,宫里住着嫦娥和玉兔。"嫦娥奔月"的故事几乎家喻户晓,抬头望月间,谁会忘记这美丽的传说呢。

远古时代,天上出现十个太阳,大地一片枯焦,大海也日渐枯竭,人类几乎无法生存。神箭手后羿同情百姓,搭弓射下九个太阳,只留下一个照明。一老道感其德行,赠不死仙丹一粒以示嘉许。后羿美丽的妻子嫦娥出于好奇,趁丈夫不在时,偷服下仙丹。顿时就飘然空中,直奔月宫而去。到月宫后,仙丹在嫦娥喘息时被吐了出来,落地而成玉兔。独处广寒宫的嫦娥思念丈夫,十分寂寞,就命玉兔日夜不停地在桂花树下捣药,以期返回地面,与丈夫团聚。

由于人们将月儿与美丽的嫦娥联系在一起,在中国人的心目中,月儿美好、静谧而可爱。早在宋代,就有"贵家结饰台榭,民间争占酒楼玩月"的记载。有的地方还兴中秋祭月,由妇女主祭。另外,出于对月神的崇拜,人们将主宰婚姻的权利赋予她,因此媒人也称"月下老儿"。一些未婚女子甚至在中秋夜秉烛燃香,祈祷美满婚姻。

5. Mid-Autumn Festival

Mid-Autumn Festival, next only to Spring Festival in importance, is celebrated on the 15th day of the 8th lunar month. As the moon seems the fullest, brightest and most attractive on that night, Chinese poets like to make it a favorite theme of their poems. For instance, *Shui Diao Ge Tou* (Tune: Prelude to Water Melody), written by Su Shi in Mid-Autumn Festival of the year 1076 and expressing the author's longing for his long-parted brother, enjoys great popularity. Whenever the festival is around the corner, few Chinese will fail to recall and recite the line of the poem "Let us wish that he would live long, though far apart, we could share the beauty of the full moon."

This poem arouses sympathy among people because the festival, like Spring Festival, is an occasion of family reunion. The full moon symbolizes family togetherness to the Chinese. As a result, the festival is also called Family Reunion Festival. On that day, women who are at their parents' home must go back to their mother-in-law's for the sake of family togetherness. For those who are far away from home, a sense of nostalgia will well up in their heart when they gaze at the full moon high in the sky.

The traditional food marking the festival is mooncake, whose round shape symbolizes both the fullness of the moon and family togetherness. But if we trace its history, we will find out that it used to be the sacrifice offered to the moon when people went outside to admire the fair moon. Only when the reunion among patriarchal clans was later stressed, did the festival embody family togetherness and happiness. A popular legend of the origin of mooncake goes like this: the common people in the late Yuan Dynasty were forbidden to use ironware. Every ten families were supposed to share one kitchen knife, and to support a Yuan soldier. The tyranny aroused people's indignation. Zhang Shicheng, a leader of the peasants' uprising from Gaoyou, established contact between people by distributing mooncakes, each with a note inside saying, "Kill the Yuan soldiers on August 15". The successful contact enabled people to revolt against the Yuan ruling class. After the overthrow of the Yuan rulers, mooncakes were eaten every year on that day to celebrate the victory.

According to a Chinese folktale, Fairy Chang E lives with her moon rabbit in the Moon Palace. Chang E's Flying towards the Moon is known to every household. The Mid-Autumn moon always reminds Chinese people of the tale.

It is said that in remote antiquity, ten suns simultaneously appeared in the sky. They scorched the earth and dried the ocean. Men could hardly survive. Hou Yi, the miraculous archer, took sympathy on the common people in disaster. He shot down nine of the suns at a stretch, leaving only one to illuminate the earth. A Taoist priest offered Hou Yi the elixir of life for what he had done for people. Hou Yi's pretty wife Chang E, however, was so curious at the pill that one day when he was not at home she took it out and swallowed it. Immediately she found herself flying up to the moon. On the moon she spat out the pill and it turned into a jade rabbit. Living alone in the Moon Palace, Chang E was so lonely and she missed her husband so much that she had the moon rabbit pounding medicine under a cassia tree day and night so that she could come back to the earth after she took it.

Due to the romantic association of the moon with the beautiful moon lady Chang E, the moon to the Chinese is attractive, quiet and lovely. It is recorded that in the Song Dynasty, to admire the glorious moon, "high officials and noble lords gather at their own pavilions while the common people vie with one another to be at the wineshop". In some places, women even perform the rite of sacrificing the moon on the night of Mid-Autumn Festival. Worshipping of the moon makes people believe that the moon is endowed with the power of deciding humans' matrimonial destiny. Hence the name Yue Xia Laor, the old man in the moon, is for a matchmaker. Some unmarried young women even light candles and burn joss sticks under the Mid-Autumn moon to pray for a happy marriage.

6. 重阳节

农历九月九日是中国传统的重阳节。《易传》中有"以阳爻为九"的记载,并将"九"定为阳数。一年中只有九月九日正好两阳相重、月日均为阳,故名"重阳"。

重阳节原是中国农民喜庆丰收的一个节日,这个节日早在战国时期就已形成,在汉代逐渐流行,到唐代诏令规定为法定节日。

古时候重阳节的活动内容主要有登高、赏菊、饮菊花酒、插茱萸、吃重阳糕等传统习俗。

农历九月秋高气爽,云淡山黛,登高远眺,蓝天白云和山川草木尽收眼底,令人心旷神怡,豪情满怀,因此从古至今都是人们游山玩水的好时节。西汉时京都长安近郊有一高台,每逢重阳佳节,很多人都要去登高台游玩远眺,观赏四周美景,故称为登高。到了三国和晋代时期,重阳主要开展登山活动,饱览山野秋色。唐代的人们则最喜欢去长安城东南的游乐园游玩。那里的西南面紧靠曲江池,隔池便是著名的大慈恩寺和大雁塔,是个观光人文景点的好去处。明代的皇帝到万寿山登高。清代在皇宫的御花园里设有专供皇帝在重阳节登高的假山。

中国是菊花的故乡,公元前5世纪的古籍上就有关于菊花的记载。唐代将菊花作为皇室御用花传到了日本。12 世纪传到了英国,17 世纪传遍整个欧洲,19 世纪传到了美国。菊花又叫黄花,属菊科,多年生草本植物,品种繁多,一般多在农历九月开放,花期很长,因此又把农历九月称为菊月,从而给每年九月九日的重阳节增添了很好的色彩。菊花还受到历代豪情满怀的诗人们所喜爱。相传晋代陶渊明退隐田园后种植了许多种菊花,每当菊花开放时亲朋好友们便陆续去观赏。唐代农民起义领袖黄巢留下了脍炙人口的《菊花诗篇》。大诗人杜甫写了十多首赏菊诗。重阳赏菊为民众所喜爱。宋代有的酒店在重阳节用菊花装饰酒店门面,让来店饮酒的顾客在菊花丛中进出,增添饮酒兴致。清代有的地方在重阳节过后举办菊花会,让人们观看菊展,参加赛诗活动,观看画家当场作菊花画。参观菊花会常常是人潮如海,热闹非常。

菊花酒有其特殊酿造工艺。据说古时候人们在农历九月九日采摘初开的菊花和青翠的菊叶,掺在用于酿酒的粮谷里,然后一同用于酿酒,存放到次年九月九日的重阳节饮用。菊花酒具有明目、治头痛、降血压、减肥、安肠胃的功效,传说喝了这种酒还可以益寿延年。

古时候人们过重阳节所插的茱萸是一种常绿小乔木,春季开紫色花,秋季结紫黑色果,其果性味酸、涩、微温,入药制成酒有止痛、理气等功效。每逢重阳节人们登高时都要摘茱萸枝插在头发上,并饮茱萸酒,据说这样可以除恶气而御初寒。

重阳糕又叫"菊糕"、"花糕"。重阳糕起源于周朝,据说最初为秋收后做的一种尝新食品,后来才发展成为重阳节的应节食品。重阳糕一般以糯米、小米和豆类制做。唐代的重阳糕上要插重阳旗,这种重阳旗很小,用五色纸雕刻成花纹,中间嵌"令"字。宋代的重阳糕十分考究,在重阳节前两三天就用糯米或小米等面粉蒸糕,上插彩旗,糕上还嵌满栗子、银杏子、松仁和石榴子等。这种重阳糕可作为馈赠亲友的节日礼品。明代的皇宫里从农历九月初一起就开始吃重阳糕。民间的重阳糕大如盆,铺枣二、三层,还要接出嫁的女儿回家一同过节。清代把重阳糕制做成像宝塔样式的九层,在上面放两只用面做的羊,以象征节日食品"重阳糕"。

今天重阳节饮菊花酒和插茱萸的习俗已成为历史,吃重阳糕的习俗也只在个别地区的民间存在。但"九九登高"活动仍然保留着,重阳节敬重老人的风气开始出现,将来有可能发展为重阳节的又一项活动内容。

6. Double Ninth Day

The Double Ninth Day is observed, as one of the traditional festivals, by Chinese on the 9th day of the 9th lunar month. It is known as chong yang jie in Chinese because "chong" means double, "yang" suggests nine according to The Book of Changes (one of the Five Classics in ancient China), and "jie" means festival.

It was originally a day for farmers to celebrate bumper harvests of crops. The festival was born in the Warring States period (475 – – 221B. C.), became popular in the Han Dynasty (206B. C.— 220A.C.), and was made an official day – off for common people by an imperial edict in the Tang Dynasty (618—907). Long ago the festival was marked by climbing heights, enjoying chrysanthemum flowers, drinking chrysanthemum flower wine, wearing in hair small cornel twigs, eating Double Ninth cake and other activities.

The 9th lunar month, with clear autumn sky and bracing air, is a good time for sightseeing. An outing lover, who stands on a height looking afar in the month, will have a panoramic view of a blue sky with pale clouds and dark green mountains, which makes him feel carefree and joyful. So people, both ancient and present, love to go sightseeing this month . People in the Western Han Dynasty (2 0 6 B.C. – 25 A. C.) liked to ascend a height in the suburbs of Chang'an (the then national capital and present Xi'an) on the 9th day of the month to enjoy sceneries, the activity being known as height ascending; people, in the Three Kingdoms period (220 – 265) and the Jin Dynasty (265 – 420), even more liked the activity to feast their eyes on the autumn country view; sightseers in the Tang Dynasty favored most a trip to the Joyous Garden southeast of Chang'an on the day, a man – made tourist attraction with the Qujiang Pool, the Ci'en Temple and the Wild Goose Pagoda to its southwest; the Ming Dynasty (1368 – 1644) emperors liked to ascend the Wanshou Hill in Beijing to mark the day; and the Qing Dynasty (1616 – 1911) emperors chose to ascend, on the day, the man-built hills in the imperial garden in Beijing.

Chrysanthemum originated in China and was recorded in some Chinese books as early as the 5th century B.C. The flower was introduced, as imperial flower, into Japan in the Tang Dynasty. Then it was introduced into Britain in the 12th century, into the continent of Europe in the 17th century, and into the U.S.A. in the 19th century. Also known as "yellow flower", chrysanthemum is of varied species in the composite family. Though its florescence lasts long, this perennial herb usually begins to bloom in the 9th lunar month, lending much festive flavor to the Double Ninth Day. That's why the month is also referred to as "the month of chrysanthemum". The flower was favored by poets through the ages. It is said that Tao Yuanming, a famous poet of the Jin Dynasty, grew many species of chrysanthemum while he lived as a hermit and the flower, when in full bloom, drew many of Tao's relatives and friends. Huang Cao, leader of the peasant uprising in the Tang Dynasty, wrote a lot of poems about chrysanthemum, which were compiled into an anthology of Chrysanthemum and, even now, are oft-quoted. Du Fu, a great Tang Dynasty poet, wrote more than ten poems singing the praises of the flower. Chinese folks were fond of enjoying chrysanthemum on the Double Ninth Day long before. The entrances of some taverns in the Song Dynasty (960 – 1279) were decorated with the flowers on the day, which was supposed to incite customers' desire for wine. Chrysanthemum displays were usually held immediately after the day in some regions of China in the Qing Dynasty. At these displays people might enjoy chrysanthemum flowers, take part in poem-composing competitions or watch painters drawing paintings of chrysanthemum flowers. The display was often lively with a sea of visitors.

The chrysanthemum flower wine is unique in brewing. In ancient times people, some say, usually picked fresh chrysanthemum flowers and leaves on the 9th of the 9th lunar month, and brewed the mixture of them and grains into the wine, which would not be drunk until the same day next year. The wine is said to have wholesome effects on sharpness of the eye, alleviation of headache, drop of hypertension, reduction of weight and removal of stomach trouble, thus contributing to longevity.

While climbing mountains on the Double Ninth Day, ancient Chinese liked to wear cornel twigs in their hair and drank the wine infused with cornel fruit. It is said that the drinkers of the wine would be free from evil and have strong physique against cold weather. The cornel is a species of evergreen arbor. It puts out purple flowers in spring and bears, in autumn, purplish-brown fruit that is sour, puckery and mild in nature. The wine, infused with its fruit, has wholesome effects on assuagement of pain and regulation of the flow of vital energy.

The Double Ninth cake is also known as "chrysanthemum cake" or "flower cake". It dates back to the Zhou Dynasty (the 11th century – 256 B.C.). It is said that the cake was originally prepared after autumn harvests for farmers to have a taste of what was just in season, and it gradually grew into the present cake for people to eat on the Double Ninth Day. The cake was usually made of glutinous rice flour, millet flour or bean flour. In the Tang Dynasty its surface was usually planted with a small pennant of multi-colored paper and bore at its center the Chinese character "ling" (order). The Double Ninth cake in the Song Dynasty was usually made with great care a few days before the Double Ninth Day, its surface planted with colored pennants and inlaid with Chinese chestnuts, ginkgo seeds, pine nut kernels and pomegranate seeds. It was a nice festive present for relatives or friends. In the Ming Dynasty, the imperial families customarily began to eat the cake early on the first day of the 9th lunar month to mark the festival, and the common people usually enjoyed with their married daughters the festive cake, which was basin-sized and covered with two or three layers of jujubes. The cake in the Qing Dynasty was made like a 9-storied pagoda, which was topped with two sheep images made of dough. The cake, so made, was called chong yang gao in Chinese, which means Double Ninth cake as "chong" means double, "yang" dichotomously suggests nine and sheep, and "gao" means cake.

Present people no longer drink the chrysanthemum flower wine and wear cornel twigs in hair on the Double Ninth Day, and only a few regions' people still follow the custom of eating the Double Ninth cake. Nearly all Chinese, however, still like to climb mountains to mark the festival. Some activities to help the aged on the Double Ninth Day are burgeoning and will probably become regular practices.

7. 中元节

　　中元节是汉族的传统宗教节日,农历七月十五举行,又称鬼节、七月半、盂兰盆节或目莲节等。

　　中元节来源于道教,原是道教祭祖的节日。道教认为,三官大帝掌管着人间的命运:上元天官主赐福,中元地官主赦罪,下元水官主解厄。正月十五乃天官诞辰,称上元节;七月十五为地官诞辰,称中元节;十月十五是水官诞辰,称下元节,其中以中元节的祭祀最隆重。

　　民间传说地官在七月十五诞辰之日,降临人间,裁定善恶。同时,由于他主宰着地狱,是日会将地狱之门打开,让众鬼魂回到人间与家人团聚。而那些孤魂野鬼就会趁机到人间兴风作浪,带来疾病和灾难。为了帮助已故祖先赦免罪愆并安抚无家可归的孤魂野鬼,人们举行各种祭祀活动,请道士作道场,普度众鬼。

　　中元节在后来的发展过程中,与佛教的盂兰盆会相互影响,最终被人们混淆在一起,因此中元节也被叫做盂兰盆节。盂兰盆节其实来源于一个广为传诵的佛教故事。盂兰盆乃梵文,意思是"解救倒悬"。佛教为宣扬其轮回教义,以"目莲救母"的故事来感化世人。据传目莲是释迦牟尼的弟子。一日禅定时看见母亲因阳世的罪业在地狱饱受饥饿之苦。目莲悲痛不已,求佛主超度母亲。佛主让他在七月十五以盆器罗列百味果食,供奉众僧,解其母倒悬之苦。由此形成了盂兰盆会。每到七月十五,为了尽孝道,各家皆备盂兰盆,施佛及僧,超度先祖,并在同一天举行祭祖仪式。

七月十五晚上还有放河灯的习俗。这也是为了祭拜亡魂。人们点燃河灯,普度那些孤魂野鬼,以免他们在人间作祟。

7. Zhongyuan Festival

The Zhongyuan Festival is a traditional religious festival for the Han nationality. Also known as the Ghost Festival, Qiyueban (the 15th day of the 7th lunar month), the Yulanpen (Ullambana) Festival, or the Mulian (Moglinin) Festival, it is celebrated on the 15th of the 7th lunar month.

The festival derives from Taoism, formerly being a day for Taoists to offer sacrifices to their ancestors. Taoism believes that the three all-powerful gods are held responsible for the fate of humans. The Heaven God of Shangyuan is in charge of bestowing good fortune, the Earth God of Zhongyuan absolution and the Water God of Xiayuan dispelling misfortune. Their birthdays, the 15th of the 1st lunar month (Shangyuan), the 15th of the 7th lunar month (Zhongyuan), and the 15th day of the 10th lunar month (Xiayuan) are observed as the Shangyuan Festival, the Zhongyuan Festival, and the Xiayuan Festival respectively. Among the three the Zhongyuan Festival has the grandest sacrifice ceremony.

A folk legend has it that on his birthday, the 15th of the 7th lunar month, the Earth God descends to the human world and judges the good and the evil. As he is in charge of the Buddhist and Taoist purgatory, the god opens its gate to let the spirits of the departed return to man's world and reunite with their families. Those lonely ghosts, however, will take advantage of the chance to present themselves on the earth and stir up trouble. They bring man diseases and disasters. On the day people make different sacrifices helping to absolve the deceased ancestors from their guilt and to appease the homeless lonely spirits, and request Taoist priests to perform rites to save the spirits.

In the course of its development, the Zhongyuan Festival and the Buddhist Yulanpen (Ullambana) Festival exerted so much influence on each other that they were confused and merged into one. Thus the Zhongyuan Festival is also called the Yulanpen Festival. In fact it can be traced back to a popular Buddhist story. Yulanpen, being a transliteration from Sanskrit ullambana, means delivering someone from the pain of being hung by the feet. Buddhism preachers employ the moving story of Mulian (Moglinin) saving his mother to educate people to accept the dogma of samsara or transmigration. According to legend, Mulian (Moglinin) is a follower of Sakyamuni, the founder of Buddhism. One day in deep meditation he saw his mother suffer from hunger in the hell due to her wrongdoings when she was alive. It grieved him to see this. He turned to Sakyamuni for the release of her. Sakyamuni said that to save his mother from the suffering of being hung by the feet he should offer sacrifices to Buddhist monks by laying out numerous kinds of fruits and food in trays on the 15th of the 7th lunar month. As a result the Yulanpen Festival came into being. On the 15th of the 7th lunar month every year, people prepare Yulanpen trays and offer sacrifices to Buddha and monks to expiate the sins for their ancestors, and hold rites offering sacrifices to their ancestors, both to express their filial piety.

There is also the custom of floating burning lamps on the rivers on the evening of the 15th of the 7th lunar month. It is to worship the spirits of the departed, and expiate the sins of those lonely and restless ghosts in case they should misbehave and haunt man.

8. 赫哲年

　　黑龙江省同江、抚远及饶河县的沿江地带,居住着中国人口最少的民族——赫哲族。过去,这个民族冬日里用雪橇出行,靠滑雪打猎为生。现在已有了很大的变化。同汉族一样,他们在正月初一过春节,即赫哲年。

　　腊月一到,赫哲人就开始为赫哲年作准备。男人推磨拉面、凿冰捕鱼,女人做李子饼、鱼毛和兽肉等节日食品,孩子们跟大人们学做贴窗和糊灯笼用的剪纸。

　　除夕夜里,家家户户都要祭祀祖先、灶神和火神。祭品通常是早上做的饺子。

　　大年初一,妇女和儿童穿上镶有五彩云边的皮衣,到亲朋好友家拜年。主人端出瓜籽糖果待客,并请客人品尝拌有蔬菜和佐料的鱼丝,有时会给客人端来一盘大马哈鱼籽。

　　村里的老人们喜欢去民间艺人家听"伊玛坎"和"说胡力"。"伊玛坎"是散文与韵文相结合的一种口头文学,以讲述男女爱情、英雄复仇和历史故事为主,语言押韵,说唱兼杂。表演者称"伊玛坎奈",意即智慧者。"说胡力"的歌词大都短小生动,主要讲述神话、寓言和民间传说。

　　节日里的娱乐活动多种多样。孩子们对"老鹰叼小鸡"这类游戏兴致勃勃;青年女子喜欢聚在一起自得其乐;小伙子们或滑雪、溜冰,或玩"叉草球"。"叉草球"由一人负责抛草球,参与者轮流用渔叉叉滚动的草球,叉中次数最多者为胜。由于玩这个游戏需要高超的技艺和快速的动作,这有利于孩子们掌握叉鱼的技巧。这一点对赫哲人很重要,因为他们曾以渔猎为生。

8. Hezhe Spring Festival

The Hezhe people, an ethnic group with the smallest population in China, live along the rivers in the counties of Tongjiang, Fuyuan and Raohe in Heilongjiang Province. These people, who used to travel by sled and hunt on skis in winter, have undergone great changes. Their Spring Festival, like the Han people's, falls on the 1st day of the 1st lunar month.

As time advances into the 12th lunar month, the Hezhe people begin their preparations for the approaching festival. Men mill flour and crack ice to fish in the river. Women busy themselves making festival food like plum cake, fish floss and dried meat of wild animals. Children, under adults' directions, cut paper to paste windows and lanterns.

On Lunar New Year's eve, each Hezhe family offers sacrifices, usually jiao zi made in the early morning, to their ancestors, the kitchen god and the fire god.

On Lunar New Year's Day, women and children, who are dressed in new leather coats with colorful laces, pay New Year visits to their relatives and friends. They are entertained with melon seeds, candies and fruit as well as fish floss mixed with vegetables and condiments, and sometimes salmon roes.

Senior villagers like to visit local folk artists and listen to them telling folktales and singing Yimakan and Shuohuli. The former is a sort of ballad, which usually tells love, chivalrous or historical stories, the words characterized by rhyme and melody. The performer is known as Yimakannai, a man of wisdom. The latter are short and lively songs covering fairy tales, fables and folklore.

Various pastimes are performed to mark the festival. Children play such games as hawk-capturing-chicken. Young ladies get together for fun. Lads are fond of skiing, skating and spearing straw-balls. In the game of straw-ball spearing, one player throws straw-balls, the others in turn throw a fishing spear to fork the balls running on the ground. He wins who forks most. As the balls are running, the lucky fellow should be deft and skillful. The game enables children to master the skills of fish spearing, which is of great importance to them as the Hezhe people used to live by hunting and fishing.

9. 那达慕大会

那达慕大会是聚居在内蒙古、甘肃、青海和新疆等地的蒙古族人民的传统节日。其庆祝活动在每年水草丰盛、牲畜肥壮、秋高气爽的七、八月份举行。会期一至八天不等。

"那达慕"又称"那雅尔",在蒙古语中为"娱乐"或"游戏"的意思。据传,那达慕大会始于汉代,王昭君出塞时,草原人民曾举行那达慕活动隆重欢迎她。据史书记载,元朝成吉思汗召集"忽力勤台"(即大聚会)首脑会议时,除了处理制定法律、任免官员和奖功罚罪等政务而外,还要举行射箭、赛马和摔跤等三项那达慕活动中的某一项活动。13世纪中期成书的《蒙古秘史》中亦有数处记载那达慕大会射箭等比赛活动的场面。到了明代,那达慕活动规模扩大。清代,那达慕大会由官方定期组织,其规模、内容和形式均有较大发展。当时蒙古的苏木(相当于现在的乡级行政单位)、旗、盟均可每半年、一年或三年举行一次那达慕大会,对获奖者的奖励也因举办单位级别的高低不同而有多寡之别,如苏木级小型比赛的摔跤冠军一般只奖给一只羊或几块砖茶;而有数百名摔跤手参加的盟级大型比赛的冠军,则可获得鼻带银环、背驮珠宝绸缎等赏赐物品的银白色骆驼,同时还要授予"猛如狮子的摔跤手"或"猛如老虎的摔跤手"。

现在,那达慕达大会的庆祝活动增加了套马、田径、拔河、篮球、排球、摩托车等体育竞赛项目。但人们最喜欢的还是最具民族特色的摔跤、赛马和射箭等传统活动。

摔跤比赛中,摔跤手一般要身着传统的摔跤服装,上身穿皮革或多层帆布制成的缀着铜钉的坎肩,下身穿三色短裙和宽大的绣花绸缎摔跤裤,脚登长筒靴。在热烈的比赛开始前,若干仿古骑士在赞歌声中大步绕场一周,唱着长调:"快一点把你们的摔跤手选出来比赛吧!"然后一对摔跤手挥舞双臂跳跃上场,互相行礼握手完毕,即在观众震耳欲聋的"加油"和欢呼声中展开争夺雌雄的比赛。

蒙古人如此喜爱摔跤有其历史原因。相传成吉思汗小时候就擅长摔跤,当了皇帝后便把摔跤作为考核任用将士的重要科目。民间也视摔跤为男儿骑马、射箭、摔跤等三艺之一。到13世纪中期,摔跤活动已超越蒙古族的范围,成为中亚不少国家的人民喜爱的体育活动。

赛马更是一项引人入胜的重要比赛活动。赛场广大,在起点和终点插上各种颜色的彩旗。骑手须是少年,比赛开始前骑手排成一字行,头裹彩巾,腰缠彩带,青春焕发,十分英武,整备并辔,令行即发。当号角鸣响,骑手们立即飞身上马,扬鞭策马。赛马如离弦之箭,驰向终点。首先到达终点的骑手被誉为"草原健儿"。

射箭比赛则扣人心弦,让人眼花缭乱。蒙古族人民世代生活在大草原上,主要以狩猎为生,因此几乎人人能骑善射。据考在元、明时期,那达慕大会进行射箭比赛时,有的蒙古部落还要朗读颂词,如甘肃省呼儿鲁克蒙古族的射箭祝颂词云:"你擎起了万钧弓啊,搭上了金色利箭……你能射倒耸立的高山，你能射穿飞翔的大雁，啊——祝福你啊，生铜熟铁般的力士。"由于现在生产技术的高度现代化，所以蒙古族人民只将拉弓射箭作为一项体育项目在那达慕大会上表演，而非谋生手段。

传统的那达慕大会都在草原上举行。随着经济发展，居住在大城市里的蒙古族人不断增加，因此现在的哈尔滨、长春、沈阳、北京等大城市的蒙古族人民也每年都要举行那达慕大会。

9. Nadamu Festival

It is a traditional festival observed by the Mongolian people who compactly inhabit Inner Mongolia, Gansu. Qinghai and Xinjiang. The festival is celebrated in July or August when the pastures there have plenty of water, lush grass, thriving herds, and fine weather. The festive celebration lasts for one to eight days.

Nadamu, also known as laya'er, is a Mongolian term, which means entertainment or game. The festival is believed to date back to the Han Dynasty (206 B. C–202 A. C). Nadamu entertainments were offered then by the Xiongnu people who lived around today's Inner Mongolia in honor of Wang Zhaojun, who was an imperial concubine and, on the Han Dynasty emperor's arrangement, came from China's inland to marry the Xiongnu Chieftain to cement a friendly tie between the Hans and the Xiongnus. According to historical records, Genghis Khan, the first emperor of the Yuan Dynasty (1206–1368), would order to hold archery or horse racing or wrestling (three of Nadamu entertainments) whenever he called a meeting of Mongol Khans to make laws, appoint and remove officials, reward the meritorious and punish the guilty. The Inside Story of Mongolia, a book that appeared in the middle of the 13th century, also describes the competitive scenes of archery and other events popular in the Nadamu Festival. In the Ming Dynasty (1368–1644), the festive items were given on a larger scale than before. In the Qing Dynasty (1616 – 1911), the Nadamu Festival celebration began to be organized regularly and officially, on a larger scale, with richer content and in new form. The governments of Sumu (township), Banner (county) and League (prefecture) might hold their own Nadamu Festival celebrations once half a year or a year or every three years. Prizes given to the winner were varied. Take for instance. A sumu-level wrestling champion was usually to be rewarded with one sheep or pieces of brick tea. A Banner-level wrestling champion, born from among hundreds of competitors, was to be given a silvery-white camel which had a silver ring fixed on its nose, and pearls, jewels, silks and satins on its back; in addition, he was to be granted such honorary titles as "a wrestler fierce as a lion" or "a wrestler fierce as a tiger".

Today's Nadamu Festival is marked by more competitive events, such as horse lassoing, track and field sports, tug of war, basketball, volleyball, motorcycling, and the like. The Mongolians, however, favor most wrestling, horse racing and archery, which are three traditional events with distinctive Mongolian flavor.

In a wrestling match, a wrestler usually wears a leather or canvas jacket dotted with bronze nail heads, a short three-color skirt, loose embroidered silk trousers and high boots. At the beginning of a match some knight-like men stride once around the arena, shouting: "The best wrestlers come and wrestle!" Immediately two wrestlers jump into the arena while waving their arms. After shaking hands, they pitch into a tough competition to deafening cheers from audiences.

The Mongolians have historical reasons for their strong interest in wrestling. Genghis Khan was said to be a good wrestler when young, and he listed the game as one of the important items for checking on and selecting military commanders when he was in the throne later; and common Mongolians viewed wrestling as one of the three skills a man should master, the other two being horse riding and archery. In the middle of the 13th century the game spread to and favored by peoples in many of the Mid-Asian countries.

Horse racing is another fascinating event during the Nadamu Festival. A horse racing ground is very big, with colorful flags planted near both the starting line and the finishing line. The competitors must be teenagers. Towards the start of racing, they stand abreast along the starting line, with horses beside, waiting for the starter's signal. Colorful turbans on heads and colorful ribbons around waists, they present a youthful and martial bearing. On the sound of the starter's horn, the young competitors mount their own horses at lightning speed and whip the animals, which gallop towards the finishing line as fast as a discharged arrow flies. The one who first reaches the line is to be granted the title "a valiant rider on the prairie".

Archery competition is very exciting. Almost all Mongolians are good archers as well as crack shots because they have been living by hunting in the vast grasslands from generation to generation. According to textual researches, the Nadamu archery competition was to be preceded by a complimentary address in some Mongolian tribes during the Yuan and Qing dynasties. For instance, the address, delivered by the Hu'erluke Tribe of the Mongolians in Gansu, reads, "Lifting your heavy bowstring with a golden arrow fitted, you can shoot a towering mountain down and your arrow can penetrate a flying wild goose. Oh, bless you, a man as strong as steel." Now, because of the advanced production and technology, the Mongolians merely view archery a sport event to mark the Nadamu Festival, not a means to make a living.

In old days, the Nadamu Festival celebrations were held merely on grasslands. But now, the celebrations are also held in big cities like Ha'erbin, Changchun, Shenyang and Beijing, as the development of economy has been bringing more and more Mongolians there.

10. 祭敖包

祭敖包,又叫祭鄂博或塔克勒恩节,是内蒙古自治区蒙古族的民间祭祀节日。"敖包"是蒙古语,意思是石堆或鼓包,本是路标或界标,后来被赋予了宗教内容,成为蒙古族牧民祭祀山神或路神的活动场所。

敖包是用石头或土块垒成的圆锥形实心塔,也有用柳条筐装上沙土垒成的,还有用树木堆成的。堆子顶端立着一根木杆,长约丈许,杆头挂着五颜六色的经文布条。早先的蒙古族信奉萨满教,认为敖包是神的居住地,对祭敖包非常虔诚。敖包通常设在地面宽阔的交通要道旁,或风光优美的山丘上。平日里,行人路过敖包时,会添加一些石块或土块在上面,以示对神的尊敬;出远门时,则会到敖包上拾一块小石头带在身边,以求平安。

祭敖包大多选在水草丰茂的春秋季节。届时,区域内的蒙古族男女老少纷纷赶往指定的敖包去参加祭祀活动。人们给敖包插上树枝,在枝头悬挂经幡,并供上佛像和各种祭品,然后由喇嘛焚香点火,颂经念词。之后由参祭者围绕着敖包转上三圈,求神降福。

祭敖包除了用牲畜血祭,还有一种礼仪是玉祭,即以玉作为供品。不过现在一般不用玉,而是用硬币和炒米等物品代替。玉祭这一习俗进一步证明了蒙古牧民们对祭敖包的虔诚。他们把贵重物品献给天地诸神,以求神灵保佑他们过幸福安康的日子。祭祀结束后,即开始传统的娱乐活动。牧民们唱歌跳舞,尽情欢乐。青年男女则利用这一时机找寻意中人,所以有"敖包相会"这种说法。

10. Aobao-Worshipping Festival

The Aobao-Worshipping Festival, also known as the Ebo-Worshipping Festival or the Takele'en Festival, is a sacrifice offering folk festival of the Mongolian nationality in Inner Mongolia Autonomous Region. Aobao in the Mongolian language means a stone pile or bulging pile, which used to be a road sign or boundary marker. As time went by, it was vested with religious implication, and became a place for the Mongolian herdsmen to offer a sacrifice to the mountain god or road god.

Aobao is a sort of solid, conical pagoda, which is piled up with stones or adobes, wicker baskets of sand, or trees. On the top of the pagoda erects a wooden pole, over three meters in length, and on its top hang colored strips of cloth with lections on them. Embracing Shamanism, the early Mongolian people believed that Aobao was the residence of gods, and thus they were extremely pious in offering sacrifices to it. Aobao was usually erected near wide thoroughfares, or on hills with beautiful scenery. Ordinarily people passing by Aobao would pay homage to gods by adding some stones or lumps of earth to it. Before going on a long journey, they would take with them a little stone from Aobao in the hope that it would bring them safety.

Offering sacrifices to Aobao is often carried out in spring and autumn when there are luxuriant grasses and abundant water. Then the Mongolian people of the area, male and female, young and old, go to the appointed Aobao and join in the sacrificing. They insert twigs in the Aobao, hang flags with lections on them, lay out Buddha portraits and all sorts of offerings, and then lamas burn incense and chant sntras. Following this, people present at the sacrificing walk around Aobao three times, praying to gods for happiness.

Apart from sacrificing livestock to Aobao, another ritual is jade sacrificing, that is, jade being used as a sort of offering. However, nowadays, coins and parched rice are substituted for jade. The custom further proves the piety of the Mongolian people towards Aobao. They offer valuable goods to gods of heaven and land, praying that the deities will bring them happiness and health. Traditional amusements follow the end of offering sacrifices. The herdsmen dance and sing to their hearts' content. Young men and women take this opportunity to look for the partner of their heart. This is how Aobao meeting derives its name.

11. 开斋节

开斋节是伊斯兰教的三大节日之一。它在阿拉伯语中被叫做尔德·费特尔,在新疆地区则被称为肉孜节("肉孜"在波斯语中的意思是"开斋")。信仰伊斯兰教的回、维吾尔、哈萨克、乌孜别克、塔吉克、柯尔克孜、塔塔尔、东乡、撒拉和保安等民族在回历十月一日庆祝这个节日,节期三天。

回历的九月叫莱麦丹月,是伊斯兰教的斋月。相传《古兰经》就是在莱麦丹月传到世间成为穆斯林行动的指引。伊斯兰教规定,每个成年穆斯林每年斋戒一个月,这是他们应守的"五功"之一。"五功"分别指念功、礼功、课功、斋功和朝功。

9月初一晚上,只要新月出现,就进入为期29或30天的斋月。斋戒期间,除小孩、孕妇、旅行者和老弱病残者外,穆斯林不可在白天进食,也不可接触烟、酒、色等,他们在斋月里要抑制私欲、消除邪念,以示笃信真主安拉。

9月27日晚是盖德尔夜。据说先知穆罕默德就是在盖德尔夜见到真主传授的《古兰经》。经书上说,盖德尔夜的修行胜过一千个月。是夜,人们通宵礼拜、圆经、赞美真主。

到了29或30日,新月的出现宣告了斋月的圆满结束,第二天即行开斋,称开斋节。如果新月被云层遮住,斋期就顺延一至三天。

穆斯林很注重卫生。他们早早地将清真寺、街头巷尾和庭院等地方清扫干净,迎接开斋节的到来。节日那天,穆斯林先"大净",再穿上漂亮的新衣服去做礼拜。据圣典记载,穆罕默德也曾在沐浴更衣后率众去荒郊礼拜。

开斋节那天,男性穆斯林身着新衣,去清真寺或郊野礼拜,祭扫坟墓,并在当天拜亲访友。女性穆斯林多在随后几天去拜访亲友。回、东乡、撒拉等民族杀鸡宰羊、炸油香、馓子并拿出杏仁、水果、茶等款待客人;维吾尔族的穆斯林则备好葡萄干、蜂蜜、杏仁、奶茶等招待来客。年轻人聚在一起进行各式娱乐活动。许多青年还选定在节日期间举行婚礼。

11. Lesser Bairam

Lesser Bairam is known as Id-Al-Fitr in Arabic and Ruz Festival (the festival of Fast-breaking) in Persian. Muslims in the Xinjiang Uygur Autonomous Region celebrates it under the name of Ruz Festival. One of the three major Islamic festivals, it falls on the 1st day of the 10th month of the Islamic calendar and lasts 3 days. The festival is observed by the ethnic groups of the Hui, Uygur, Kazak, Uzbek, Tajik, Kirgiz, Tatar, Dongxiang, Salar, Bonan, etc., where Islam has a large following.

Ramadan, the 9th month of the Muslim year, is a holy month of fast. It is said that the Koran is revealed in this month as guidance for Muslims. The Muslim canons require that every Muslim adult fast in Ramadan. This is one of the five Pillars of Islam, the other four being Profession of faith, Salat (the daily ritual prayer), Alms tax and hajj (pilgrimage to Mecca).

The 29 or 30 days of fast begins when the crescent of the new moon is seen on the 1st night of Ramadan. Through the fast days, no food or water may be taken from sunrise to sunset. But children, pregnant women, travelers, the sick and the aged are exempt. Muslims must abstain from smoking, drinking and conjugal relations during the fasting hours. They are required to resist selfish desires and rid themselves of evil thoughts in this holy month to demonstrate their filial piety to Allah.

The 27th night of Ramadan is referred to as Al-Gadr. Since God revealed the Koran to the prophet Muhammad on this night, the Koran says that Muslims who cultivate themselves according to the Islamic canons that night benefit more than those who do the same for 1000 months in other times. As a result of this, Muslims spend the night repeating the prayers, reading the Koran and giving praise to God.

The appearance of the new moon on the 29th or the 30th of Ramadan marks the consummation of the fast and the beginning of the Lesser Bairam, which celebrates breaking of the fast. If the moon happens to be shadowed by clouds, the fast is to be prolonged one to three days.

Muslims are particular about sanitation and hygiene. They clean up mosques, streets and courtyards to usher in the Lesser Bairam. On the first day of the festival, they bathe themselves well, put on new and beautiful clothes and go for festival prayers. The practice traces so long back that some Islamic classics record that the prophet Muhammad once headed his followers to a field for special prayers after be took a bath and put on new clothes.

On the very first day of the festival, male Muslims, in their holiday best, go to the field or assemble in the mosque for special prayers. They visit the tombs of their kin and friends and call on each other to exchange holiday greetings. Female Muslims visit their friends and relatives in the following days. The Huis, Dongxiangs and Salars usually entertain their guests with such festival food as chicken, mutton, fried cakes, deep-fried dough sticks, almonds, fruit and tea. The Uygurs prepare for their guests raisins, honey, almond and milk tea. Young people of the nationalities give various festival performances and some of them favor the Lesser Bairam as their wedding day.

12. 古尔邦节

古尔邦节是伊斯兰教重要的传统节日,每年于伊斯兰教历的十二月十日开始庆祝,节期三天。居住在中国西北的新疆、青海、甘肃、宁夏等省区的维吾尔、哈萨克、回、乌孜别克、塔吉克、塔塔尔、柯尔克孜、撒拉、东乡、保安等信仰伊斯兰教的少数民族都过古尔邦节。

古尔邦节在阿拉伯语中称为"尔德古尔邦",也称"尔德艾祖哈","尔德"意为"节日","古尔邦"和"艾祖哈"则含有"宰牲"、"献牲"的意思,汉语通常取其义译作"宰牲节"、"献牲节"。

历史悠久的古尔邦节源于一个古老的阿拉伯传说。相传阿拉伯人的先知易卜拉欣于伊斯兰教历十二月十日夜里梦见真主安拉,启示他杀自己的儿子伊斯马依献祭,以表示对真主的忠诚。虔诚的易卜拉欣不愿违背安拉的命令,准备杀儿子献祭。当他杀儿子的时候,安拉被他的忠诚所感动,便立即派遣特使牵着一只黑绵羊匆匆赶到现场,让易卜拉欣以宰羊替代献子。为感激安拉的仁慈,从此在阿拉伯民族中逐渐形成了每年十二月十日宰牲献祭的古尔邦节。到7世纪穆罕默德创立伊斯兰教后,仍沿袭了这一风俗习惯,并把古尔邦节定为伊斯兰教的重要节日。

过节前夕，家家户户都要把房屋清扫干净，炸馓子、烤饼子、做蛋糕、宰杀牛羊。节日清晨穆斯林们就沐浴净身，严整衣冠，去清真寺参加会礼。在嘹亮、悦耳的乐曲声中穆斯林们互相握手、拥抱、问候、祝福。然后在教长（伊玛目）带领下诵着赞词步入礼拜大殿，举行节日会礼，观看宰牲仪式，听阿訇朗颂《古兰经》。礼毕家庭经济条件较好的一些人家要宰一只羊，有的要宰牛或骆驼。按照习惯，宰杀的牲畜肉不能出售，要按规定将部分送给清真寺和宗教职业人员，剩余部分用来赠送亲朋好友，并把骨头和血埋于地下，以防玷污。在节日里人们都要拜访亲友，馈赠礼品，主人则要按照传统礼节以丰盛宴席接待，宾主共享羊肉、油炸糕点和果品，并互相祝福，亲切交谈。青年男女们则在庭院或广场上载歌载舞，从白天到深夜，久久不愿离去。

中国新疆的维吾尔族要在城镇或乡村的广场上举行盛大的群众性文娱活动（即麦西来甫歌舞集会）。他们在广场的四周布满五彩缤纷的伞棚、布帐和夹板房，在里面陈设着各式各样的木桌、地毯、毛毯、方巾，上面放着花色品种繁多的小吃，如烤包子、烤羊肉串、炸馓子、凉粉、冷面，以及葡萄、核桃、石榴、桑葚、桃、杏等，这些可口的食物供参加节日活动的人们享用。群众性文娱活动的主要内容有"撒那"、"赛乃姆"和"多朗赛乃姆"等三种舞蹈。"撒那"是一种古老淳朴的男子集体舞，舞者身着各色民族服装，手拉手围成大圈小圈，腰间系着红绿三角围巾，随着舞步有规律有节奏地摆动，在清脆悦耳的鼓乐伴奏中不时齐声喊着"嘿！嘿！"声助兴。"赛乃姆"舞姿优美，富于抒情，是妇女们喜欢跳的舞。参加跳舞的维吾尔族妇女们戴着图案美丽色彩鲜艳的绣花帽，穿着丝绸裙和丝绒短坎肩，佩戴晶莹闪光的头饰，随着节奏多变的曲调欢歌起舞。"多朗赛乃姆"舞则是大型群体舞，男女老幼均可参加。其特点是具有典型的民族风格，以及形式多样的旋转和跳跃。

在节日期间，新疆的哈萨克、塔吉克、乌孜别克和柯尔克孜等民族还要举行叼羊、摔跤、赛马等比赛活动。在叼羊开始前，要由一位长者祈祷，参加叼羊比赛的人则骑在马背上向长者祝福。其后长者把一只小山羊放在预先指定的地点上，待号令枪一响，骑手们便催马飞奔去争夺小羊，夺得小羊的骑手在把小羊带到指定的地点之前，他将遇到其他骑手的奋力追赶、争夺。经过多次争夺后最终把小羊带到指定地点的骑手便是获胜者。那只小羊煮熟后的羊肉被称为"幸福肉"，供大家聚餐。

在古尔邦节日里，新疆的哈萨克族还有"姑娘追"的娱乐活动，为节日增添了极尽欢乐的气氛。"姑娘追"在哈萨克语中称为"克孜库瓦尔"，是男女青年们最喜爱的游戏，也是他们彼此表白爱情的一种特殊方式和良好机会。"姑娘追"开始时一对对男女骑马向指定的地点徐徐前进，小伙子对姑娘说着诙谐俏皮的话语或表示求爱，不论小伙子的话是否中听，姑娘都不能作任何反对的表示。到达指定地点返回时，小伙子骑马在前面跑，姑娘在后面拼命追。当姑娘追上小伙子时，如果对他不满意可以用鞭子抽打他，小伙子不得还手；如果姑娘对他有意，则只是晃几下鞭子，或象征性地轻轻抽几下。这时小伙子不再催马奔跑，双双倾吐爱慕之情。活动到此结束。

12 . Corban Festival

It is an important Muslim festival, which lasts three days from the 10th of the 12th month according to the Islam calendar. The festival is observed by the minority peoples of Uygur, Kazak, Hui, Uzbek, Tajik, Tartar, Kirgiz, Salar, Dongxiang and Bonan, all being Islamism believers who live in Xinjiang, Qinghai, Gansu and Ningxia in northwestern China.

The Corban Festival is known as Erde Corban or Erde Aizuha, spelt according to Arabic pronunciation. Here, "erde" means festival, "corban" means slaughtering sacrificial animals and "Aizuha" means offering sacrificial animals; hence the festival is also called Zai Sheng Jie (Festival of Slaughtering Sacrificial Animals) or Xian Sheng Jie (Festival of Offering Sacrificial Animals) in Chinese.

The time-honored festival derives from an Arab legend. According to the legend, Ibrahim, the Prophet of Arab people, dreamed on the 10th of the 12th month of the Islam calendar that Allab ordered him to kill his son as a sacrifice with the intention of testing his loyalty. Very devout, Ibrahim decided to do as he had been ordered. Just as he was about to kill his son, Allab, who was moved by his devoutness, had a black lamb sent to him and told him to kill it instead. From then, Arabs celebrated the Corban Festival on the 10th of the 12th month of the Islam calendar to express their gratitude to Allab for his kindness. The festival was made an important festival of Islam after the religion was founded by Mohammed in the 7th century, and is celebrated every year now.

Just before the festival all Muslim families sweep their houses, fry dough rings, toast pancakes and slaughter sheep or cattle, to mark the occasion. Early on each morning of the festival days Muslims bathe, dress neatly and go to mosques for services. When they meet there amid clarion and melodious music, they shake hands, embrace and exchange words. Then they follow an imam into the mosque hall while chanting along, where they are to hold the festive rite, watch the sacrificial animal slaughter and listen to the imam chanting Koran. After the rite, better-off families each slaughter a sheep, one head of cattle or a camel. The custom has it that part of the animal meat is to be offered to imams and other Muslim leaders, the rest is to be offered to relatives or friends, and the bones and blood are to be buried to keep them sacred.

During the festival Muslims usually visit their relatives or friends, presenting gifts, while the hosts treat them to mutton, deep-fried cakes, and fruit. Both parties cordially exchange blessings while they take the foods. Young Muslims sing and dance in courtyards or on grounds, late into night.

Xinjiang's Uygurs particularly hold grand entertainments on grounds in both urban and rural areas. They set up around a ground colored canopies, cloth tents and wooden board sheds. Under the canopies, and in the tents and sheds are wooden desks, or spread carpets, woolen blankets and kerchiefs; displayed on them are various refreshments, such as roasted stuffed buns, shashliks, deep-fried dough rings, bean jelly, cool noodles, grapes, walnuts, pomegranates, mulberries, peaches, apricots, and so on. All these foods are for holidaymakers. The entertainments are, in the main, three ethnic dances, which are named sala, sailem and duolang-sailem in the local language pronunciation. The sala is an old group dance for men; the dancers, in different-sized rings, wearing colored costumes and red-green-striped triangular aprons, hand in hand, make rhythmical movements now to the left and now to the right, while shouting "Hey! Hey!" to melodious drumbeats and other musical strains. The sailem is a graceful and lyric dance, mainly performed by female; the dancers dance to varied musical strains, wearing colorful embroidered hats, silk jackets, silk skirts and glistening head ornaments. The doulangsailem is a group dance; it is performed by any people, men or women, old or young, and featured by distinctive Uygur flavor, of varied whirling or leaping movements.

During the festival, Xinjiang's Kazaks, Tajiks, Uzbeks and Kirgizs usually offer sports, such as goat wresting, wrestling and horse racing. Before the goat wresting begins, a venerable elder prays for the success of competitors while the competitors on horseback give their blessings to the elder. Then the elder places a small goat at an appointed spot. On the crack of a starting gun, the goat wresters whip their horses ahead for the animal. The one, who has seized the goat, has other competitors behind trying to wrest away the goat. The winner is the one who reaches the appointed spot, with the goat in hand. And the winner would treat all competitors to the mutton, known as the mutton of happiness.

Xinjiang's Kazak people offers another entertainment known as guniangzhui in Chinese or kezikuwaer in the Kazak language, meaning a girl pursues a boy. It lends much joy to the festival and is most favored by young people as it provides good chances for them to express love. In the first half of the entertainment, young men and girls on horseback ride abreast towards an appointed spot, slowly and in male-female pairs. While moving on, the young man would make witty remarks to the girl or say courting words to her, and the girl must not act anyway to express her opposition. After they have reached the spot, the young man gallops back fast and the girl runs on horseback after him at full speed. The girl, who has caught up with him, may whip the man if she will not give her heart to him, and he must not whip back; the girl, if she takes a fancy to the man, just pretends to whip or gently whips him. In the latter case, the young man would stop galloping so as to have more talks about love.

13. 诺劳孜节

诺劳孜节是新疆柯尔克孜族人民的传统节日,于每年春季白羊星在天空正南方第一次出现的第二天过节,这一天是柯尔克孜族太阳历的元月初一,因此诺劳孜节即是柯尔克孜族人民的新年,大约在公历的三月二十二日前后。

"诺劳孜"一词来自古伊朗语,意为"春雨日"。柯尔克孜族人民选定这一天过诺劳孜节的原因与他们的祖先信仰原始的萨满教有关。他们的祖先认为天神是万物之主,太阳是人类的主父,月亮是主母,星神是掌握人类命运的主神,其中的白羊星是造福于人类的主神之一,它让太阳调节气温和季节,使大地解冻,万物复苏,草木萌发,羊群产羔;而双鱼星则是使人遭灾遇祸的根源。因此柯尔克孜族人民就在双鱼星降落消灾,白羊星升起得福的第二天举行祭奠仪式,向祖先和神灵供献祭品,欢度新年。

在节日那天,柯尔克孜族的男女老少都要穿上华丽的民族服装,举行形式多样的节日活动。

依照柯尔克孜族人的传统习惯,把一天分为黎明更、日出更、午时更、日落更、星现更、午夜更等六个时辰,节日仪式从黎明更开始举行。黎明更时分一到,各家的家长首先起床,穿戴完毕后在堂屋的正中位置处点燃一堆松柏树枝,并手持冒着烟的松柏枝在每个人的头上转一圈，预祝他们在新的一年里平安无事，生活愉快。最后再把冒着烟的松柏枝带到畜圈门口，赶着牲畜在烟上通过，以祈求牲畜兴旺，膘肥体壮。在他们信仰伊斯兰教之后，在诺劳孜节的此时又增加了念《古兰经》的内容，其用意仍为祝福人畜两旺。有些地区的柯尔克孜族人的每家门前用芨芨草生一堆火，首先让家里的男孩和女孩，其次是成年的男人和女人，——从火堆上跳过，最后再赶着全家的牲畜也从火堆上跳过，其用意也是为人畜消灾除祸，平安度过新的一年。

日出更以后各家都要杀一只羊。然后做"诺劳孜"饭，即新年饭。其做法是把炒熟去皮的小麦和大麦加上牛羊肉等七种以上的食品煮成粥，再加上盐、葱和各种野生调味佐料。柯尔克孜族人把这种类似汉族人的"腊八粥"的饭称为"克缺"或"冲克缺"，意为丰盛粥。做这种饭要用往年剩余的陈粮食和其他食物，而且要求做得很丰盛。吃克缺饭不仅是为了祈求在新的一年里兴旺平安，也是对家庭生活水平和家庭主妇烹调技艺的检验。

从午时更起，柯尔克孜族人们成群结伴地骑着马互相去各家各户拜年。然后汇集在草滩、平地或广场上，举行赛马、马上取物、打靶、叼羊、摔跤、拔河、捉迷藏、荡秋千、唱歌、跳舞等娱乐活动。人人都发挥各自的一技之长，尽兴游玩，欢悦至极。

到日落更畜群归来进圈前，每家的毡房前再次用芨芨草生一堆火，首先由全家人从火堆上跳过去，然后再赶着畜群跳火堆，再次表示祈求消灾除祸，祝福人畜两旺。这时各家都要请客吃饭，互相做客。饭后男女老少分别举行跳舞、唱歌等活动。在柯尔克孜族乐器"考姆兹(三弦琴)"、"克雅克(拉琴)"、"却奥尔(牧笛)"等的伴奏声中,演唱优美动听而又极富民族特点的"诺劳孜歌",其大意是:驱走了缠身的魔鬼,迎接新的一年来临,共同祝福我们月月都顺利,全年都平安。

13. Nuolaozi Festival

The Nuolaozi Festival is a traditional festival celebrated by the Khalkhas people in the Xinjiang Uygur Autonomous Region. It falls on the day after the Aries first rises in the due south sky in spring. The day was made the first day of the first month of the Khalkhas calendar, coinciding with March 22 by the Gregorian calendar, and hence is observed as New Year's Day by the Khalkhases.

Nuolaozi originates from an archaic Iran expression which means "spring rain day" literally. The Khalkhases' ancestors chose this day as their New Year's Day because they believed in a primitive religion named Saman. According to the religion, the Heavenly God was the supreme ruler of the universe, the sun was the father of human beings, the moon was the mother of human beings, and the stars decided human beings' destiny. The Aries, one of the stars bringing benefits to mankind, is said to help the sun speed up the coming of spring by regulating temperature, thus promoting the land to thaw, plants to sprout, sheep to produce lambs and all other living things on earth to revive. Hence the Khalkhases observe their New Year's Day and offer sacrifices to their ancestors and gods on the day when the Pisces, said to be a source of disasters or misfortunes, sets and the Aries rises.

On the festival day the Khalkhases, men and women, old and young, in gorgeous ethnic costumes, take part in different festivities.

According to the traditional Khalkhas way of counting time a day is divided into six periods successively named the dawn watch, sunrise watch, midday watch, sunset watch, star-rise watch, and midnight watch. The festive ceremony begins when the dawn watch comes in. According to the ceremonial practice, the head of a family gets up before all others at daybreak; then he lights a pile of pine twigs or cypress twigs placed at the center of the main hall and waves a smoking pine twig or cypress twig around the head of each family member once, an expression to wish them safe and happy in the new year; finally, he puts the smoking twig on the ground before the corral and leads his domestic animals to cross the twig, an emblem to pray for thriving, plump and sturdy herds. The Khalkhases chant the Koran as an additional item of the festivity after they began to believe in Islam. The Khalkhas families in some parts of Xinjiang, on the occasion, each build a fire of splendid achnatherum before their houses instead of the fire at the center of the main hall; then all family members successively jump over the fire; finally domestic animals are led to cross it. Both embody the wish to ward off misfortunes and disasters.

When the sunrise watch begins, every Khalkhas family slaughters a sheep for the Nadun porridge, also known as New Year porridge. It is a kind of assorted porridge made of parched barley, parched wheat, beef, mutton, and so on, which is spiced by salt, chopped green onion and some wild condiments. The porridge is called keque or chongkeque in the local language, both meaning sumptuous porridge, which is something like the Han people's laba porridge (rice porridge with beans, nuts and dried fruit eaten on the 8th day of the 12th lunar month). It should have cereals from past reserve and other things as its ingredients and be sumptuous. The Khalkhases eat the festive porridge not only to pray for a prosperous and safe year to come, but also to demonstrate a family's well-to-do life and the mistress's good cookery.

When the midday watch comes in, the Khalkhas holidaymakers go, on horseback and in groups, to pay New Year calls to their neighbors. Some time later, they gather on a grass flat, or a ground, to take part in entertainments, such as horse racing, picking up objects on the ground from horseback, shooting, sheep wresting, tug of war, hide-and-seek, playing on swings, singing, dancing and so on. Every participant gives full play to his skill in a particular line and enjoys himself to his heart's content.

When herds come back to the corral at the start of the sunset watch, every household makes a fire of splendid achnatherum in front of its yurt; all its members jump over the fire and its domestic animals are led to cross it, both also to symbolize warding off misfortune and disaster, and to express the hope for thriving herds in the coming year. Then all households entertain each other to dinners; after dinner, they all gather to sing and dance to the accompaniment of the kaomuzi (a Khalkhas three-stringed plucked instrument), keyake (a Khalkhas two-stringed instrument) and queao'er (a Khalkhases flute). The most beautiful and Khalkhas-flavored is "The Song of the Nuolaozi Festival", whose gist goes that we all sing to wish for happiness and safety in the coming year after we have driven off evil spirits.

14.花儿会

　　花儿会是青海、甘肃、宁夏一带土、回、撒拉、东乡、保安等民族传统的节日。花儿会常与当地的庙会以及朝山活动连在一起,各地举办花儿会的时间并不统一,但大都在春、夏季节。届时,成千上万不同民族的人们从四面八方赶赴花儿会,在花儿会上纵情歌唱。

　　花儿是一种典型的民歌,其内容以抒发年轻人的感情为主。因为在唱情歌时,女孩被称作"花儿",男孩被称作"少年",遂以"花儿"或"少年"代称这种民歌。

　　花儿由句、令、调组成。句是一个完整意思的语言表达,花儿通常有三至六句组成,前两句起比兴作用,后几句切入正题。令是花儿的曲名,花儿的令多达两百多种。有以内容命名的,如红花令;有以民族命名的,如撒拉令;还有以地区命名的,如河州令。调指花儿的旋律曲谱,花儿的调式多为商调式和徵调式。

　　民族不同,地区不同,演唱花儿的形式和风格也有所不同。像受藏族民歌影响的撒拉花儿,普遍带有颤音;以歌舞著称的土族人唱的花儿则旋律独特优美,节奏感极强。

　　花儿持续三至六天。花儿多为即兴演唱,故有很强的竞赛性。花儿会上,花儿爱好者们自动组成歌摊,先在歌摊内比唱花儿,然后由各歌摊涌现出的优秀歌手进行比赛,角逐"案首"(第一名)。对花儿歌手来说,能荣获"案首"是莫大的荣耀。但在组歌摊时,要注意"躲唱",即年轻人不能与长辈同在一组。只有当长辈不在同一组时,才能随心所欲地唱花儿。

关于花儿会的由来,各地说法不一。一些著名的花儿会,如农历二月初二的青海互助县雷台花儿会、四月二十八的甘肃夏松鸣岩花儿会、五月十七的甘肃岷县二郎山花儿会、六月初六的青海互助五峰山花儿会、六月初一至初六的甘肃康乐莲花山花儿会等都有各自关于花儿会的传说。著名的莲花山花儿会流传着一个动人的民间故事,相传仙人广成子带着莲花仙女通过甘肃康乐县时,莲花仙女爱上了当地的一位青年,广成子大怒,将莲花仙女变成了一座山。人们被莲花仙女的真情感动了,决定为她建一座庙。六月初一庙成之时,从莲花山上冉冉升起了一对青年男女,女的手持莲花,男的手摆彩扇,两人唱着动听的花儿。一阵风过,吹落了莲叶,他俩便以"花呀,莲叶儿"作为花儿的尾声。于是,持花摆扇,以"花呀,莲叶儿"作词尾就传为习俗了。

通往莲花山的路上有人拉起绳子拦路问歌,答得上的方可通过。花儿会上最精彩的是花儿对唱。对唱在五至八人的班子间进行,各班子间一唱一和,一问一答。每个班子设有一名指挥,负责提问和答唱,答唱必须紧扣主题,否则会被嘲笑。花儿会上的优胜者叫"花儿把势"。花儿会期间,商贸会等活动的举行使参加花儿会的群众多达五六万人。

14. Hua'er Festival

Hua'er (flower) Festival has been celebrated for generations among the Tus, Huis, Salars, DongXiangs and Bonans in Qinghai and Gansu provinces and the Ningxia Hui Autonomous Region. As the festival joins the local temple fair and pilgrimage, the celebration time varies from place to place, but mostly in spring and summer. At the festival, thousands upon thousands of people come to the fair from all directions and sing their fill.

The "Hua'er" is sung in a typical folk tune and mainly expresses the emotions of young people. Girls are addressed as Hua'er and boys Shaonian (youth) in those love songs. Hence the name of the folk tune Hua'er or Shaonian.

The Hua'er is marked by rhymed lines, tune and tone. A line is an expression of a full meaning. The Hua'er usually consists of 3 to 6 lines with the 1st two functioning as a metaphor and the rest revealing the subject matter. Tune means the tune names of the Hua'er. Of the existing 200 – odd tune names, some are named in accordance with subject matters, like the Tune of Red Flowers, others after nationalities, such as the Tune of Salar, and still others after places, like the Tune of Hezhou. Tone refers to the melodious notation of the Hua'er, which falls on the 2nd and the 4th scale among the 5 scales of ancient Chinese music.

In different nationalities and regions, the performance style and form are different. For instance, the Salar Hua'er is presented with a sweet trill tone under the influence of the Tibetan folk songs, while the Tu people, who are renowned for their singing and dancing, sing the Hua'er with beautiful and peculiar melodies and accented rhythms.

The festival lasts 3 to 6 days. The Hua'er is in most cases sung impromptu. Consequently, it promotes competition. The Hua'er singers form singing groups voluntarily. Top candidates will stand out after some time of singing inside the groups. The singing contest is thereafter carried out among those outstanding singers striving for the title of Anshou, the 1st place in the contest. To a Hua'er singer, it is great honor to be entitled the Anshou. While forming a singing group, it is a taboo for the young Tu people and their elders to sing in the same group. Only when there are no elders in the same group, can the young people sing freely.

There are different versions about the origin of the festival. Some renowned Hua'er Festivals have their own legends, say, the Leitai Hua'er Festival in Huzhu County of Qinghai held on the 2nd day of the 2nd lunar month, the Songmingyan Hua'er Festival in Linxia County of Gansu held on the 28th of the 4th lunar month, Mount Erlang Hua'er Festival in Min County of Gansu celebrated on the 17th day of the 5th lunar month, Mount Wufeng Hua'er Festival in Huzhu County of Qinghai celebrated on the 6th day of the 6th lunar month, and Mount Lotus Hua'er Festival in Kangle County of Gansu observed from the 1st to the 6th of the 6th lunar month. The story of Mount Lotus Hua'er Festival goes around that when Lotus the fairy passed Kangle County with Guang Chengzi the celestial being, she fell in love with a local young man. In his fury, Guang Chengzi changed the fairy into a mountain. Deeply moved, people built a temple in memory of her infatuation. The 1st of the 6th lunar month, the day of the completion of the temple, saw a young couple rising from the mountain. With lotus in the woman's hand and a colored fan in the man's, the couple were singing the Hua'er. A gust of wind blew down the lotus leaf, the couple therefore ended off their Hua'er with "Oh flower, the lotus leaf ". The later people sing as the couple did, lotus bloom and colored fan in hand.

On the way to Mount Lotus, a rope is set across to stop a passer-by and invite him to answer the Hua'er. Unless he sings in reply, they won't let him go. The competition of singing Hua'er in a dialogue style is the highlight of the festival. The contest is carried out between groups, each consisting of 5 to 8 people. The groups echo each other, raising and answering questions by singing. In each group a conductor is designated to be in charge of raising and answering questions. He must strictly relate the answering Hua'er to the subject matter, or the group led by him will be sneered at. Winners at the festival are entitled master Hua'er singers. Trade fairs are held during the festival, which may draw as many as 40 to 50 thousand people.

15. 藏历年

　　藏历 12 月 29 日至 1 月 15 日是藏族同胞欢庆藏历年的日子。藏历已有千年的历史,虽曾受汉族和其他民族的影响,却依然保持着自身的特色。藏历一年有十二月份,分四季,依次为冬、春、夏、秋;并以木、火、土、金、水等五行替代汉历的十天干,以鼠、牛、虎、兔、龙、蛇、马、羊、猴、鸡、狗、猪等十二生肖替代十二地支。

　　按照惯例,各藏民家从 12 月中旬就开始为节日准备酥油、奶茶、酥油茶、羊肉等食品。12 月 29 日晚,各户都做大扫除并把垃圾倒在十字路口,意在将危害家人幸福安康的脏东西一起倒掉。当晚他们吃一种名叫"古突",或叫"土粑"的面食,并把石头、羊毛、木炭、辣椒等包在"古突"里预测家人在新年的情况:吃到石头的人,新年里心硬如石,吃到羊毛的心软,吃到木炭的心黑,吃到辣椒的嘴辣,如此等等。家里的每个人都要吃上九碗年饭,而且每碗要有剩,并将剩余物倒入盆里。晚饭后就端上这只盆,举着火把查看各房间。这在旧时叫"驱鬼",其实是检查房间的清洁和布置情况。除夕夜里,人们打扫庭院,给地面洒水,在门窗上悬挂色彩绚丽的香布,在桌上放置"切玛"、羊头、青稞酒和水果等。"切玛"是木制五谷斗,木板上刻着花、象牙、宝石等图案。节日期间,须往"切玛"里装入酥油糌粑、炒麦粒、炒蚕豆之类的东西,并在上面插上青稞穗。藏族同胞以这种方式表达他们祈祷五谷丰登、人畜两旺的良好心愿。

藏历正月初一,天还没亮,藏民就在房顶燃起松脂,放上染色的青稞和麦穗,以求来年富足如意。妇女们早早起床去河边背回一桶"吉祥水",其他尚未起床的人就在床上等着用"吉祥水"洗脸。洗过脸,喂过牲口后,全家穿上新衣:男人们穿崭新的藏袍和藏靴;女人们系艳丽的"帮典"(围裙),戴缀有珊瑚、玛瑙和珍珠的头饰。母亲把"切玛"端到家人前,让每人取食一点糌粑并互道"扎西德勒"(万事如意)和"格莎尔桑"(新年好)。这一天不能外出访客,全家聚在一起享用节日食品。

新年的第二天,人们开始到亲朋好友家串门拜访。客人向主人道声"扎西德勒",主人则回应一声"格莎尔桑";客人从主人端来的"切玛"中抓出少许糌粑粉洒向空中,反复三次后,才拈少许吃下;主人随后给客人敬上一杯青稞酒,客人以无名指在酒里蘸三下,弹向空中,然后分三口喝完这杯酒;关系亲密的朋友间要敬献哈达——一种色彩多样的半透明绫罗织品,多为纯白色,长可达六、七米,宽三、四米,哈达越长,敬意越深。礼仪结束后,主客可尽情地饮酒、进餐、叙谈、唱歌和跳舞。藏民喜欢跳欢快的踢踏舞(藏语叫"堆谐")以及"锅庄"和"弦子"舞。跳踢踏舞时,舞者随音乐的节奏踏地顿足;"锅庄"舞因人们最初是围着灶塘跳这种舞而得名;"弦子"舞则源于藏族独特的民族乐器——弦子(藏语叫"白旺")。

藏历年间,有的地方要举行赛马、摔跤、射箭、赛牦牛、拔河和民歌赛等活动。傍晚时分,人们燃起篝火,狂欢到深夜。1月15日后,藏历年宣告结束。

15. Tibetan New Year

The Tibetan New Year is celebrated from December 29 through January 15 by the Tibetan calendar. The calendar, with a history of 1000-odd years, has retained its peculiarities although it was greatly influenced by the Han and other nationalities. According to the calendar, a year is divided into 12 months in four seasons, which go in the order of winter, spring, summer, and autumn. The Tibetans designate the years by the five elements (wood, fire, earth, metal, water) or by the 12 animals (rat, ox, tiger, hare, dragon, snake, horse, sheep, monkey, cock, dog and hog), unlike the Hans who do that by the 10 Heavenly Stems and the 12 Earthly Branches.

Traditionally all Tibetan families start, in the middle of December, to prepare butter, milk tea, buttered tea, Qingke wine, mutton and some other holiday food. On the night of December 29, they do a thorough cleaning and dump all the waste at crossroads, believing that the dirty things harmful to the health and happiness of the family members are thrown away with it. Also on that night, they eat Gutu (or Tuba), a kind of flour food. The dumplings of Gutu contain surprising objects like stones, wool, charcoal, chili, etc. He who happens to have Gutu with stones will be seen stonehearted in the year to come; with wool, kind-hearted; with charcoal, cruel-hearted; with chili, sharp-tongued. At the dinner on that night, each family member should have 9 bowls of food, and each bowl must contain some leftovers, which are to be put into a basin. After dinner, the family, with the illumination of a torch, holds the basin and inspects every room. This custom was known as driving-away-ghosts, which is actually a check of the cleaning and decoration of rooms. On New Year's eve, the family clean up their courtyard and spray water on it. They adorn the doors and windows with colorful fragrant cloth, and display on a table a Qiema (a container), a sheep head, Qingke wine, fruit, etc. Qiema is a kind of rectangular wooden container engraved with the design of flowers, tusks, jewels and so on. During the festival, Qiema is fully loaded with buttered Zanba, roasted wheat, roasted broad bean and the like, into which ears of Qingke barley are planted. In this way, the Tibetans express their wishes for flourish of crops and fecundity of men and livestock in the new year.

Before daybreak on Tibetan New Year's Day, people burn pine rosin and place dyed Qingke barley and ears of wheat on the roof, a wish for a prosperous new year. Women get up early to carry home buckets of auspicious water from the river. The other family members stay in bed, waiting to wash their faces with the water. This done and livestock fed, men put on new Tibetan robes and boots while women are dressed with colorful Bangdian (that is, aprons), and headdress dotted with corals, agates and pearls. The mother of the family then places the Qiema before everyone and each takes a little Zanba out of it while saying prayers like Zhaxidele (all the best) and Geshaersang (Happy New Year). Visits not allowed, all the family members stay home and enjoy holiday food and drinks.

On the 2nd day of the New Year, relatives and friends visit each other. A visitor greets a host by saying Zhaxidele, while the host says Geshaersang as a reply. The visitor takes a fistful of Zanba powder out of a Qiema carried by the host and scatters it in the air. He repeats this three times and eats the fourth fistful. He is then offered a glass of Qingke wine and is supposed to drink it up in three mouthfuls after he dips his ring finger three times in the wine and flicks it in the air. Among very close friends, Hadas, a kind of semi – transparent, colorful damask silk, are presented. The most commonly seen ones are pure white. Some Hadas are 6 or 7 meters long and 3 or 4 meters wide. The longer the Hada, the more respectable the receiver. After all the etiquette, the host and the guest are free to drink, eat, chat, sing and dance. They love to dance a cheerful tap dance known as Duixie in the Tibetan language. In the dance, dancers tap their feet on the floor to the music rhythms. Guozhuang dance and Xuanzi dance are also very popular. The former originated from people's dancing around a cooking stove, while the latter earned its name from a unique Tibetan musical instrument: Xuanzi (in Tibetan language Baiwang), a 3-stringed plucked instrument.

In some places, people celebrate the festival by holding activities like horse racing, wrestling, archery, yak racing, tug-of-war, and folk song competition. In the evening people make bonfires and revel late into night. After January 15, the Tibetan New Year comes to an end.

16. 旺果节

旺果节又称"望果节"或"丰收果",是西藏自治区藏族人民预祝丰收的传统农祀节日。"旺"在藏语中指"田地","果"的意思是"转圈"。"旺果",即"转地头"之意。过去一般是在大雁南飞的季节到来之前庆祝该节,现在则是各藏区根据农事安排来确定具体时间,由于是预祝丰收的节日,故大都选在秋季青稞麦成熟之际,即藏历七月举行,节期三至五天。

旺果节距今已有1500多年的历史。据《笨教历算法》等藏族文献记载,早在公元五世纪末,雅砻一带就已经兴修水利,开始用犁耕地,农业生产比较发达。但是,面对风、霜、雹、雪、旱、虫等自然灾害,人们无能为力,只能求助于神灵。为了确保粮食丰收,笨教教主根据教义,教村民们在青稞麦穗成熟之前,举行"旺果"仪式。仪式上,人们以村寨为单位,在教主的带领下,手捧香炉,举着经幡,手拿青稞麦穗,绕田间地头转圈,求神灵保佑庄稼丰收。仪式后还开展角斗、斗剑、耍梭镖等娱乐活动。14世纪末,佛教的格鲁派(俗称黄教)成为西藏的主要教派,掌握了地方实权。受其影响,旺果节的内容发生了变化。绕田间地头转圈时,改为手举佛像,背诵喇嘛教经文,求佛保佑农业丰收。仪式后,还增设了赛马、射箭、演藏戏等娱乐活动,使节日内容越来越丰富,成为仅次于藏历年的传统节日。

解放后,旺果节的规模更加宏大。届时,各村寨的村民们都换上节日的盛装。人们打着各色彩旗,举着青稞穗,抬着用青稞、麦穗扎成的系有洁白哈达的"丰收塔",手擎标语,举着经幡、佛像,敲锣打鼓,载歌载舞地绕着田间地头转圈,一派热闹景象。

转地头的仪式结束后,欢乐的人们携带帐篷、青稞酒、酥油茶等涌向林卡,饮酒喝茶,谈笑风生。节日期间,有的地方还举办赛马、射箭、赛牦牛、演藏戏和跳踢踏舞等传统娱乐活动。

16. Wangguo (Ongkor) Festival

The Wangguo (Ongkor) Festival, also known as the Bumper Harvest Festival, is a traditional sacrifice offering day, which the Tibetan people in the Tibet Autonomous Region celebrate to anticipate a bumper harvest. In the Tibetan language wang (Ong) means field or land and guo (kor) circling or walking around. So Wangguo (Ongkor) is walking around the fields. The Wangguo Festival used to be observed before the season when geese fly to the south. Nowadays it is fixed in accordance with the farming arrangements in different parts of the region. An occasion to expect a good harvest, it is usually celebrated in autumn when barley is ready to get in, that is, the 7th month of the Tibetan calendar. The celebration lasts three to five days.

The Wangguo Festival has a history of over 1500 years. The records in the chronicle of the Bon Religion show that as early as the end of the fifth century people in the area of Yalong began to construct irrigation works and plough the land, reaching a relatively advanced level of farming. However, in the face of such natural calamities as windstorm, frost, hail, snow, drought and pests, people could do nothing but pray to gods. To ensure a bumper harvest, the hierarch of the Bon religion summoned the villagers to observe the Wangguo ritual before the ripening of barley. Led by the hierarch and with incense burners, flags and barley ears in hands, people from the same village as a unit walked around the fields, praying to gods for a bumper harvest in the ritual. Afterwards other entertainments like wrestling, fencing and dart – throwing were carried out. At the end of the 14th century the Gelugopa (Yellow) sect of the Tibetan Buddhism came to power. Consequently some changes were made to the Wangguo Festival. When people circled the fields, they held portraits of Buddha in hands and chanted the sutras of Lamaism, praying to Buddha for a bumper harvest. After the ritual horse racing, archery contests, Tibetan operas, et cetera, were added to the repertoire of the festivities, which made the festival only second to the Tibetan New Year in significance.

After the liberation of Tibet, the Wangguo Festival becomes even grander. Holding multicolor banners, barley ears, slogans and Buddha portraits, carrying on shoulders a Bumper Harvest Tower made from barley and barley ears and dressed up with white Hada (a piece of silk used as a greeting gift, etc.), people from different villages, clad in festal attire, play the gong and drum and dance around the fields merrily.

After the ritual of circling the fields, the cheerful people, bringing along tents, barley wine and buttered tea, stream into woods to drink and enjoy themselves. In the course of the festival, some traditional amusements are performed in parts of the region such as horse racing, archery competition, yak racing, Tibetan opera and tap dance.

17. 火把节

　　火把节是中国西南地区彝、白、傈僳、纳西、普米、哈尼等少数民族的传统节日,农历六月二十四日前后举行。

　　节日这天,在云南大理的彝族和白族村寨里,村村都要做一枝宝塔状的大火把。火把由干柴和松枝层层包裹而成。村民们还在自家门前立起一枝枝小火把。黄昏时分,他们带上小火把,聚在大火把周围,等待着点燃火把那一激动人心的时刻到来。点燃火把后,人们高举小火把,绕着房屋转悠,那些燃烧的火把使黑夜亮如白昼。之后,人们聚到篝火旁,歌舞饮酒,通宵达旦,预祝来年好收成。

　　当地还有火把节泼火的习俗。人们在袋里装满松脂,追逐泼火。迎面碰上行人时,他们就从袋里抓出一把松脂粉洒在火把上,火苗遇上松脂,"呼"地冒出一团火焰。据说这样能驱邪除病,当地人称为"泼火祝福"。

　　有些地方的彝族人要举行宗教活动,彝民们宰杀猪牛鸡等献祭神灵。

　　摔跤也是庆祝火把节的一项重要活动。在鼓乐和音乐声中,摔跤手们赤膊上阵,获胜者往往成为姑娘们理想的择偶对象。

　　云南纳西族的火把节为期三天。第一天,主妇们准备节日食品,男人们制作火把。第二天,人们白天串门互访;晚上则举着火把在田间地头走动,意在为庄稼照明、驱赶虫害。第三天的庆祝活动最盛大。是日,人们用火把烧掉屋内蜘蛛网之类的污秽东西,意在驱邪除害,祈祷来年丰收;晚上,村民们围着大火把歌唱跳舞。哈尼人将各类水果用彩线挂在火把上,待火烧断彩线,水果就会掉下来。哈尼人认为,火把上掉下来的果子能给人带来好运,因此,在场的每个人都争抢落下的果子。

　　四川凉山一带的傈僳人在火把节举行群众性的火把游行,人们高举火把,在田间地头漫游。

　　民间流传着各种有关火把节起源的传说。白族人认为火把节与公元8世纪时发生在奴隶制国家"南诏"的悲剧有关。南诏国王皮罗阁野心勃勃,要征服云南的其他五个王国。他设下一计,邀约五国的首领前来他新建的松明楼开会。登睒国王的妻子慈善夫人竭力阻止丈夫赴约,但登睒国王执意前往,她只好在丈夫临出发前给他戴上一只铁手镯。不久,传来登睒国王与其他四个国王在松明楼被焚的消息,慈善夫人赶往松明楼,凭着铁手镯,认出了丈夫的遗骸。皮罗阁被她的美貌和智慧打动,要娶她为妻。但慈善夫人埋葬丈夫后就命人关闭城门,绝食身亡。为了纪念她,白族人民把6月25日定为火把节。又因为慈善夫人曾用双手在松明楼的灰烬中搜寻丈夫的遗骸,白族妇女在节日期间采集凤仙花染指甲来纪念她。彝族庆祝这个节日则是为了纪念摔跤英雄额其拉巴战胜天神。据说额其拉巴是摔跤能手,且天下无敌,连天神派来的比赛者都被他打败了。天神一怒之下,放出万千害虫下界糟蹋老百姓的庄稼。额其拉巴带领彝族人民制作松枝火把,并带领众人高举火把,先绕田走一圈,再将火把插在田埂上诱杀害虫,从而使那年的庄稼获得丰收。从那以后,彝民们每年都在6月举行火把节以示庆贺。

其实各少数民族的祖先庆祝火把节是出于对火的原始崇拜和对庄稼丰收的期盼。便是今天,虽然节日里有摔跤、赛马、斗牛、秋千和射箭等活动,但是"举火把、烧天虫、盼丰收"仍是火把节的一项重要内容。

17. Torch Festival

Torch Festival, a traditional festival of the Yi, Bai, Lisu, Na xi, Pumi, Hani and some other minority nationalities inhabiting southwest China, falls around the 24th of the 6th lunar month.

On the day of the festival, the Yis and Bais of the Dali Bai Autonomous Prefecture in Yunnan Province would build in villages big, pagoda-shaped pine torches wrapped up with layers of dried firewood and pine branches. In addition, there stand small torches at the doorway of every household. At dusk, carrying small torches, villagers gather around a big torch and wait for the exciting moment to come when the big torch is lit. Then, holding their flaming torches high, the villagers walk around their houses and fields. The flaming torches make the night a bright day. People then meet at a bonfire, singing, dancing or drinking through the night in the hope of bountiful crops in the coming year.

Flame spreading is another local custom to observe the festival. People run after one another and spread flames. Whomever they encounter, they will take a handful of rosin powder out of the bags they carry and spread it into the fire. Once the rosin powder meets the fire, it bursts into flames. This is said to help them avert and get rid of evil spirits and diseases. It is locally called blessing one by flame spreading.

The Yis in some places carry out religious activities, and they sacrifice pigs, cattle, roosters and the like to the god on the day of the festival.

Wrestling is an important activity celebrating the festival. To the accompaniment of drumming and music, wrestlers go into battle barebacked. Winners in the contest are very likely to be chosen by maids as candidates for their spouses.

The festival lasts three days to the Naxis in Yunnan Province. On the 1st day, housewives prepare holiday food while men make torches. On the 2nd day, people visit each other in the daytime. When night falls, holding flaming torches, they walk around the fields to illuminate the crops and drive away vermins. Celebrations on the 3rd day are the grandest. On this day, spider webs and some other filthy things inside a house are burnt off, a sign of warding off ill luck and evils, and a prayer for a smooth and healthy year. At dusk all villagers sing and dance around a huge lit torch. The Hanis like hanging on a torch various fruits with colorful threads. When the threads are burnt, the fruits fall. According to the Hanis, luck is with those who catch any of the fruits. As a result, every one strives for them.

On the day of the festival, holding torches aloft, the Lisu people of Liangshan Yi Autonomous Prefecture in Sichuan Province would stroll around the fields and enjoy mass torch parade.

There are various legendary stories about the origin of the festival. The Bais associate it with a tragedy that happened in the slave state of Nanzhao in the 8th century. Piluoge, King of Nanzhao, burned with conquering the other five states in Yunnan Province. He designed a scheme, and whereby invited the five kings to meet at the Songming Building he newly built. Lady Cishan, Queen of the Dengdan State, having failed to persuade her husband from going, put an iron bracelet on his arm at his departure. Before long, Dengdan King, together with the other four kings, was burnt to death at the Songming Building. At the news, Lady Cichan hastened to the site and recognized her husband by the iron bracelet. Impressed by her beauty and wit, Piluoge yearned to marry her. Lady Cishan, however, having buried her husband, had the gate of Dengdan city closed and starved herself to death. In memory of her, the Bais designate June 2 5 of the lunar calendar as the Torch Festival. As Lady Cishan was said to have sifted through the ashes of the Songming Building with both hands for her husband's remains, the Bai women dye their nails red with balsams during the festival to honor her. The Yis, however, celebrate the festival to commemorate the victory won by Eqilaba the hero over the god. Having no rivals in the world in wrestling, Eqilaba beat the wrestler sent by the god. The god was so enraged that he let out millions of pests to ruin the crops. Pine torches made and held aloft, Eqilaba, followed by the other Yis, walked around the fields and planted the lit torches into the field ridges to lure the pests to death. The Yis had a good harvest that year. In celebration of the victory, they hold a torch festival every year in June.

Actually, it was out of their primitive worship of the fire and prayer for bumper harvests that the forebears of the ethic groups observed such a festival. Even today, holding torches to burn pests in the hope of a bountiful year remains a predominant part of Torch Festival though there are other activities such as wrestling, horse racing, bull fighting, swinging and archery.

18. 三月街

　　三月街又称观音市,是云南大理白族人民的盛大节日。节期在农历三月十五至二十日,这期间要举行赛马、射箭、歌舞等活动,还要举办具有浓厚民族特色的物资交流会,届时云南和邻近各省的客商云集于大理城西点苍山东麓的三月街,进行物资交流和文体活动。

　　关于三月街的来历,在当地民间有一个美好的传说。据说在大理国时期,洱海岸上住着一位姓赵的老渔翁,他惟有一子名阿善,父子相依为命,艰苦度日。阿善勤奋、忠厚、善良、勇敢,乐于助人,为人所喜爱;洱海龙王的三公主阿香则勤奋简朴,平等待人,受人尊敬。阿善为了缴"渔月捐",在一个月明风静的夜晚去洱海捕鱼,连撒数网均无所获,便放下渔网垂头丧气地坐在船头抱着三弦,弹唱着渔家的苦难与辛酸。三公主听见了阿善那凄苦哀伤的曲调后也心酸落泪,于是变成一位美丽的姑娘来到阿善的船上细问缘由。三公主听后十分同情,为了帮助阿善,阿香和他私定了终生。八月十五日晚上,阿善和阿香正式结为伉俪。翌年三月十五日是月亮上赶街的日子,阿香复现为一条小龙,驮着阿善到月亮上去赶街。他们在那里游览了广寒宫,会见了嫦娥和吴刚,见到了美丽的玉兔,最后才去大青树附近赶月亮街。街上的珍珠、宝石、白玉和金银器物金光闪烁,各种穿、戴和家用物品琳琅满目。但是他们既无货币,又无物品,无法同他们进行交换,带不回人间来,只得空手回到了大理。

村里的人们听阿善阿香说到月亮街市的盛况后深受启发,翌年三月十五日便在点苍山东麓的三棵大青树附近搭棚店,摆摊点,交换农副产品,形成街市。这一消息不胫而走,在周围的村村寨寨广泛传播。从此,每年三月十五日,四面八方的人都到大青树下来赶街。因街市日期在三月,故称三月街。赶街的习惯也一代又一代地沿袭至今,而且越赶越兴旺。

传说毕竟是传说。据史籍记载,三月街起源于盛唐时期的云南大理。当时,大理一带农业、畜牧业、手工业、商业和交通运输业比较发达,先后出现一些经济中心城镇。为了推动经济发展,大理及这些中心城镇要定期举行庙会。其中,大理城三月街的庙会规模最大,后来逐渐发展成今天的三月街。

每年三月街市期间,白族人民在三月街的入口处竖立一个用松枝扎的七、八米高的大牌坊,上书"大理三月街"五个大字。赶街市的有来自云南的白、藏、纳西、怒、汉等各族人民及邻省的客商。天刚亮,通往三月街的大路小道已是车水马龙,人如潮涌,从大理古城至会场的二、三里长的大路两旁已摆满了各种土特产品,其中有苍山竹器,洱海弓鱼,腾冲玉器,鹤庆陶器,迪庆皮张,丽江骏马,还有雕刻精美的木器,花纹美丽的大理石制品,各种美味食品,名贵中药材,颇具民族风味的草帽,反映白族人民劳动与爱情的刺绣品,三弦、笛箫等民族乐器,造型别致的花盆、杯、碟等器皿。

街市期间的文娱体育活动令人向往。入夜之后,优美动听和曲调多变的白族大本曲,高亢婉转的藏族民歌,以及其他民族清新悦耳的歌声和乐器声等彼此交融,互相参和,通宵达旦,愉悦至极,使整个街市沉浸在节日的欢乐气氛之中。体育活动有赛马和射箭等。

　　三月街市也是白族青年男女谈情说爱和对歌挑选伴侣的场所。他们互相对歌传情,表白自己,了解对方,在一唱一答中逐渐接近,情投意合者,便可到僻静处去倾诉爱慕之情,确定终生相伴相随。

18. Third Month Fair

The Third Month Fair, also known as Avolokitesvara (Guanyin) Fair, is a festival grandly celebrated by the Bai people living in the Dali Bai Autonomous Prefecture of Yunnan Province. It lasts from the 15th to the 21st of the 3rd lunar month. The festival is marked by horse racing, archery competition, singing, dancing, and a commodity fair with a distinctive national flavor. The Third Month Fair is held in the Third Month Street, located at the eastern foot of the Diancang Mountains west of Dali Town, and often draws lots of businessmen from other parts of Yunnan and even its neighboring provinces.

The Third Month Fair hangs a lovely legend which circulates among the locals. It is said that an old fisherman named Zhao lived with his only son named Ashan on the shore of the Erhai Lake near Dali in the Dali State period (937 – 1253). The son was very popular among his neighbors because he was diligent, honest, brave and always ready to help others. Axiang, the third princess of the Dragon King dwelling in the Erhai Lake, was also held in esteem because she was diligent, thrifty and treated others as equals. On a moonlit and quiet night, Ashan tried to catch some fish in the Erhai Lake to pay the monthly fishing tax. When his several net casts were rewarded with nothing, he stopped fishing and sat on the bow playing the sanxian (a three – stringed plucked instrument) to pour out the miseries of him and other fisherfolks. At the plaintive strains Axiang, was moved to tears, so she incarnated herself from a yellow dragon into a beautiful girl and came to Ashan's fishing boat to ask the reason. She became very sympathetic, after she had known his plight, and secretly betrothed herself to him so as to help him more. They got married on the 15th evening of the 8th lunar month that year. The 15th day of the 3rd lunar month the next year was the day for the Moon Fair held on the moon, so Axiang reincarnated herself to the yellow dragon and carried Ashan on her back to the Moon Fair on that day. On the moon the couple first met Chang'e (a legendary moon goddess), Wugang (a legendary moon immortal) and Jade Rat (a legendary animal) while they visited the Guanghan Palace, and then went to the fair near a big lush tree. At the fare were many pearls, gems, white jade objects, gold or silver utensils, dresses and house articles, all a feast for their eyes. The couple, however, went back down to Dali, empty – handed, as they had neither money to buy nor anything of their own to barter.

Enlightened by Ashan's account about the prosperity of the Moon Fair, his fellow villagers set up store sheds and stalls near three big trees at the eastern foot of the Diancang Mountains near Dali Town on the 15th of the 3rd lunar month the next year after the couple's return. There they bartered and sold their agricultural products, and thus a fair came into being. This news spread like wildfire in the neighboring villages. From then, the villagers came to the fair on that day every year. The fair was called the Third Month Fair because of its time. It has been regularly held since then, and increasingly prosperous at that.

Legend is probably untrue. According to some historical records, the Third Month Fair originated in Dali during the flourishing period of the Tang Dynasty (618 – 907). Then, the Dali area enjoyed fairly developed farming, animal husbandry, handicraft industry, commerce, communications and transportations, which gave birth to a number of towns. Dali and other towns in the area regularly held temple fairs so as to promote the development of local economy. The temple fair held in the Third Month Street of Dali Town, the biggest of all, gradually grew into the present Third Month Fair.

A gateway of pine branches is to be put up at the entrance of the Third Month Street by the Bais just before the Third Month Fair begins. The gateway, seven or eight meters high, bears five big Chinese characters Da Li San Yue Jie, which dually mean the Third Month Street of Dali and the Third Month Fair of Dali. Those who go to the fair are the Bais, the Yis, the Tibetans, the Naxis, the Nus, the Hans and other nationalities, from Yunnan and its neighboring provinces. Early at daybreak in the fair session, all the roads to the Third Month Fair are thronged with fair participants and on both sides of the road from the old district of Dali Town to the fair, about 1.5 kilometers long, are crowded with shops and stalls which sell different special local products of Yunnan. Of them are the bamboo articles from the Cangshan Mountains, the fish from the Erhai Lake, the jade objects from Tengchong County, the earthenware from Heqing County, wooden articles with exquisite patterns, marble artifacts with fine designs, delicious foods, rare medicinal herbs, straw hats with national flavor, embroideries with patterns describing the Bai people's labor and love, national musical instruments like sanxian, shen (a reed pipe wind instrument) and xiao (a vertical bamboo flute), and unique-shaped utensils like flowerpots, cups and small plates.

The entertainments and sports during the fair session are a great invitation to holidaymakers. When night falls, the fair seethes with a joyful atmosphere brought about by the melodious and varied strains of the Bais, the sonorous and sweet folk songs of the Tibetans, and the songs of other nationalities. The sports include horse racing, archery competition and the like.

The Third Month Fair provides good opportunities for unmarried Bais to talk love and choose marital partners through antiphonal singing. The young men and girls get to know each other while doing the singing. The pair, who take a fancy to each other, would go to a secluded place to talk further and even decide on their marital relation.

19. 年收扎勒特节

　　年收扎勒特节是云南省哈尼族的哈尼历新年,在农历十月庆祝。按哈尼历法,一年有十二个月,每月三十天,各天分别以十二生肖(鼠、牛、虎、兔、龙、蛇、马、羊、猴、鸡、狗、猪)命名。其中"龙"居第五位,这样每月有三个"龙日"。根据哈尼族的习惯,他们可以从每年农历十月的任何一个"龙日"开始过新年。节期没有统一规定,有的山寨五、六天,有的山寨七、八天。

　　关于年收扎勒特节的由来,在哈尼族人民中有多种传说,其中一种较为普遍的说法是在古时候,现在的云南地区有位阿妈生了三个儿子,大儿子长大后变成了豹子,老二长大后变成一股风,老三长大后变成一条龙,而且他们变化后都离开了阿妈。阿妈年老后孤孤单单,无依无靠,就到处寻找自己日夜思念的儿子们。她找到了大儿子豹子,但他说:"阿妈,我成天在山林里找野兔野羊过活,还经常饿肚子,无法照顾你了。"阿妈又去找到了老二风,他也说:"阿妈,我来去无踪无影,弄不到任何东西给你,怎能和你住在一起呢?"阿妈最后找到了老三龙,龙无可奈何地说:"阿妈,我已无法离开江河了,不能回家同你一起生活。我这里有三包宝贝,你带回家去就能自己生活下去了。"

阿妈带着三包宝贝离开三儿子龙,艰难地往回走。她越走越觉得腰酸腿痛,便在离家不远的路边坐下来休息。阿妈坐了一会儿,觉得身子舒服些了,就小心翼翼地打开一个小包,原来里面装的是些用泥土捏的猪、牛、羊、鸡、鹅、鸭等动物玩意儿。阿妈心想,肚子饿着,哪还有心思摆弄这些东西呢,就随手放在地上。她又打开一包来看,里面包的则是一些金黄色的稻谷。阿妈正惊奇之际,忽然一股暖风吹来,稻谷都洒在了地上,迅速长成金黄色的稻穗,那些泥土玩意儿也在地上翻滚,变成了活的家畜家禽。阿妈看到后十分高兴,但随即又发愁地说:"龙儿啊,你给了我这么多东西,却没有人来陪伴我度日和持家呀!"话刚说完,从那还没有打开的小包里走出了三个大姑娘和三个小伙子,他们六个人满面春风地上前拉着阿妈的手,亲切地说:"阿妈,我们都是你的孩子,你不用发愁,我们共同侍候你老人家。"这事发生在农历十月的一天。阿妈想到龙儿最有孝心,就把这一天定为龙日,以后成为哈尼族新年的第一天。

在节日前夕,哈尼族居住的各村寨都要清扫得干干净净,男青年穿黑色对襟上衣和长裤,包黑色头巾,束绣花腰带;女青年则穿缀满闪光发亮的银珠、银链的新衣,头裹靛青色头巾。在节日第一天黎明时的铓鼓声中,哈尼族各村寨都已糯米饭飘香,妇女们忙碌着做汤圆、糯米粑粑和其他美味食品;男人们则忙着宰猪宰羊。各家都要在门前的院坝里杀一只大红公鸡,并就地煮熟,全家人就地共进早餐。全家成员都必须吃上鸡肉,即使回娘家去过新年的儿媳也要给她留一块,因为传说吃不上鸡肉的人死后将成为漂泊不定的野魂。

有些地区的哈尼族人过节日的第一天要举行隆重的荡秋

千仪式。仪式开始时,主持人"莫叭"端着一碗糯米团子,其中三个白的,三个黑的(外面有黑芝麻),首先念一段辞旧的话,念完后将三个黑团子倒在他身后的地上;接着念一段迎新的话,念完后将三个白团子倒在他身前的地上。这时许多人一齐朝天鸣放火药枪,擂响铓锣和大鼓。在全村寨男女老少的热烈欢呼声中,"莫叭"用双手使秋千摆动三次,欢乐的荡秋千活动正式开始。在场的男女老少都要参加荡秋千活动,他们认为这样可以使人在新的一年里幸福安康。同时荡秋千也是男女青年们谈情说爱的好机会,姑娘小伙子在欢笑中互相增进了解和认识,其中许多甚至定下终身。节日将结束时,人们再度聚集在秋千旁,"莫叭"在铓锣、大鼓声中将秋千砍倒,然后众人各自散去。

在整个节日期间的早晚饭前,家家都要将一盅酒和三个糯米团子在村口倒掉,以示敬献祖先。接着又给同宗辈份最高的人家送去一点熟肉和三个糯米团子,表示尊敬长辈,不忘亲情。

过节时哈尼族人还要邀请附近其他民族甚至过路的陌生人去家里做客,敬酒祝福,离别时主人还要送一包腌肉、豆腐团子和一块或几块糯米粑粑等物品,客人不得拒绝,以表示对主人的尊敬。

有些地区的哈尼族村寨把所有的人家按户分成三大组,从节日的第三天开始轮流于每天傍晚举行盛大的村头酒宴——"资乌都"(意为互相轮流喝酒),一组一天,在节日的第五天结束。每天下午太阳偏西时,做东道主的那组人家就将各种最拿手的美味佳肴和焖锅酒按顺序摆在早已铺垫好的村头竹席上。有的宴席长达百余米,场面极为盛大、热烈、奇特,气氛非常融洽、和谐、亲近。到时全村人自动聚拢来,按规定人数自由组成一桌。由大家推举的两位"阿窝"坐在宴席的上方。"阿窝"必须是德高望重的男性长者,儿孙健在,不曾再婚,勤劳耕作,善于治家理财。"阿窝"在宴席上诵完简短的祝词后,大家一齐高喊"沙——收——罗",共同饮酒,庆祝新年,然后在铓锣和皮鼓伴奏下,两位"阿窝"踩着鼓点,手摇棕扇,耸肩扭腰,尽兴舞蹈。其他人边喝酒边喝采助兴,宴席中的"沙——收——罗"的祝福声也持续不断,气氛热烈非常。

节日夜晚各村寨的活动场地燃起一堆堆篝火,人们再次聚集在一起,在哈尼族乐器的伴奏下,围着熊熊篝火继续唱歌跳舞,直至兴尽而散。

19. The Hanis' New Year

Known as Nianshouzhalete in the Hani language, the festival is celebrated by the Hani people in Yunnan Province in the 10th lunar month. According to the Hani calendar, a year has 12 months and a month has 30 days. The days are cyclically denoted by 12 symbolic animals of rat, ox, tiger, hare, dragon, snake, horse, sheep, monkey, cock, dog, and hog; hence each month has three "dragon days". The custom has it that the Hanis' New Year may begin on any of the three "dragon days" of the 10th lunar month and its length varies from 5 to 6 days or 7 to 8 days in different regions.

The festival's origin has behind a number of legends. Here is the most popular one. Long long ago, a mum in the present Yunnan had three sons. Later, the first one grew into a leopard, the second one into a wind and the third one into a dragon. They all left their mum when they grew up. Lonely and helpless, the mum went to many places trying to find them she missed day and night. One day she found Leopard, but he said, "I myself often go hungry though I am busy all day long looking for hares and goats as food in the mountains. So I can't look after you, mum." Then she continued to look for and found Wind, but he said, "Mum, I am on the go all the time without leaving a trace. How can I stay with and support you?" Finally she found Dragon, but he said in utter helplessness, "Mum, I can't live with you since I have to be in rivers, yet I give you three packets of treasures which will help you."

With the packets, the mum trudged wearily for home. The farther she walked, the more aching she felt her back and legs. So she sat down for a rest by a roadside when she was near her home. In a while the mum felt her ache much alleviated, so she cautiously unwrapped one of the packets. What met her eye were some clay-molded figurines inside: pigs, oxen, sheep, chickens, geese and ducks. She casually put them on the road, yet too hungry to take a fancy to them. Then the mum opened up another packet and saw bright yellow grains of rice inside. She was wondering about the occurrence when a warm wind scattered the grains, which instantly grew into paddy stalks with long ears all over the nearby ground; and the clay-molded figurines became animate, turning about on the road. This made the mum elated, but soon she felt worried, saying, "My dear son, I have had so many things from you, but none of them can keep me company and help me with house chores." No sooner had she finished speaking than six people, three girls and three lads, emerged out of the third packet. The strangers, all beaming with happiness, walked up and took her hands, saying cordially: "Mum, we are all your children and will attend on you." This happened one day in the 10th lunar month. The mum named the day "dragon" after the name of her third son, as she thought he was filial to her. Later, the dragon day was made the first day of the Hani people's New Year.

Towards the festival, celebrators are to give a thorough cleaning to their houses. Young men are to wear black Chinese-style jackets, black trousers, black turbans, and embroidered waist belts while girls are to wear new costumes decorated with tiny silver balls and silver chains, and indigo-blue scarves. The dawn of the first day of the festival sees a strong festive atmosphere. Drumbeats resound in the air; men are busy slaughtering pigs and sheep; women busy themselves preparing stuffed dumplings made of glutinous rice flour, cakes made of the same flour, and other nice foods, the sweet smell wafting over all villages. For the breakfast of the day, all of a family are to have, in their courtyard, a big red-feathered rooster which must be killed and cooked likewise in their courtyard. Anyone, who has not had the chicken, would supposedly be a wandering soul after death; hence even the daughter-in-law, absent from the breakfast for a New Year visit to her parents, is to eat some of the chicken reserved after she comes back home.

The Hani people, in some regions of Yunnan Province, begin their New Year celebration with a ceremony of playing on the swing on the first day of the festival. In the beginning of the ceremony a presider, locally known as moba, chants a message bidding farewell to the old year and throws, from a bowl onto the ground behind him, three black balls which are made of glutinous rice and covered with black sesame; and then he chants message ushering in the new year and throws, from the same bowl onto the ground before him, three white balls which are also made of glutinous rice. As soon as he has finished the procedures, many celebrators unanimously fire hunting guns at the sky, and beat gongs and drums. Amid the crowd's cheers, the presider swings the swing three times with both hands to mark the beginning of the game. All present, men and women, old and young, will join the game as they suppose that it would bring them happiness and health in the new year. The game also provides good opportunities for young celebrators to talk love, some of whom are even lucky enough to have their marital partners. Towards the end of New Year, celebrators gather again around the swing and the same presider cuts off the swing amid the sounds of gongs and drums to mark the close of the celebration.

The custom has it that before each breakfast and supper during the festival, every family has to sprinkle a cup of wine over and throw three glutinous-rice balls on the ground at the entrance of the village as sacrifices to ancestors, and present some cooked meat and three glutinous-rice balls to the venerable elder of the clan to show respect.

During the festival, the Hani people like to invite home, as guests, neighbors of other ethnic groups and even strange passers-by and treat them to wine and food. The guests are to be given beacon, bean-curd balls and one or nine cakes made of glutinous rice when they leave for home; and their acceptance of the gifts demonstrates their respect for hosts.

There is a unique custom in some Hani regions. There, the families of a village are divided into three groups. The groups take turn to hold a grand wine party, known as ziwudu in the Hani language, at the entrance of the village from the 3rd to the 5th day of the festival. Towards dusk, the families of the host group lay their own most delicious foods and wine on a strip of bamboo-mat-covered ground at the entrance of the village. The strip is, sometimes is over 100 meters long, presenting a scene of grandeur and uniqueness as well as an atmosphere of harmony and intimacy. All villagers sit along the strip in groups of an equal number, each group with two venerable elders (known as awo in the Hani language) seated at the seats of honor. The two men, apart from being hard-working and good at the management of family property, must have children and grandchildren who remain alive, and have never remarried. After one of the two elders finishes chanting a blessing message, all shout in chorus "Sa-Shou-Luo". The words in the Hani language mean to drink, and celebrate New Year. Then, to the accompaniment of gongs and drums, the two venerable elders joyfully dance, drawing up shoulders, swaying hips and waving a fan each. In the meanwhile, others drink and shout "Sa-Shou-Luo". The party is a very lively scene.

Bonfires are ablaze on public grounds in all villages when night falls during the festival. Celebrators dance around the bonfires to the accompaniment of the Hani instruments. They will not go home until they enjoy themselves to their heart's content.

20.苦扎扎节

苦扎扎节又叫"六月年"或"六月节",是云南哈尼族的传统农祀节日。"苦扎扎"是哈尼语,意思是预祝庄稼成熟,人们有个好收成。一般在六月二十四日前后举行,节期二至五天。节日的主要活动是杀牛祭神。

根据哈尼族的民间传说,每到五、六月,天神就要到各村寨巡查,保佑庄稼丰收,人畜两旺。为了迎接天神,人们架起"磨秋"充当"天梯"。打磨秋是节日的主要娱乐活动之一。这是一种"丁"字形的木架,人骑坐在木架的两端,用脚蹬地就能使它上上下下旋转飞动。哈尼青年特别喜欢这种活动,磨秋场上人头攒动,大伙儿争先恐后玩磨秋。磨秋场上除了磨秋,还有秋千。荡秋千也是哈尼人喜欢的活动。据说,架秋千也是为了迎接天神,因为秋千被认为是天神的坐骑。节日的磨秋场上一片欢声笑语,往往是全寨的人聚在一起,载歌载舞,共庆节日。

节日的最后一晚,一些哈尼人家燃起松明火把,照亮屋子的各个角落,并扫除杂物。之后,将火把集中在村口烧掉,以示驱邪除恶,保护家人的身体健康。

20. Kuzaza Festival

Known as the June Festival, the Kuzaza Festival is a traditional sacrifice offering day for the Hani nationality in Yunnan province. In the Hani language Kuzaza means a wish to have early ripe crops and a bumper harvest. The festival falls on the days around June 24 in general and lasts two to five days, the major activity of which is to sacrifice bulls to gods.

The Hani folklore has it that in May and June of each year gods inspect every Hani village so as to bless people and livestock and to ensure a bumper harvest. To welcome gods, people erect Moqiu as a ladder leading to heaven. Moqiu is a T-typed wooden structure, and riding Moqiu is now one of the main entertainments of the festival. People ride on both ends of the structure and step down on the ground, thus making it turn up and down. The amusement is popular with the Hani youth, who crowd the Moqiu ground and vie to play with it. Aside from Moqiu, there are swings, on which people play jubilantly. According to legend, swings are supposed to welcome gods as well, for swings are believed to be gods' horses. The merry festival sees on the Moqiu ground the gathering of the entire village people, who dance and sing to celebrate the happy day.

On the last night of the festival, some Hani families light pine torches to illuminate every corner of the house and rid trash of it. Afterwards, they burn all the torches at the gate of the village, symbolic of evils being exorcised and the family's health protected.

21. 泼水节

泼水节是中国云南省傣族的新年,也是傣族一年中最盛大的传统节日,节期三至五天,一般在傣历六月初至七月初之间举行,故傣语称之为"傣历新年"或"六月新年"。但云南省德宏地区傣族的泼水节在中国农历的正月初一,与汉族的春节同期。

泼水节始于印度。印度婆罗门教(即印度教的前身)有一种宗教仪式,即每年公历的四月二十日或二十一日,教徒们要到河里去沐浴,以洗去身上的邪恶。年高不能去河里洗澡的,则由子女或亲友们挑水回去为他们泼水洗澡。随着受婆罗门教影响较大的佛教传到缅甸、泰国、老挝和中国云南省傣族居住地区,此宗教仪式也随着传到了上述国家和地区,并逐渐形成为泼水节。可见傣族的泼水节与佛教有着密切的联系。但民间对于泼水节的来历则有着多种传说,其中流传较广的一种说法是在很早以前,有个恶魔霸占了云南省勐巴拉纳西地区,给当地人民制造了深重灾难。恶魔呼气成大风,风到之处邪火熊熊;它吐出的口水如汹涌的江河,若谁得罪了它,大水就立即冲垮他的竹楼。傣族许多勇士想除掉它,但反而被它所害了。

恶魔不仅凶残,而且好色,它抢去傣家十一个如花似玉的姑娘为妻。她们无比痛恨恶魔，打算把它杀掉，为乡亲们报仇雪恨。有一天恶魔又抢来了一个叫侬香的美丽姑娘，她聪明、机智、勇敢，但无力与恶魔拼个你死我活，要想为乡亲们报仇除害，只能行韬晦之计，等待时机。于是侬香装出一副满足现状，寻欢作乐的模样，成天和恶魔接近周旋。在傣历六月的一天夜里，侬香趁恶魔高兴的时候陪它喝酒，劝它喝了一坛又一坛美酒，并用甜言蜜语奉承道："大王，你本事高强，水火刀剑都伤害不了你，你一定长命不死，祝贺你啊！"恶魔在沉醉中说出了自己惟一的弱点，叹道："其实不然，如果有人拔下我的一根头发来勒住我的脖子，我的脑袋也会掉的……"。侬香听罢若无其事地说："大王，你喝醉了，快去躺下睡觉吧！"恶魔睡熟后，侬香轻轻拔下它头上的一根头发，套在它的脖子上，双手用力一勒，恶魔的脑袋立刻掉到地上。原来恶魔是个火魔，它的头落地后到处乱滚，滚到哪里火就烧到哪里。为避免引起大火，十二个姑娘轮流抱住滚烫的魔头，并不停地泼水降温，直到魔头最后死去。当地的傣族人民于第二年的傣历六月举行泼水节，他们将清水泼在亲友熟人的身上，以纪念姑娘们斩魔除害的功绩和表达企盼太平盛世的愿望。此后年年举行泼水节，最终形成为傣族人民辞旧迎新的隆重节日。

在节日前夕，孩子们都要砍竹做水枪，并在水枪上雕刻花纹；各家各户的门上都贴着五彩缤纷的剪纸，装饰一新；姑娘们把一束束芬芳馥郁的鲜花浸在水桶里，备好节日泼洒的香水；每家都要做具有浓郁民族风味的食品。

泼水节的第一天在每年的岁末。这一天不泼水，人们早起沐浴后，青年男女们穿上美丽的民族服装成群结队上山采摘野花，装饰房间；善男信女们则到寺庙去拜佛，在寺庙中用沙堆成几座四、五尺高的宝塔形沙堆,在塔尖插八根缠着彩纸的竹枝,围塔坐着聆听诵经和讲历史传说;中年妇女们将清水泼在佛像上,为佛洗尘。然后人们都到江边去观看紧张激烈的龙舟比赛。

第二天是泼水日,是最热闹的一天,男女老少一起出动,人们提着桶、端着盆来到大街上,街道两旁早已备好了加入香水或放入花瓣的清水。参加活动的人把水泼在亲友、熟人身上,以示祝福,消灾除病。但由于人与人之间存在着亲疏长幼等不同的关系,所以泼水时又可分为文泼与武泼两种形式。文泼是对长者,泼水时先舀起一勺净水,说着祝福的话语,再拉开长者的衣领,把水倒进去,让水顺着脊背往下流,被泼者还得高兴地接受祝福,不得拒绝。武泼则很随便,人们可以用瓢、盆、勺、桶等互相泼洒,迎着头脸或身上泼过去。身上泼的水越多,说明自己受到的祝福越丰,因而越高兴。人们在水花中跳舞、唱歌、欢笑,忘记过去的一切烦恼,全身心都沉浸在欢乐之中。有的小伙子还闯进姑娘的竹楼,以泼水表达爱慕之情。

泼水节的第三天是丢包、放火花、放高升和放孔明灯等活动,也十分精彩热闹。丢包是青年男女们的一种求爱活动。"包"是内装棉籽等物品的一种约十六公分见方的布包,丢包时未婚青年人按性别排成两行,相向而站,中间相隔七至十米左右。刚开始时各自将手中的布包向对面乱掷,等到各自意中有属时,逐渐变成双双对掷。在这一过程中,女方可以伺机抢走意中人身上的佩刀或头巾等物品,然后跑回家去备好酒菜,等小伙子来索取时便互相倾诉衷肠,订下终身。

放火花是把一根两米多长的圆木挖空,里面装满火药,接上引线,固定在架上,夜间点燃引线,绿色火焰自空心圆木中喷出,火花可高达数十米,蔚为壮观。这时青年们伴随着铓锣、象脚鼓和芦笙的节奏尽情起舞。

高升是傣族人民创造的一种独特焰火,即在一根长长的竹竿顶端绑上一圈竹筒,竹筒里装满火药,置上引线,一旦点燃便尖啸着飞向蓝天,在高空中喷发出绚丽多彩的焰火。在放高升达到高潮时,要在一个最大的高升里放进五种物品,待高升在空中炸开后那五种物品就徐徐降落在地面上,抢到那些物品的人被视为幸运者。

放孔明灯也在节日晚上进行。孔明灯是用竹篾和韧性纸糊成的长圆形灯,高约七米,直径为两米,下面留有一个孔,将十字架上缠着浸透了燃油的布条点燃,插在孔下的竹圈上,热气进入灯内,加热后产生浮力,孔明灯就徐徐上升,就像一盏明灯悬浮在空中,缓慢移动,十分壮观,象征着人间的光明与祥和。

在泼水节日里还有群众性的歌舞活动,不分男女老幼,凡是能上场的人都到广场上去围成一圈,伴着铓锣和象脚鼓点欢快地唱歌跳舞。有的跳象征吉祥的孔雀舞、篾帽舞,有的跳"依拉贺"舞。民间歌手们则演唱十分感人的有关泼水节的传说。总之人人都沉浸在节日的欢乐气氛之中。

除傣族外,云南省的德昂和阿昌等民族也过泼水节,而且各有自己的民族特色。

21. Water-Splashing Festival

The Water-Splashing Festival is the New Year, as well as the most important traditional festival, observed by the Dai nationality in Yunnan Province of China. The festival usually lasts 3-5 days somewhere between early the 6th month and early the 7th month of the Dai calendar; hence it is also known locally as the New Year of the Dai calendar or the New Year of the 6th Month. The Dais in Yunnan's Dehong Dai and Jingpo Autonomous Prefecture exceptionally celebrate the festival on the 1st of the 1st lunar month, the same day as the Spring Festival of the Han people.

The Water-Splashing Festival originated in India. According to one of the rites of Brahmanism (the predecessor of Hinduism of India), the believers were to bathe in rivers on the 20th or the 21st of April to supposedly wash all evils off them. Those who were too old to bathe personally in rivers were to be bathed by their children, relatives or friends. With Buddhism, which was greatly influenced by Brahmanism, the rite was introduced into Burma, Thailand, Laos and the Dai-inhabited regions of Yunnan, and later grew into the present Water-Splashing Festival. This shows the close tie between the festival and Buddhism. Many folk tales, however, claim their own origins of the festival. Here is the most popular one. Long long ago, a demon forcibly occupied the Mengbalanaxi region of Yunnan and inflicted untold misery upon the locals. His puff would be a strong gust of wind, which would bring about an evil raging fire. His spitting would bring about a turbulent river, which would wash away the bamboo dwelling houses of those who offended him. Therefore, many of the brave Dai men, who tried to kill him, were killed by him.

A lecher and a cruel murderer as well, the demon forcibly took eleven beautiful Dai girls as wives. The girls, filled with bitter hatred, secretly planned to kill him as to avenge their fellow villagers. One day another beautiful girl named Nongxiang was forcibly taken by the demon as his 12th wife. She was bright, witty and brave, but too physically weak to subdue the demon through fistfight; hence she chose the tactics of concealing her intention and biding her time for revenge. Accordingly she was wallowing pleasure all day together with him, in a pretended satisfaction. One night in the 6th month of the Dai calendar when she accompanied him in drinking wine, Nongxiang urged the demon to drink one jug after another, and flattered him, saying: "My Lord! You are certainly immortal since you are all-proof. Congratulations!" In tipsiness the demon sighed his sole vulnerable spot: "No. My head would be cut off if someone ties a hair from my head around my neck and increasingly tightens it." Pretending to take no interest in the secret, Nongxiang said, "My Lord! You are drunk and go to bed to have a rest." When the demon was fast asleep, she gently plucked out one of his hairs and tied it around his neck. The moment she forcibly tightened the hair, his head dropped to the ground. The head kept rolling about and set fire to whatever it touched, because he was the demon of fire. To avoid a conflagration, the twelve girls grasped the flaming head and splashed water over it by turns until the head became lifeless. The local Dai people began to hold the Water-Splashing Festival in the 6th month of the Dai calendar the next year to commemorate Nongxiang and express their wish for times of peace and prosperity by splashing water over any of their friends, relatives or other folks around. Since then the Dai people have observed the festival every year to bid farewell to the outgoing year and to usher in the new year of the Dai calendar.

The preparations for the festival begin days before it: Children make bamboo water throwers with patterns; all households have their doors decorated with colored paper-cuts; girls have sweet-smelling flowers soaked for fragrant water to be splashed; and all households make foods with distinctive Dai flavor.

The first day of the festival is generally the last day of the old year. On this day, all people get up early in the morning and take baths. Then, young men and girls, who are dressed in attractive Dai costumes, go to the mountains for wild flowers to decorate their rooms; Buddhism believers go to temples, where they worship Buddha and sit around sand heaps listening to sutra recitation and lectures on historic tales, each of the sand heaps being about 1.5 meters high, pagoda-shaped and planted atop with eight bamboo branches wrapped by colored paper; middle-aged women clean Buddhist images with clear water. Still then, all go to watch the exciting dragon boat race.

The second day of the festival, which is the liveliest, sees water splashing. All people, men and women, old and young, taking along buckets or basins, come to broad streets. The streets are lined, on both sides, with containers of clear water which is scent or has petals floating on. When the entertainment begins, festival celebrators splash the water over their relatives, friends or acquaintances, wishing that they would be lucky and free from adversities or diseases. The ways to splash water fall into gentle splashing and violent splashing, depending on how intimate the target is to the splasher and how old the target is. The gentle splashing is done to venerable elders. In doing it the splasher, while speaking some blessing words, pulls away an elder's collar and gently tips into the opening a ladle of clean water which flows down the target's back, while the target should willingly accept the splashing and reciprocate the splasher's good wishes by blessing. The violent splashing is done to others but the elder. In doing it the splasher is free to splash water, from a gourd ladle, a basin or a pale, over a target, and the target likewise splashes back. The more water one bears, the happier he feels. All the amusement makers dance, sing, and laugh heartily while splashing, entirely lost in pleasure. Some young men even go to bamboo dwelling houses and splash water over girls there, a symbol of love.

The third day of the festival sees tossing bags, setting off sparks, setting off Gaosheng, flying Kongming lanterns and other entertainments.

The bag tossing is a game for young people to court marital partners, and the bag used in the game is a cloth one with cotton seeds inside, about 16 centimeters square in size. Before the game begins, young unmarried players stand face-to-face in two lines according to sex, 7 – 10 meters apart. When it begins the players toss their bags to the opposite players blindly and, after some time, they toss them merely between two, who take a fancy to each other. In the game, a girl may snatch away the sword or the head cover of a lad she loves, and run home. At home the girl prepares nice food and wine for the lad who is sure to come for thing he has lost. The pair, while taking the food and drinking, pour out their feelings and even decide their engagement.

The sparks are set off by a thrower, which is made by filling a hollow log, over two meters long, with gun powder which is then connected to an infuse; and this log is fixed on a stand. When the infuse is lit at night, bluish-red showers of sparks eject dozens of meters up into the sky, quite a magnificent spectacle. Meanwhile young people dance to their heart's content, to the accompaniment of the Dai gong, the elephant-leg-like drum and the lusheng (a reed-pipe wind instrument).

The Gaosheng is a unique kind of fireworks created by the Dai people. It is a long, erect bamboo pole, its top being fixed with a number of short gunpowder-filled bamboo pipes which are each connected to an infuse. Once lit at night, the pipes soar up into and explode in the sky, producing brilliant fireworks. When this entertainment reaches its climax, the biggest Gaosheng's pipes containing five different objects are fired into the sky. When they explode, the objects fall down, and those who are quick enough to have any of them are seen as fortune's favorites.

The Kongming lantern is to be flown at night, too. The lantern is made of thin bamboo strips and tough paper, pillar-shaped, about seven meters tall and two meters in diameter. At its bottom is a round opening with a bamboo strip ring, and the ring is fixed with a bamboo cross twined with oil-soaked cloth pieces. When the cloth pieces are lit, hot air sends the lantern up into the sky, where it slowly drifts about. The magnificent view is a symbol of brightness and auspiciousness in the world.

The Water Splashing Festival is also marked by singing and dancing. All festival celebrators, men and women, old and young, are lovers of the entertainments. Usually the performance stand in rings, heartily singing and dancing to the accompaniment of the Dai gong and the elephant-leg-like drum. The most popular dances are the Peacock Dance, the Bamboo Hat Dance and the Yilahou Dance. Folk singers sing songs on the legend of the Water-Splashing Festival. All celebrators are lost in pleasure.

Beside the Dais, the De'ang people and Achang people, both ethnic groups in Yunnan, celebrate the festival in their own ways.

22.盍什节

　　盍什节是云南傈僳族人民庆祝新年的节日,"盍"和"什"在傈僳语中分别代表着"年"和"新"。各地庆祝节日的时间并不统一,大致在农历 11 和 12 月之间。

　　节日期间,傈僳人通常用杵和臼舂籼米和糯米做粑粑、酿制水酒。人们把籼米粑放在桃树和李树上,并让狗先品尝糯米粑,目的是祈求来年风调雨顺,粮食丰收。根据傈僳民间传说,古时洪水泛滥,人类濒临灭绝。有一对兄妹从洪水中逃生,并按上天的意愿结为夫妻,繁衍后代。他俩辛苦地挖掘沟渠、疏导洪水,在荒原上耕种。未料来了一场洪水,庄稼全给卷走,粮食颗粒未收。黄狗飞上天为他们讨来谷种,才使农业生产恢复。从此,傈僳人民开始祭狗并世代沿袭。

　　节日庆祝活动繁多。打靶比赛是其中的一项:小伙子们拿出心爱的弓弩朝百步开外的靶子射击。这些弓弩由桑木或其他硬木做成,弩线则用牛筋制成。姑娘们将绣好的荷包挂在竹竿上,在树梢间晃动,让小伙子们射击。谁射下荷包,谁就能喝到姑娘们斟上的美酒。

　　怒江沿岸的傈僳人在节日到来时会给耕牛喂盐,以示对它们终年辛勤劳作的尊敬。当地的傈僳人还保留着温泉沐浴的习俗。传说山神每年都在正月初一和十五来温泉沐浴洁身。出于对神的膜拜，当地人争相效仿，只要有温泉的地方，就有成群结队的人在此沐浴。为了沐浴，人们带上节日食品，在温泉附近搭上帐篷或者就在岩洞里住上三五日。为了消除病患，有的人一天要沐浴五六回。

傈僳人能歌善舞。他们在琵琶等乐器的伴奏下载歌载舞，所唱歌曲涉题广泛，所跳舞蹈刚劲、富有节奏。节日期间要举行传统的赛歌会，届时，男女分开站立，女的手拉手组成一圈，男的以手搭肩组成一圈，他们的脚步和着一定的节奏来回移动。赛歌会的主题出自一首流传至今的长诗，其内容是讲述一对恋人三年三次相聚温泉的故事。除了现成的诗，人们还即兴创作歌词，悠扬的歌声远远飘扬。赛歌会上，傈僳人品尝着美酒，晚上则升起篝火继续歌唱。歌会持续十几天，是男女青年约会的好时机。根据傈僳族传统，男女青年不管相识与否，即使在田野上相逢，也可邀请参加对唱。

22. Heshi Festival

Heshi Festival is the New Year of the Lisus, most of whom live in Yunnan Province. "He" and "shi" respectively mean "year" and "new" in the Lisu language. The time for the festival varies from place to place, approximately between November and December of the lunar calendar.

During the festival, the Lisu people usually make cakes by pounding polished long-grained rice and glutinous rice with mortar and pestle and brew wine. They lay on peach and plum trees long-grained rice cakes and feed their dogs with glutinous rice cakes before people eat them. This is to pray for good weather and bumper harvests in the year to come. The Lisu folk legend goes that in ancient times, the world was inundated with flood, which put man in peril of extinction. A young man and his sister escaped the deluge and became husband and wife for the reproduction of human beings in compliance with God's wishes. They industriously dug channels to dredge water and reclaimed wasteland to grow crops. Unfortunately, a flood destroyed all crops. Their yellow dog flew to the heaven and brought back down some grain seeds, thus the farming was restored. From then, the Lisus began to worship dogs, which has been handed down from generation to generation.

There are diversified festivities that highlight the festival. The archery competition is one of them. Young men, each with his treasured bow and arrow, shoot at a target about one hundred steps away. Their bows are made of mulberry wood or other hard wood and the strings cattle's sinew. Girls hang on the top of bamboo poles their embroidered pouches and sway them among treetops for young men to shoot at. Whoever shoots down a pouch wins a cup of good wine presented by a girl.

The practice of bathing in hot springs has had a long history and is still popular among the Lisus along the Nujiang River of the Yunnan Province. These people also feed the cattle with salt on New Year's Day in honor of their assiduous labor in the past year. According to legend, the mountain god comes to the world for a bath in Hot Springs on the 1st and 15th of the 1st lunar month. Worshipping the god, the Lisu people follow suit. Where there is a hot spring along the Nujiang River, throngs of people are seen bathing. The bathers eat festival food they bring and stay in tents they put up or in caves near the hot springs. Usually, they stay there for 3 to 5 days. Some bathe 5 or 6 times a day in the hope of curing themselves of their diseases.

The Lisus are good at singing and dancing. They sing folk songs of different subject matters to the accompaniment of pipa and other musical instruments, and dance energetically and rhythmically. In some places, the traditional singing contest is held. In the competition, women, hand in hand, form a circle while men form another with hands upon each other's shoulders. They move their feet in harmony to certain rhythms. The singing competition comes from a long poem that, still popular, tells the love story of a lad and a girl who met 3 times by a hot spring in 3 years. Apart from ready-written poems, people compose impromptu words for songs. Their melodious sound spreads far and wide. The singing contest is punctuated by delicious food and good wine. When night falls, people make bonfires and continue their singing. The contest lasts over 10 days and offers young Lisu people chances to date. The Lisu tradition allows young men and women, whether acquaintances or not, to invite each other to participate in antiphonal singing even when they meet in the field.

23．刀杆节

刀杆节，云南傈僳族民间传统节日。傈僳语称"阿堂得"，意即"爬刀杆"，每年农历二月初八举行。

节日那天，人们穿上节日盛装，汇集到刀杆场观看爬刀杆表演。场上的刀杆架由两根20多米长的粗木杆搭成。木杆之间绑着36把或72把锋利的长刀，刀口朝上，构成刀梯。刀杆的顶端挂着小红旗和鞭炮。爬杆者多为健壮的中青年男子。他们经过训练，有爬刀杆的特殊本领。每个爬杆的人都头缠红布，身穿红衣，赤着双脚。

上"刀山"之前，爬杆者先进行下"火海"表演。刀杆场上燃起了几堆熊熊的烈火，在铓锣声和人们的欢呼声中，表演者赤足跳进"火海"，在火堆中来回跳跃，进行着"打火滚"（赤足在火堆中跳来跳去，称为"打火滚"）、"拉火链"（将烧红的铁链在手上传来传去，称为"拉火链"）、"洗火脸"（双手捧着火焰往脸上压，称为"洗火脸"）等绝技表演。之后，这些下过"火海"的勇士纵身跳上刀杆，赤脚踩在刀刃上，手攀着刀口爬到刀杆顶端，点燃鞭炮，把小旗子抛向人群，引来阵阵的欢呼喝彩声。

刀杆节体现了傈僳人敢于上"刀山"，下"火海"的勇敢精神。相传这一节日是为了纪念有恩于傈僳族的王骥。王骥是明朝的兵部尚书，受朝廷的派遣，来到云南，帮助傈僳人民驱逐外敌,夺回领土,过上安定的生活。为了保障当地的安宁、巩固边防,他组织傈僳青年习武练兵,准备随时抵御外敌入侵。这时,当朝的皇帝却听信奸言,以为王骥组织边民习武是要造反,将他召回京城,并在农历二月初八把他毒死。消息传来,傈僳人民悲愤不已。为了纪念王骥,他们把他的忌日定为自己的节日,并以上刀山、下火海的仪式来表达愿为他赴汤蹈火的感激之情以及傈僳人保卫家园、抵御外敌的坚定决心。

23. Knifeladder-Climbing Festival

The Knifeladder-Climbing Festival is a traditional folk festival for the Lisu nationality in Yunnan Province. It is called Atangde in the Lisu language, which denotes climbing the knifeladder and is observed on the 8th of the 2nd lunar month.

On that day, people dressed in their holiday best converge on a ground to watch the performance of climbing the knifeladder. The knife rack erected on the ground consists of two thick wooden poles over twenty meters high. With their edges facing upwards, 36 or 72 long, sharp knives bound between the two poles form a ladder of knives. On the top of the knifeladder hang tiny red flags and fire-crackers. Generally the climbers are robust young men. Being trained, they have special skills to climb it. With his head wrapped with red cloth, each climber is barefooted and in red.

Before climbing the knifeladder or the so-called knife mountain, the climbers first perform plunging into a sea of fire. On the ground a few raging fires are made. In the drumming of Mangluo (a sort of musical instrument), and cheers of people, the performers jump to and fro between the fires in barefeet, showing such unique skills as jumping barefoot in the fire, passing around a red-hot iron chain, and washing their face with flames in both hands. Having performed plunging into a sea of fire, these brave men jump onto the knife ladder and step on the knife edges in barefeet. They climb up the edges hand over hand, light firecrackers and scatter the tiny flags among the crowds, arousing peals of laughter and cheers.

The Knifeladder-Climbing Festival reveals the spirit of the Lisu people's daring the knife mountain and the sea of fire. It is said that the festival is celebrated in memory of Wangji, who was kind to the Lisu nationality. A minister of War Ministry in the Ming Dynasty, Wangji was sent by the court to Yunnan Province, where he helped the Lisu people drive out the invaders, recapture the land and lead a peaceful life. To safeguard tranquility in the area and consolidate the frontier defense, he organized young men of the Lisu nationality to practise martial arts and trained soldiers, preparing them to resist foreign invasion. At that moment, the emperor, however, recalled Wangji to the capital city and poisoned him on the 8th of the 2nd lunar month, as he believed the treacherous officials' words that Wangji organized the frontiersmen to practise martial arts to rebel. Word of Wangji's death filled the Lisu people with grief and indignation. To memorize him, they designated the date of his death as their festival and performed the rites of climbing a mountain of knives and plunging into a sea of fire to show their gratitude towards him, their willingness to go through hardship for him and their determination to defend their homeland and resist foreign invaders.

24. 大 过 年

　　大过年是云南省普米族人民最隆重的节日,节期从腊月三十日开始,一般为三至十五天。

　　腊月三十这天,各家都要把房屋内外清扫干净,贴对联辞旧迎新,青年男女们把松毛撒在火塘周围和院子里,将腊梅插在房屋门前。各家都把熟肉切成块,一块送给家族中的长辈,一块留给家里出远门未归的亲人,一块送给已出嫁的女儿。普米族人把腊月三十吃猪头肉当作家人团聚、和睦、兴旺的象征,若过了大年三十家里还挂着猪头肉,表明这家人过年时未能团聚。

　　普米族人在除夕晚上家家团聚会餐,各村寨的鞭炮响个不停。会餐前要在火塘旁举行祭祖仪式,将三杯酒、三块肉、三块粑粑分别放在火塘的铁三角顶端,以示思念祖先;给狗喂点饭团。吃饭时如有客人在座,要让客人吃第一块猪头肉和鸡头。但客人应揭开鸡头骨,取出鸡舌软骨叉,并朝东方凝视片刻,然后客气而又庄重地对主人说:"你们的幸福和欢乐就要降临了。"主人全家则齐声道谢:"托你的洪福!"

　　除夕夜各家要留一人守岁,通宵不睡觉,到次日鸡叫头遍时放炮三响,然后吹海螺报岁。天明时家长用松枝、蒿叶、酒菜、牛奶等上房顶祭祀房屋,意为迎新年、请祖先、驱鬼蜮、求平安。青年男女们竞相去河里背水,以首先得到净水者为吉祥。最后合家一起吃酥油糯米饭。

普米族人还有初一未请不进邻居家庭院的习俗,但每家必须请一位客人去做客。客人必须身体健壮、性情温和、为人诚实、办事稳妥。去请客的人不能进庭院,只能在门外喊。被邀请者将受到盛情接待。兰坪县的普米族人还有在大年初一请过路人去家里做客的习俗。这天他们早早带上酒菜去村口等,遇有过路行人就先敬一碗酒,喝完后就往家里请,请到第一位客人者感到很自豪,因此常常出现多人争请一位客人的情景。被请的人进屋前说:"祝你家丰衣足食,和睦兴旺!"主人答道:"托你的洪福!"客人离别时主人还要赠送猪头肉、黄酒和糯米粑粑等食品。

初二各家赶牛去地里犁上一犁刀后停下来,人们相约在山上放牧。牛群进入牧场后大家就将各自带去的酒菜拿出来一同享用,共祝新年。

能歌善舞的普米族人民在节日期间自然要举行多种歌舞活动。他们最喜爱的舞蹈是舞步刚健明快的四弦琴舞和羊皮舞,这些舞蹈多反映他们耕作、狩猎、纺织等生产内容,用芦笙、笛子、唢呐等乐器伴奏,气氛欢快、热烈、奔放,唱歌的歌词内容则多以男女青年的爱情生活为主,形式主要为叙事歌。在节日期间还要举行赛马、跳高、摔跤、踢毽子和"打粑粑"等文娱体育活动。"打粑粑"是把粑粑和肉挂在树上,轮流用弩射击,以比赛优劣。

节日最后一天,男女青年各自带着玉米、青稞、小麦等爆花,到山上去举行"灭虫"仪式。他们把各种爆花倒进一个大簸箕里,姑娘们又把各自的手镯取下来埋在爆花里。爆花视为"小虫",手镯当作"大虫",然后大家围拢吃爆花,即象征消灭虫子。谁的手镯先露出来,大家就用手指轻轻地弹一下她的手背,寓意大虫被消灭了,地里的庄稼不会遭虫害。晚上男女老少都要打扮,盛装上山露营,举行隆重的篝火晚会,尽兴欢乐,愉快地度过节日的最后一个良宵。

24. The Pumis' New Year

It is the festival most grandly celebrated by the Pumi people in Yunnan Province. The festival lasts 3 – 15 days, from the 30th of the 12th lunar month.

On the first day of the festival, people make ample preparations to bid farewell to the outgoing year and usher in the new year. Every household gives a thorough cleaning to the house and puts up couplets on doorposts. Young people of a family scatter pine needles around their fire pit and over their courtyard, and plant branches of winter sweet flowers before the front gate of their house; every family prepares three pieces of cooked pork, one for the venerable elder of the clan, another for someone of the family who happens to be away from home on that day and the third for the married daughter. The Pumi people see it a symbol of family reunion and prosperity to eat a pig's head on the day; hence a pig's head, if it is found hanging in a house after the 30th of the 12th lunar month, demonstrates the absence of the family reunion at the festival.

On New Year's Eve, every family has a dinner of reunion while firecrackers keep going off with crackles. The dinner is preceded by a short ceremony. At the ceremony, three cups of wine, three pieces of meat and three cakes are respectively placed on each end of a three – angled iron stand beside the fire pit to commemorate ancestors. Also before the dinner, cooked rice balls are offered to dogs. At the dinner, the host should first offer the guest, if any, a piece of meat from a cooked pig head and a chicken head. Before he eats the chicken head, the guest should take off its tongue and, staring in the east direction, say, "You will be blessed with happiness." The host family would unanimously reply, "We owe it to your great blessing!"

One member of a family is to stay up all night on New Year's Eve and announce, at the next daybreak, the arrival of the New Year by setting off three gunshots and blowing the conch. Then the head of the family holds a sacrificial rite on the roof to usher in the New Year, invite ancestors, exorcise evil spirits, and wish for a safe and sound life, the sacrifices being pine branches, wormwood leaves, dishes, wine and milk. Meanwhile young people run to fetch clear water from a river, and the one who has first got the water is supposed to be lucky. Still then, all of the family together have buttered glutinous rice for breakfast.

The custom has it that every Pumi family would try to invite home a guest on the 1st of the 1st lunar month, though no one should get into a neighbor's courtyard without invitation. The guest should be robust, gentle, honest and reliable. Once he is invited home, the guest is to be accorded with lavish hospitality. The Pumis in Lanping County of Yunnan Province like to invite a passer-by as guest. Early on the morning of the 1st of the 1st lunar month, the villagers would stay at the entrance to their village, with wine and dishes beside, waiting for a passer-by. They would offer wine and dishes to the first one they meet and invite him home. He who has had a guest home feels honored; hence many villagers are often found trying to invite the same guest. Before he gets into the host's house, the guest would say, "Wish you ample food and clothing, and a peaceful life." And the host would reply: "We owe them to your great blessing." Towards his departure, the guest is presented a piece of meat from a pig's head, rice wine and cakes made of glutinous rice flour.

On the 2nd of the month, all families symbolically plow a bit in their own fields and then drive their farm cattle into the mountain to graze. While their animals graze, people sit together, enjoying wine and dishes they take along, in celebration of the New Year.

The Pumis, of course, see the festival a good opportunity to sing and dance as they are good singers and dancers. They favor most the Sixuanqin Dance and the Sheepskin Dance, which both reflect farming, hunting, spinning, waving and other labors. They dance in vigorous and sprightly movements, to the accompaniment of the lusheng (a reed-pipe wind instrument), the flute, the suona horn (a wind instrument) and other instruments, creating a lively and unrestrained atmosphere. They often sing narrative ballads on young people's love affairs. The festival is also featured by sports like horse racing, high jumping, wrestling, shuttlecock kicking and shooting, a competitive game in which competitors shoot arrows at a cake or a piece of meat hanging from a tree.

On the 3rd of the month, young people, taking along popped corn, highland barley and wheat, hold a rite in the mountain to express their determination to exterminate insect pests. At the rite, they put their popped grains, supposed to be small insect pests, in a bamboo winnower, and the girls of them bury their bracelets supposed to be bigger insect pests in the grains. Then all begin to eat the grains, suggesting that they are eating small insect pests. And all would flick the hand back of a girl when her bracelet first appears from the grains, to mean that a bigger insect pest has been killed and crops will not suffer its harm. On that night most of villagers, in their best clothes, hold a campfire party in the mountain, enjoying themselves to their heart's content all night.

25. 苗　年

　　苗年是我国苗族的传统节日,具有浓郁的民族色彩。由于我国的苗族分布在贵州、云南、四川、湖南、广西等广大地区,因此,苗族人民过苗年的日期也就有所差别,总的日期范围在稻谷入仓和秋种完毕后的每年农历十月至十二月之间。

　　苗年前夕家家都要杀鸡、买肉、精制酸鱼、酿酒、做糯米糍粑和豆腐等,备好应节食物。其中,精制的酸鱼别有风味,是用来祭祀祖先或招待亲友的食品。除夕日各村寨都要打扫除尘,搞好卫生,准备迎接节日。

　　节日早晨,各家要举行"敬牛"和"敬田"仪式。"敬牛"是各家长者在牛鼻子上抹些酒,表示对牛辛苦耕地的犒赏。"敬田"是由各家长者在田地里摆好酒、肉、香、烛和纸钱等祭品,说些"敬田熟谷、敬土收棉"一类的吉祥话语。之后,各家把饭菜摆在火塘边的灶上,举行简短的仪式祭祀祖先,怀念亡灵。再后,全家开怀痛饮,美餐一顿,庆祝节日和丰收。

　　早餐后人们身着新装走村串寨,探亲访友,或去参加内容丰富多彩的节日活动,其中主要有斗牛、踩芦笙、走寨和游方等。斗牛是一项极富民族特色的群众性娱乐活动,不少苗寨设有斗牛场,斗牛场是一块长约50米,宽10余米的坝子,四周有山坡成为天然看台,观众依山观看。参加比赛的牛一般都要打扮一番,在牛的峰包上套一个双龙抢宝或双虎搏斗的精雕深红色峰架,架上插着五面小红旗,犄角插上五颜六色的纸花,脑门上拴一个护头草团,从峰包到尾根两侧拴布条,布条上系彩带和响铃。斗牛前要举行简短的仪式。仪式开始时由一名有威望的老人把葫芦酒洒在斗牛场上,然后宣布斗牛开始。这时寨子里身着民族服装的高大健壮的勇士把两头膘肥体健的蒙上眼睛的犍牛牵入场内,当两牛走到相距不远时,勇士迅速取下牛头上的眼罩后随即闪开,两头犍牛便奋力搏斗起来。这时观众吹呼雀跃,呐喊助兴。经过数个回合决出胜负。获胜者头顶红花,身披红绸,昂首嘶鸣,十分威风,四周观众也一齐欢腾。苗族人非常喜欢看斗牛比赛,有时一场观众可达万余人。

"踩芦笙"即跳芦笙舞,也是苗年的传统重点活动内容,一般多在斗牛结束后举行。苗族青年们成群吹起节拍轻快、雄浑有力的芦笙合奏曲,使整个舞场都沉浸在美妙的旋律之中,盛装的苗族姑娘们翩翩起舞,尽情欢乐。这种舞会还有"讨花带"的习俗,即当外村寨的小伙子到本村寨的芦笙场吹起"讨花带"的芦笙时,姑娘们就把花带挂在小伙子的芦笙上表示感谢。小伙子们得到花带后还要再回场中吹奏一、二次,以向姑娘们表示谢意。

"走寨"更是苗年一种极富民族特色的节日活动。一般由二、三十个身着艳丽民族服装的青年男女组成一个芦笙队,由一位德高望众的老人带领,去邻近的各村寨"走寨子"(即拜年),所到之处都在芦笙场上跳芦笙踩堂舞,舞罢观众齐声欢呼"务啊、务啊!"(即好啊,好啊!)表示热烈欢迎,然后分别邀请客人到家里做客,并热情款待。

"游方"也是节日期间青年男女们的一项重要活动,大多数村寨都有固定的游方场或游方坡,只限于本村寨的未婚女子和外村寨的未婚男子参加。一般是青年男子们事先约定,在天快黑时成群结伴去其他村寨的游方场。到达后就吹起悦耳的木叶哨,并大声呼喊:"妹妹快来游方啊!"村寨里的姑娘们听到哨声和呼喊,就穿戴好漂亮的服饰,三五成群地来到游方场。一般是两男两女对歌,互相唱答或故意逗乐。唱过数轮后姑娘们走到男方身边逗乐取笑。通过游方交往,若双方都有意,男方就将头巾赠与姑娘,姑娘则以金银饰品或腰带回赠,以示定情。

　　在游方场外,夜幕降临后节日喜庆仍在继续,各村寨的楼阁上传来的铜鼓声和歌声响彻夜空。

25. The Miaos' New Year

The Miaos' New Year, with distinctive national flavor, is the traditional festival of the Miao nationality of China. Because they are distributed over the wide areas of Guizhou, Yunnan, Sichuan, Hunan, and Guangxi, the Miao people celebrate their New Year on different days. In general, the festival is observed somewhere from the 10th lunar month to the 12th lunar month after paddy rice is harvested and autumn sowing finished.

Towards the festival, all families are busy preparing festive foods, like chicken, pork, sour fish, wine, glutinous rice cakes, bean curd and so on. Of them, the sour fish, tastes unique, good for worshipping ancestors and entertaining relatives and friends. On New Year's Eve, all families are busy cleaning their houses.

Early on the festive morning, every family is to hold an ox-worshipping rite and a field-worshipping rite. At the former rite, the venerable elder of a family applies some wine to the ox's nose as a reward for its toil in the past year; at the latter rite, the same elder sets out wine, pork, burning sticks, burning candles and sacrificial paper in the fields, and chants some auspicious words like "sacrifice to my paddy fields for better harvests of rice" and "sacrifice to my dry land for better harvests of cotton". Then, every family holds a short rite to worship ancestors, with varied foods set out on the kitchen range beside the fire pit. Still then, all members of a family sit together, drinking and eating to their heart's content in celebration of the festival and bumper crops as well.

After breakfast people, in their holiday best, call on their relatives and friends or join in varied festival activities: mainly bullfighting, the Lusheng Dance, Group New Year Call and Outdoor Antiphonal Singing.

The bullfighting is an entertainment with distinctive Miao flavor. Many Miao villages have grounds for the game. About 50 meters long and 10-odd meters wide, the ground is a stretch of flatland surrounded with hills, which provide natural bleachers. The bull for the game is usually so adorned: its bump is fixed with a crimson rack engraved with the patterns of two dragons struggling for a pearl or two tigers fighting each other, and is planted with five red pennants; its horns are hung with colored paper flowers; its forehead is covered with a round straw pad; its two sides from the hump to the tail are stretched with two cloth strips tied with colored ribbons and small bells. A bullfight is to be preceded by a short ceremony. At the ceremony, a venerable elder sprinkles wine over the ground and then announces the start. Instantly two robust men, in the Miao-style costumes, each leads into the ground a sturdy bull whose eyes are covered. When they are led close to each other and their eye covers are taken off, the bulls immediately plunge themselves into a fierce fight. Meanwhile the spectators burst into cheers and jump for joy. The winner is decided through several rounds of strength trial. With red flowers on its head and red silk draped over its body, the winner holds its head high, neighing in satisfaction to the cheering spectators around. The Miao people are so fond of the bullfighting that spectators for one fight, sometimes, total over ten thousand.

The Lusheng Dance is a dance performed to the accompaniment of the lusheng (a reed-pipe wind instrument), and usually after a bullfight. The girl dancers, in their best costumes, dance trippingly to the lively and forceful strains of the lusheng played by a crowd of young men, throwing all present into joy. The dancing is, sometimes, interspersed by an episode if some of the spectators are young men from neighboring villages. The episode has it that the young men play musical strains on the lusheng to ask for colored ribbons from the girl dancers and the latter readily hang them on the young men's lusheng in appreciation. The young men reciprocate the girls' kindness by playing more strains.

The Group New Year Call is of distinctive Miao flavor. The custom has it that scores of young people, dressed in colorful costumes and headed by a venerable elder, go to neighboring villages to express their New Year greetings while playing the lusheng. When they arrive at a village, they dance to the accompaniment of the lusheng. The dance always ends amid the shouts "Ah! Ah!" (good) from spectators. The guests are to be cordially entertained.

The Outdoor Antiphonal Singing is an important festivity. Most of the Miao villages have their own grounds or hill slopes for the game. Its participants must be unmarried girls from one village and unmarried young men from other villages. According to the custom, groups of young men go to the ground of the girls' village at dusk. On their arrival, the young men whistle a melodious tune on tree-leave whistles and shout: "Sisters! Come to join us in amusements." On hearing the whistles and shouts, the girls in their best come to the ground in threes and fours. Then the two parties begin to do antiphonal sing. After several rounds of antiphonal singing, the girls walk over to the young men to make fun of them. If a young man and a girl take a fancy to each other, he will present a scarf to her and she will reward him with one of her gold or silver ornaments, or waist belt, as a keepsake.

Matching the amusements on the ground, bronze-drum beats and sounds of singing from towers outside the ground resound across the heavens even after nightfall.

26. 四月八

　　四月八节是贵州省贵阳附近苗族人民的传统节日,每年农历四月初八举行。

　　节日那天,贵阳、惠水、龙里一带的苗族群众身着鲜艳的盛装,汇集到贵阳市喷水池旁,举行各种节日活动。小伙子们吹起芦笙、短笛、唢呐,姑娘们则跳起芦笙舞,并展开富有民族特色的山歌对唱活动;除此之外,还有舞狮、赛马、比武、唱花灯等活动使节日热闹非凡。

　　关于这个节日的由来,民间流传着一个动人的传说:早先的贵阳一带由苗族祖先开拓。他们在此安居乐业,管当地叫"格洛格桑"。但官府为了侵夺当地,派兵前来攻打。有位名叫"亚努"的苗族首领骁勇善战,他带领苗族群众与官府战斗,不幸战死,被埋在"嘉八许",即今贵阳喷水池一带。为了纪念这位民族英雄,每到他的忌日,即四月初八,苗族群众纷纷汇聚喷水池旁,举行各种活动祭奠他。这个日子后来逐渐演变成了一个传统节日。

　　另一个流行于贵阳一带的传说也与这个节日的由来有关。据说很早以前,住在"格洛格桑"的一位叫做格波绿的苗族老人带领子孙后代把这一带开垦成了一个苗家人的乐土,不料却招来另一个部落首领胡丈郎的妒馋。奸诈的胡丈郎设计攻占了苗族人民居住的地方,格波绿老人也在战斗中英勇牺牲。

苗族人离开故土后,逃到坡坝沟,在那里建立了自己的家园。但胡丈郎经常欺诈压迫他们。苗族群众忍无可忍,决心起兵攻打胡丈郎,夺回故土。在一位名叫祖德龙的后生带领下,他们与胡丈郎的部落进行了一场战斗,不幸的是祖德龙在战斗中身亡。与格波绿相同的是,他也是在四月初八牺牲在"嘉八许"这个地方。后来,苗族群众为了纪念这两位英雄祖先,每到四月初八,就身着盛装,带上芦笙,结队赶往嘉八许,在那里唱歌跳舞怀念祖先。

26. Siyueba Festival

The Siyueba Festival is a traditional festival observed by the Miao nationality near Guiyang in Guizhou Province, on the 8th of the 4th lunar month which means Siyueba in Chinese.

On that day, in gaily-colored attire people from the areas of Guiyang, Huishui and Longli gather around the Fountain in Guiyang to perform various festival activities. Lads play the reed-pipes, piccolos and suona horns while girls love to dance the reed-pipe dance. They also sing folk song antiphons with Miao characteristics. Moreover, other events like lion dance, horse race, and festive lantern singing add great fun to the festival.

The origin of the festival can be traced back to a moving legend popular among the people, which goes that the area of Guiyang was first cultivated by the ancestors of the Miao nationality. They settled down there and gave the place the name of Geluogesang. Nevertheless, the local authorities sent for troops to occupy this place. A chieftain by the name of Yanu, brave and battlewise, led the Miao people to fight the invaders. Unfortunately he was killed in the battle and was buried at Jiabaxu, which is near the present Fountain area in Guiyang. In memory of the national hero the Miao people converged around the Fountain and performed different events to make sacrifices to him on the date of his death, that is, the 8th of the 4th lunar month, out of which the traditional festival evolves.

Another legend circulating around the area of Guiyang relates to the origin of the festival as well. It is said that long ago Gebolü, an old man of a Miao tribe living in Geluogesang, led his children and grandchildren to cultivate the place so that it became an earthly paradise of the Miao people. Unexpectedly it incurred the covetousness of Huzhanglang, a chieftain of another tribe. Huzhanglang, a treacherous man, captured the place of the Miao people by design, and Gebolü died a heroic death in the battle.

The Miao people had to leave their homeland and flee to Bobagou, where they established their home. Being often bullied and oppressed by Huzhanglang, they came to the end of their forbearance and determined to rise up against him and seize back their native land. Led by a young man named Zudelong they fought against the tribe of Huzhanglang. Unfortunately he died in the battle. Like Gebolü Zudelong sacrificed his life at the place of Jabaxu on the 8th day of the 4th lunar month. To commemorate the two heroic forefathers, the Miao people, with their Lusheng and in their holiday best, go to Jiabaxu in crowds on the the 8th of the 4th lunar month every year, where they sing and dance.

27. 姊妹节

　　"姊妹节"的原意为"吃姊妹饭",是贵州省清水江流域苗族青年男女聚会的传统节日,从每年的农历三月十五日开始,节期一至三天。

　　关于姊妹节的来历,在当地流传着一个美好的传说:据说在很久很久以前,清水江畔有一群聪明、美丽、活泼的苗族姑娘,她们丰衣足食、生活愉快。但美中不足的是当地缺少青年小伙子,又很少和外界接触,因此她们中的大多数人成年后还未找到如意郎君。为了自己的婚事,她们就聚集在一起商议,通过分析比较,她们认为自己居住的地方山清水秀,土地肥沃、物产丰富、气候宜人,而且她们一个个都生得如花似玉、聪慧伶俐,谁也不愿意离开家园,远嫁他乡。于是她们为了生活得更加快乐幸福,决定一人准备一份美味饭菜,在三月十五日这天大家相聚会餐,唱歌跳舞,痛痛快快地玩耍。谁知到了姑娘们联欢会餐的那天,知道消息的远方近处的小伙子们都去看热闹,使其会餐的清水江畔挤满了英姿飒爽的青年小伙子。姑娘们非常高兴,请他们一同会餐,邀请他们一道唱歌跳舞,大家都玩耍得很痛快。分别时,热情好客的姑娘们又用自己的帕子包了糯米饭送给他们。小伙子们受到了热情款待,非常高兴。过了数日,小伙子们仍然留念着那群美丽的姑娘,就以还帕为名,又送给姑娘们一些彩色绣花线,以示感谢。从此便经常寻机会来找姑娘们玩耍,唱歌跳舞,增进了彼此之间的感情。不久姑娘们都找到了自己称心如意的心上人。姑娘们为了永远不忘那个聚集会餐的日子,继续传播爱的种子,就决定每年的农历三月十五日都聚集会餐。久而久之,便演变为独具民族特色的姊妹节,成为青年男女们谈情、说爱、择偶的共同佳节。

在节日里,苗族的每户人家都要吃姊妹饭。姊妹饭是用野生植物的鲜花和嫩叶汁把糯米染成五颜六色,然后再放在木甑子里蒸熟而成,其色鲜艳,晶莹透亮,清香悦目,松软可口,其中的黄色饭团是用当地产的一种野生植物的黄色花朵染成的,苗族人称这种花为"姊妹花",是姊妹饭里必不可少的一种颜色。

节日的一大早,清水江畔就聚满了穿戴一新的人群。苗族姑娘们身穿绣着美丽花纹图案,缀满银牌和银铃的民族服装,头上戴着鸾凤银冠,颈上戴着项圈银链,两耳佩戴银质耳环,手腕上戴着各式手镯;小伙子们则穿着青、蓝、紫等各色对襟衣服,头上包帕,显得格外潇洒利索。青年男女们在江岸上参加或观看各种娱乐活动,如踩鼓、跳芦笙舞、斗牛、划船、鸣锣、击鼓、吹芦笙、唱山歌等。其中斗牛是最热烈的场面。在斗牛场上,随着芦笙的欢快演奏,一头体健硕大的雄牛被牵进赛场。它一听见了芦笙响,就吹鼻刨蹄,不停地转圈,好像是在迫不及待地期待着进行战斗。接着赛场上又鞭炮齐鸣,另一头高大壮实的雄牛也健步入场。待两头牛相距不远时,双方主人即解开牛的缰绳,在牛屁股上拍打几下立即闪开,两头牛就开始步步逼近,怒目出击。它们在争战中时而互相猛冲猛抵,时而挥角低头撞击,在相互进进退退、冲冲打打的搏斗中,牛角撞得砰砰作响,战斗十分艰苦激烈。通常要进行较长时间的反复决斗才能分出胜负。若双方势均力敌,决不出输赢时,人们就上前去把两头牛分开。这时四周的观众一齐涌进斗牛场,往牛的背上和头上抹泥巴,表示向双方牛主人祝贺。牛的主人也极高兴,双脚不停地欢跳。同时全场持续不断地响彻着"吁——吁——吁……"的欢呼声。

黄昏时分,中老年人陆续离开清水江畔,宽阔的草地和沙滩就成为了青年男女的世界。他们的活动内容主要是唱音调高昂的"飞歌"(即山歌)和社交恋爱的"游方歌"(即玩耍)。在夜幕下,到处是自由对歌的青年男女,嘹亮激越与温柔多情的悦耳歌声在夜空中荡漾,使歌场上的青年男女们沉浸在歌与爱的无比欢乐与幸福之中。大约唱到夜间十点时分,有些小伙们集体邀请姑娘们回到村寨灯火通明宽敞的房子里赴宴对歌。室内的中央摆着几张方桌,桌面上摆满了鲜鱼、腊肉、腌鸭蛋、荷包蛋、大块豆腐、大粑粑、炒花生、煮熟公鸡及其他一些美味佳肴。宴会开始前,首先由一位"小伙子头"和一位"姑娘头"配成一对带头入席。其余的青年男女则各自邀约配对后相继入席就座。这时凑热闹的观众已围满了一屋,为宴席助兴。对歌宴开始时,小伙子头首先举杯,唱着充满深情厚意的优美的敬酒歌,向"姑娘头"敬酒。姑娘头可以接过酒杯一饮而尽,也可以不接酒杯,继续与小伙子头对唱,有时要对唱一个多小时姑娘头才接杯饮酒。姑娘头干杯后,立即向小伙子头回敬一杯,小伙子头干杯后,接着向下一位姑娘敬酒,于是又展开一场新的对歌饮酒。如此往返,人人都要对歌饮酒,因此在宴席间掀起一个又一个欢乐的浪潮。桌旁围观的人群也随着宴席上的浪潮一同欢呼、喝彩、鼓掌,使室内始终洋溢着欢乐的气氛,直到雄鸡啼鸣,东方破晓,对歌宴会才宣告结束,姑娘小伙们才尽兴而归。

27. Sister Festival

The Sister Festival, derived from the Sister Dinner, is a traditional festival especially celebrated by young Miao people living along the Qingshui River in Guizhou Province. It lasts from one to three days starting from the 15th of the third lunar month.

The festival hangs a beautiful legend, which is popular among the locals. According to the legend, a long, long time ago there lived some Miao girls on the bank of the Qingshui River. Though they were bright, beautiful, vivacious, well-fed and well-clothed, most of them had not married either because the local young men were insufficient for choice or because the girls had little contact with outside areas. So the girls put their heads together, trying to find a solution to this problem. Through discussions they concluded that they would not marry anyone living far away from their homeland since the place had green hills, clear waters, good soil, abundant products and delightful weather, and that they would hold a dinner party on the 15th of the 3rd lunar month to come, each contributing an appetizing dish, to enjoy themselves to their heart's content by eating, singing and dancing. It was unexpected that the dinner party drew many handsome young men far and near to watch the girls' performance. Very delighted, the girls invited the young men to dine, sing and dance with them. They all had a very good time that day. At departure the hospitable girls gave the guests each some steamed glutinous rice wrapped with their handkerchiefs, and the boys left in great satisfaction. Yearning to see the beautiful girls, a few days later the boys came to the girls on the excuse of returning the handkerchiefs, and sent the latter each some colored silk threads for embroidery in thanks for their hospitality. After that they often came to play, sing and dance with the girls, bringing them closer in affection. Not long afterwards all the girls had chosen their beloved. To mark the day and provide chances for other girls and boys to establish ties of love in the future, the Miao girls made it a regular practice to have a dinner party of the kind on the day every year. In the course of time, the party evolved into the present Sister Festival, which is a golden chance for the young to court their future spouses.

During the festival, every Miao family would eat Sister Rice, a kind of glutinous rice balls dyed colorful with different juices of wild plants' leaves and flowers, and steamed in a wooden steamer. The rice is crystal, fragrant, soft and appetite-inviting. The yellow rice ball, which is an indispensable variety of Sister Rice on the dining table, is dyed with a local wild plant's flowers known as Sister Flower.

Early on the morning of the first day of the festival the Miaos, clad in their holiday best, crowd the bank of the Qingshui River. The girls wear costumes decorated with beautiful designs, silver trinkets and silver bells, and adorn themselves with silver head ornaments, silver necklaces, silver earrings and various bracelets. The young men wear collarless jackets in black, blue or purplish and turbans, looking natural and brisk. Both girls and boys pitch in or watch various entertainments, such as the drum dance, lusheng dance, bullfight, boat rowing, gong striking, drum beating, lusheng (a wind instrument) playing, folk song singing, and so on. Of them, the bullfight is the most exciting. As the fight begins, a big and strong bull is led into an arena to the cheerful music of the lusheng. At the music, the animal keeps mooing, hoofing and walking around, as if to challenge any opponent. A while later another bull, big and strong likewise, is led into the arena amidst the pop of firecrackers. When the bulls are not far from each other, their owners unrein them and tap their hips to urge them to fight. Staring, the animals walk towards each other and begin to fight, locking their horns or attacking each other's horns, which causes clatters. Usually the victor comes out only through a number of fierce fights. If victory hangs in the balance anyway, the bulls would be disengaged by men. At this moment some spectators crowd into the arena and plaster mud on both bulls, an expression of congratulating both bull owners on victory, while the owners keep jumping with great excitement. At this moment all spectators keep shouting "Whoa-whoa-whoa", making the scene even more hilarious.

Towards evening only young people remain there. They engage in singing folk songs and love songs locally known as youfang in antiphonal style. Their voices, clear and loud or soft and pleasant, linger in the dark air for long and all merry makers are immersed in great joy and happiness. About ten o'clock at night, some of the young men would invite some of the girls to a well-lit and spacious room; there they continue to do antiphonal singing while enjoying a feast. In the center of the room are tables laid with many appetizing foods, such as fish, cured meat, salted duck eggs, fried eggs, bean curd, cakes, roasted peanuts, cooked roosters, and the like. In the beginning of the singing a girl and a boy, two supposed leaders, first pair off and take their seats at a table. Then other young people follow suit while spectators crowd around to cheer for them. Still then, the boy leader proposes a toast to the girl leader while singing an affectionate song. The girl leader may either take over the cup and drink the wine down in one gulp or merely serenade her partner without taking over the cup. In the latter case, the antiphonal singing sometimes lasts over an hour before the girl takes over the cup to drink at last. In either case, the girl leader would propose a toast, in return, to the boy leader. After the first round, the boy leader would do the same to another girl. They keep so singing and drinking, bringing about one surge of excitement after another. Meanwhile the spectators keep shouting and clapping their hands, making the atmosphere more hilarious. The merry-making lasts until cocks crow at daybreak.

28. 六月六

六月六,或称六月街,是布依族的传统节日。布依族主要分布在贵州南部和贵阳地区,语言从属汉藏语系壮侗语族。布依人在农历六月六庆祝自己的节日,也有在六月十六或二十六的。

节日那天,他们给祖先供奉猪、牛、鸡、粽子等祭品。布依人庆祝这个节日就是为了纪念祖先反压迫斗争所取得的胜利。

同一天,人们吃糯米饭和糯米粑,喝糯米酒并将米团染成五色象征五谷丰登。村民们把涂有鸡血和猪血的纸三角旗插在田地里预防虫害。这一风俗起源于一个民间传说:

从前,勤劳勇敢的青年六六从一口直通龙宫的水井汲水时,捉回一只好看的虾。当晚,六六梦见了月亮女神寻找女儿。第二天,他干完农活儿回家,发现有位美丽的姑娘在为他做饭,这姑娘就是月亮女神的六公主,她对勇敢的六六倾慕已久。他俩成了亲,一年后喜得一子,邻里叫他天王。天王长得很快,是种庄稼的能手。可惜好景不长,国王垂涎月亮公主的美貌,派士兵来抢她。在去王宫的路上,公主飞上月宫,六六也跟去了,留下天王孤零零一人。当地官员眼馋天王的庄稼,为了霸占庄稼想杀死他,但穷苦的伙伴们放走了他,让他飞往月宫去。临走前，天王告诉大伙儿他会让蝗虫下界糟蹋贪官污吏的庄稼以示惩罚，老百姓的庄稼就以烧香、祭祀同他们的区分开来。由于月亮公主掌管六月雨水，从那以后，每年六月不是暴雨就是干旱，并且蝗虫猖獗。人们记起天王的话，赶紧杀猪、烧香祈求风调雨顺、粮食丰收。每到天王升天的六月六日，老百姓就晾晒衣服预防虫蛀。小伙子们则去河边唱起动听的情歌，盼望像六六一样找到自己的"月亮公主"。

　　节日那天，妇女们挎着满篮的粽子，走村串寨的拜亲访友；年轻人身着民族服装，聚集在广场参加如对歌、丢花包或赶表这样一些活动。对歌通常分组进行，人数不限，可以是两人，也可以是十来人。丢花包在清初就已流行。花包内缝小豆、米糠、棉籽等，过去只向自己倾心的人投掷，现在则可用来表达敬意。赶表是布依年轻人找对象的活动：青年男女聚集在一起，通过"雀子"（即媒人）的介绍，俩俩相识。如果彼此情投意合，就找个地方对唱情歌；如不中意则委婉拒绝。

28. Double Sixth Festival

Double Sixth Festival, also known as the Sixth Month Fair, is a traditional festival of the Buyi Chinese, who live in Guizhou Province, especially in southern Guizhou and around the city of Guiyang. These people whose language belongs to the Zhuang-Dong subfamily of the Sino-Tibetan language family celebrate their festival on the 6th of the 6th lunar month, or the 16th or 26th of that month in some places.

On the day of the festival, the Buyi people sacrifice to their ancestors pigs, cattle, chicken, glutinous rice dumpling and the like. The festival is celebrated to commemorate their forbears' victory in the struggle against oppression.

On that day, not only do people eat cooked glutinous rice and glutinous rice cake, but they also drink glutinous rice wine. They dye the rice in five colors to symbolize an abundance of crops. Villagers in some areas plant into their farming land paper pennants soaked with the blood of roosters and pigs to prevent their crops from insect pests. This custom originated from the following legend.

Long long ago, there was a brave hard-working young man named Liu Liu ("liu" in Chinese is the figure 6). One day when he drew water from a well that was connected with the Palace of the Dragon King, he caught a good-looking shrimp and brought it home. That night Liu Liu dreamed about the Moon Lady's looking for her daughter. When he came home from the fields the next day, Liu Liu found a pretty girl cooking for him. The girl who had long before fallen in love with Liu Liu for his bravery was the Moon Lady's 6th daughter. They got married and had a son a year later. The boy, who was called Tian Wang, the god, by the neighbors, grew up fast and was expert at farming. The good days, however, didn't last long. Coveting the Moon Princess's beauty, the king sent his soldiers to take her away. The princess flew to the moon on the way to the palace and Liu Liu followed, leaving Tian Wang alone on earth. Local officials intended to kill him so as to seize his crops. Luckily, Tian Wang was set free by the poor. He had ensured, before he flew to the moon, that he would punish the cruel officials by sending locusts down to destroy their crops and requested that the poor mark their crops by offering sacrifices and burning incense. As his mother, the Moon Princess, was in charge of the 6th lunar month's rain, every year in that month, there were either storms or droughts, and more and more locusts. The poor, remembering Tian Wang's words, slaughtered pigs and burned incense to pray for good weather and bumper harvests. Every year on the 6th of the 6th lunar month, the day when Tian Wang flew to the moon, Buyi families will air their clothes to rid them of pests. Young men, on the other hand, like to sing sweet love songs along the riverbanks in the hope that they might find their own moon princesses like Liu Liu.

On that day, women, carrying baskets of zongzi, pay visits to their relatives and friends from one village to another. Young people, dressed in their folk clothing, crowd the square to participate in such games as antiphonal singing, silk ball throwing and lover seeking (Ganbiao in the Buyi language).

Antiphonal singing is often done between groups, but the number of singers is not limited, ranging from 2 to 10 odd. Silk ball throwing has been a popular game ever since the early Qing Dynasty. The ball, filled with red beans, rice bran and cottonseeds, used to be thrown to a desirable partner but is now used either to show respect or love. Ganbiao is a game by means of which young Buyi people seek lovers. The game goes like this: a large crowd of young men and women gather at a square and are introduced to one another by a que zi, a matchmaker. A young man and a young woman find a place to sing love songs in the antiphonal style if they are congenial to each other. Otherwise one will tactfully refuse the other.

29.歌墟节

　　歌墟节是广西壮族农村中一种群众性的唱歌活动,也是他们的传统节日。节期在每年的春秋两季,每期数日。春季的歌墟节多在农历三月三日前后举行,秋季的歌墟节则多选在中秋节前后举行。

　　歌墟节是汉语的叫法,壮语却有多种称谓,如有的地方叫"欢龙洞",意为到田间去唱歌;有的地方叫"圩蓬",意为欢乐的节日;有的地方叫"欢窝敢",意为在岩洞外唱歌……壮族人民认为唱歌可以沁脾乐神,防病治病,延年益寿,消灾除祸,所以经常选择吉日去野外唱歌,久而久之逐渐发展为定期举行的歌墟节。

　　但关于歌墟节的来历,在民间却有多种传说。其中一种说,从前有一对美丽的壮族青年男女,他们情深意笃,擅长唱歌,因此常以唱歌表达诚挚的感情。但由于受到双方父母的干预,不能结为伉俪,最终酿成以身殉情的悲剧。那天正是农历三月三日壮族歌仙刘三姐遇害的日子。从此以后,壮族青年们为了反抗不合理的婚姻习俗,追求婚姻自主,在每年的三月三日这天就集中在一起唱山歌三天三夜,挑选自己的意中人。

　　关于歌墟节的历史演变的确是有据可考的,如北宋《太平寰宇记》中就有"男女盛服,聚会作歌"的记载。《说蛮》中也说及壮族每逢春秋男女聚会唱歌。明代的歌墟节已和现代相近,壮族青年男女在春秋两季携带礼物,在风光秀美的山上旷野去吹箫奏笛,女子三五唱歌,男子成群来和,歌声持续不断。歌墟节还是他们谈情说爱的好机会,且出现了抛绣球的游戏。歌墟节在清代得到了进一步发展,有的村寨常达数千人,活动内容也更为丰富。到民国时期,广西举行歌墟节或类似活动的范围已达二十六个县,几乎遍及广西壮族人民所居住的各个地区。

据传说与文献记载,历史上的歌墟节多以"依歌择配"为主要内容,如广西横州一带每年歌墟节前一个多月,男子将布帕送给他看上的女子,如女子有意,就在布帕上绣花归还,叫做"抛帕";宾州一带在每年春秋歌墟期,男女聚会时各自拿着扇子和手帕互相拍着玩,物色意中人,称为"博扇"。

在歌墟节前夕,歌墟附近的村寨各家都要扫房设铺,备好酒菜和五色糯米饭,待到歌墟节时接待远道而来的亲朋好友。有的地方还要为对歌搭彩棚,凡是未婚姑娘都必须每人拿出一匹10米至几十米长的布来搭歌棚,这些布将作为姑娘们日后出嫁时的嫁妆之一。

每到歌墟节时青年男女们都穿戴打扮得十分漂亮,集中到旷野或山头或竹林或草坡,再按男女分组互相对歌,从白昼到夜晚,到处都响彻着动人的歌声。歌墟场上唱的歌有多种,其中有情歌、盘歌、叙事歌、农事歌、故事歌等。正规的歌墟节还有自己固定的一套程式,不能任意唱歌。程式规定开始时唱"见面歌和赞美歌",以示互相问候;接着唱"求歌"(也称"请歌"),即请对方唱歌;然后唱"盘歌",盘歌的内容十分丰富,天文、地理、历史、哲学、文学、社会生活、劳动生产等均可作为一问一答的内容；最后唱"倾慕歌"(初交歌)、"盟誓歌"(深交歌)。此外，对歌者应按不同对象的身份特征来确定歌的内容，否则会被视为失礼。

在对歌的同时，有些青年男女们在各自的布棚里隔棚互相抛掷绣球，接绣球是对自己聪明才智的一种考验，当把绣球抛到对方场内时若接不住，说明接绣球的人不灵巧，不敏捷，有时还要罚他唱歌或表演节目。因此抛掷绣球时双方都很投入，以致有的人过于慌乱而逗引人捧腹大笑。绣球也是未婚青年男女们传播爱情的信物，当未婚的女青年把绣球悄悄送给她选中的意中人，对方又回赠毛巾，手巾等物品后，双方再通过对歌增进了解，即可进而结为秦晋之盟。

有些地方的歌墟节活动还各有特点，例如平果、马山等地的歌墟节还有放花炮的活动，每场歌墟先放三炮，然后唱歌，因此称为"花炮歌墟"。再如都安一带的歌墟节有碰蛋的习俗。节前各家都把鸡、鸭、鹅蛋煮熟，染成鲜红色，用绳子连成一串。在歌墟节日里青年男女们提着蛋串在人群中物色对象，看中时就用自己手里的红蛋去碰对方的红蛋。如果对方同意，就用蛋碰蛋，双方即可以到人少的地方去交谈，以增进互相了解，建立友谊甚至爱情。如果对方不同意，便以手掩蛋。

歌墟节给壮族人带来欢乐，给壮家青年带来爱情，必将越来越热闹。

29. Singing Festival

Featured by mass singing, the festival is celebrated as one of the traditional festivals by the rural people in the Guangxi Zhuang Autonomous Region. It is observed twice every year; usually the first takes place around the 3rd day of the 3rd lunar month and the second around the Mid – autumn Festival (the 15th day of the 8th lunar month), each spanning a couple of days.

The Singing Festival, known as "Gexujie" in the Chinese language, is called differently in the Zhuang language in different regions: "Huanlongdong" in some regions, which means singing in the fields; "Xupeng" in other regions, which means a joyous festival; "Huanwogan" in still other regions, which means singing outside a grotto. The early Zhuang people thought that singing could refresh mind, gladden hearts, prevent and cure diseases, prolong life and ward off misfortunes, so they often gathered outdoors on an auspicious day to sing songs. This activity gradually grew into the present Singing Festival.

The origin of the festival, however, has different folk legends behind. One of them tells that long ago a young man and a girl of the Zhuangs, both good singers, often did antiphonal singing to express their deep and sincere love for each other. However, they could not get married due to their parents' interference, and died for love. Their death day happened to be the 3rd day of the 3rd lunar month, on which Third Sister Liu, a Zhuang singing star, was murdered. After their tragical death, the young Zhuangs gathered outdoors, on that day every year, to sing folk songs for three days and nights on end, expressing their resistance against the loathsome convention of arranged marriage as well as their determination to choose their beloved ones of their own will.

The true development of the Singing Festival is recorded in historical books. Here are two examples: Notes on Geographical Conditions and Local Customs of China, a book in the Northern Song Dynasty (960 – 1127), describes how the Zhuangs, dressed in their best, gathered and sang; Notes on the Savage Tribes, a book in the Yuan Dynasty (1206 – 1368), describes how the Zhuangs gathered and sang in spring and autumn. In the Ming Dynasty (1368 – 1644) the festival was somewhat like what it is today in terms of celebration. Usually, young Zhuang people, bringing along gifts for singing partners, went to scenic mountains or fields. There they, grouped on the basis of sex, played wind instruments, did antiphonal singing, and played the game of casting colored silk balls to court marital partners. In the Qing Dynasty (1616 – 1911) the festival grew a lot in scale, often several thousand participants in a village, and was much richer in content. In the period of the Republic of China (1912 – 1949), the festival spread up to 26 counties, almost covering all the regions inhabited by the Zhuangs of Guangxi.

The festival in the past, according to historical documents and legends, was featured by the choice of marital partners. Take Guangxi's Hengzhou and Binzhou counties for example. A

Hengzhou young man, who took a fancy to a girl, would meaningfully give her a handkerchief over a month before the festival; the girl, if she loved the man, would embroider the handkerchief with patterns and give it back at the festival. This was called "a handkerchief tactic". In Binzhou a young man and a girl, the former holding a fan and the latter a handkerchief, would tap each other with the things in their hands at the festival, trying to find a beloved one. This was called "a fan tactic".

The custom has it that all families, in the villages near a festival celebration site, are to clean up houses, put up makeshift beds, and prepare wine, food and colored steamed glutinous rice, shortly before the festival, for their relatives and friends who come from afar for the occasion. Colored-cloth canopies would be put up for antiphonal singing in some regions; each unmarried girl has to offer a piece of cloth, from ten to dozens of meters long, for the canopies, and later the cloth is to be returned to the offerer as trousseau.

At the festival young people, dressed in their best, gather in the fields, atop hills, among bamboo groves or on grass-covered hillside, and do antiphonal singing in groups based on sex. They sing from morning to night, with strains resounding far and wide. The songs cover a wide variety of contents, such as love, inquiries, narration, farming, stories, and so on. The singers, engaged in formal antiphonal singing, should sing songs according to the priority of contents: first the songs of meeting and praise, which are for greeting; then the songs of invitation, which are given to invite partners of the opposite sex to sing; still then the songs of inquiries, which are designed to ask partners of the opposite sex to answer questions of astronomy, geography, history, philosophy, literature, social life, labor, production and the like; last the songs of admiration, which express the initial establishment of friendship between singers, and the songs of devotion, which express the establishment of profound friendship between singers. And the singers should consider their partners' status when they decide the exact contents of songs, or they would be seen as breachers of etiquette.

While the antiphonal singing is going on, some other young men and girls may be busy casting colored silk balls from one canopy to another. How well one can catch the ball is the measurement of one's intelligence. Whoever fails to catch the ball is seen as clumsy, and even made to sing a song or give a performance as a forfeit. Hence, the players so cautiously concentrate themselves on the game that some of them set audience roaring with laughter for their panic manner. The colored silk ball is also seen as a keepsake by the Zhuangs. An unmarried girl often secretly gives such a ball to a young man she takes a fancy to, and the latter usually reciprocates the embodiment of love with a towel or a handkerchief, thus establishing a tie. Later, the two may get to know more about each other through antiphonal singing at the festival and even get married still later.

The festivities in some regions have other features. Take Pingguo and Mashan counties for example. Their antiphonal singing at the festival is preceded by firing three fireworks, hence the festival there is known as "the Singing Festival of Fireworks". Take Du'an

County for another example. The Singing Festival there is featured by, besides others, egg-touching. The custom has it that young unmarried Zhuang people dye red, boil and string eggs of hens, ducks or geese before the festival. They would walk about among celebrators at the festival gathering, each holding a string of eggs, and trying to find a desirable young one of the opposite sex. If any of them finds one, he or she would touch the opposite one's egg string with his or hers. The touched one, if in consent, would touch back the same way. Then both would go to a secluded place to talk over friendship and even love. The touched one, if in discontent, would shield his or her egg string with hands from more touches.

The Singing Festival celebration will be livelier and livelier each year, as it lends joy to all the Zhuangs, and opportunities to the young to court.

30.达努节

"达努"意为"瑶人",达努节是瑶族人民的传统节日,即瑶年,又称盘古节和祖娘节,于每年的农历五月二十六日开始过节,节期为四天。

关于达努节的由来,在瑶族人民中还有一段十分感人的故事。据说远古时候,在如今的广西和广东一带有两座一样高大秀美的山峰,左边那座叫布洛西山,右边那座叫密洛沱山,这两座山会相向移动,每年靠近一步,经历 1995 年后,它们靠近了 1995 步。又过了 5 年,它们靠拢了,就在这年的农历五月二十九日,大地上一声巨响,两座山同时裂开了,布洛西山的裂缝中走出一个身材魁伟的男子,他就叫布洛西;密洛沱山的裂缝中走出一位身材苗条的女子,她就是密洛沱。他们就把这一天作为自己的生日,不久他们又结为幸福的夫妻。他们生了一个俊俏的女儿,名叫瑶台。瑶台长大后母亲密洛沱给了她一袋稻种,教她上山开荒种地,自谋生路。瑶台很勤劳,种的庄稼长得很好。可是从播种到收获前的过程中,都不断遭到鸟兽的毁坏,辛苦一年,几乎颗粒无收。第二年母亲密洛沱又给了瑶台一袋稻种,还给了她一面铜鼓,说:"你烦恼时敲敲铜鼓,就会愁云消散,高兴起来。鸟兽听见铜鼓响就吓跑了,不敢来吃你的庄稼。"从此瑶台在山里安居乐业,丰衣足食,心情愉快,成为了瑶族人民的祖先,铜鼓也成为了他们的传家宝,人人喜爱它。密洛沱年老后,有一天她把女儿瑶台叫回家说:"五月二十九日是我的生日,我不要你什么礼物,到时候你给我带一坛小米酒和四两新麻来就行了。在我生日前三天,你拿铜鼓来闹场。"瑶台遵照母亲的吩咐一一照办了。至今瑶族人民的达努节都是从农历五月二十六日开始,到二十九日结束。而且家家户户都用四两新麻作为祭祀品,表示永远记住民族母亲的生日和恩情。

瑶族人民在达努节人人都梳妆打扮,穿戴一新。家家都要杀鸡宰羊,喝香喷喷的陈年米酒。在节日里还有丰富多彩的各种活动,其中主要有"铜鼓舞"、"兴郎铁玖舞"、点冲天炮、对歌、笑酒等活动。

铜鼓是流行于广西、广东、云南和贵州等地区少数民族的打击乐器,大约出现在春秋中期。铜鼓大小不一,鼓腔中空,无底,两侧有铜耳环,鼓面鼓身雕刻有精美的花纹。铜鼓舞则是一种极富有民族特色的舞蹈,也是一个比赛项目。比赛时一般每次出场二男一女,其中一名男子敲悬挂在木架上的铜鼓,并按习惯鼓点和节奏边敲边舞;另一名男子站在场边敲皮鼓,而且要表演多种不断变化的优美舞姿;女的则拿着草帽在铜鼓手后面边舞边扇,两人的动作必须配合协调,共同表演出优美的舞蹈。各组出场表演完后要评出一组最佳鼓手,并向最佳鼓手敬酒祝贺,颁发纪念品,赠予鼓王称号。

"兴郎铁玖舞"是为庆祝达努节而跳的纪念舞,在节日的夜间举行。当夜幕降临时,瑶族男女老少便提着灯笼,打着火把聚集在广场,欢快地跳舞。"兴郎铁玖舞"由十个单独成舞的段落组成,其先后顺序为:猴鼓舞、藤拐舞、猎兽舞、开山舞、南瓜舞、采茶舞、丰收舞、牛角舞、芦笙舞、花伞舞等。这些舞蹈粗犷泼辣、节奏轻快,生活气息浓厚,极具民族风情。

点冲天炮也是达努节的一项娱乐活动。冲天炮是瑶族人民把自制的火药装到一个铁筒里,再装上炮捻。节日时在广场里按一定距离放置,数量最少数十枚,最多可达数百枚。放置完后由若干名男女放炮手来点燃,比赛谁点燃的多。

瑶族人民过达努节也有对歌的活动,一般都在跳舞后举行。青年男女们唱的是情意深长的"趣话歌",对歌后又邀请意中人到他处去唱情歌,通过对歌选择伴侣。中老年人唱的是饶有风趣的"醉酒歌",每唱完一段就全体举杯饮酒欢呼。对歌直到午夜方散。

另外都安瑶族人民在达努节时还有"笑酒"的习俗。就是喝酒的人一边喝酒一边对讲一段简短的笑话或对唱一首简短的歌,这些笑话和歌都运用了比喻手法,含有讽刺对方的意味,让人听后哈哈大笑,当然被讽刺的人也不示弱,用同样的手段来回敬对方,于是又引起一场哄堂大笑,因此人们把过达努节时这样饮酒说唱的习俗叫做"笑酒"。

30. Danu Festival

The Danu Festival, in which Danu means the Yao people in the local language, is the Yaos' New Year. Also known as the Pangu Festival and the Zuniang Festival, it lasts four days from the 26th of the 5th lunar month.

Its birth hangs a touching legend, which circulates among the Yaos. In ancient times, the legend says, there stood two mountains in the areas of present Guangxi and Guangdong provinces of China. They were equally high and scenic. The one on the left was called Buluoxi and the one on the right Miluotuo. They kept moving towards each other, bringing them a step closer a year. So, 1995 years' movement had brought them 1995 steps closer. Another five years' movement had brought them together. On the 29th of the 5th lunar month that year, the two mountains spilt at the same time with a thunderous crack. Out of the left mountain's opening came a stalwart young man named Buluoxi while from the right mountain's opening came a slim girl named Miluotuo. Both took the day as their birthdays. Some time later, they got married and had a beautiful baby girl named Yaotai. Miluotuo gave her daughter a bag of paddy rice seeds and asked her to reclaim wasteland on the mountain for cultivation of paddy rice, when the latter grew up. Thanks to her hard work, Yaotai's crops in the first year were coming along fine. Unfortunately they were often damaged by birds and beasts during their growth, with the result that her hard work of one year was almost rewarded with nothing. The next year, Miluotuo gave her daughter another bag of paddy rice seeds and a bronze drum, saying: "It will be helpful to beat the drum as the drumbeats can dispel your worries and frighten birds and beasts away from your crops." From then on, Yaotai lived a life of peace, contentment and plenty. She is supposed to be ancestress of the Yao people, and the drum had been later handed down as an heirloom. One day in her old age, Miluotuo recalled her daughter home and said to her: "My birthday is the 29th of the 5th lunar month. I expect from you, as birthday gift, nothing more than a jar of rice wine and four liang (a unit of weight, each about 50 grams) of hemp. Besides, I hope you come to beat the bronze drum in celebration on the 26th, three days before my birthday." Yaotai did all as she had been told; hence the present Danu Festival lasts four days from the 26th of the 5th lunar month, and every household offers four liang of newly reaped hemp as sacrifice to the Yao people's ancestress for her birthday and kindness.

To mark the festival, all celebrators dress smartly, eat chicken and mutton, and drink long-reserved rice wine. The festival is also featured by varied entertainments. The main ones of them are dancing Bronze Drum Dance and Xinglangtiejiu Dance, setting off rockets, doing antiphonal singing, and "joking in drinking".

The bronze drum is a percussion instrument popular among the minority nationalities in Guangxi, Guangdong, Yunnan and Guizhou. Its birth dates back to the middle of the Spring and Autumn Period (770–476 B.C.). The drum is painted all over with exquisite patterns and fixed with a bronze ring on either side, its body hollow and bottom open. The Bronze Drum Dance is of distinctive Yao flavor and often presented as a competitive item. The dancers are divided into groups for competition, each consisting of two males and one female. One of the males dances to rhythmical drumbeats while beating a bronze drum hung on a wooden stand; the other male dances in graceful movements while beating an oxhide-headed drum to accompany other two dancers just outside the performance court; the female dances behind the first male while waving a straw cap, the cooperation between them being well in harmony. The best group is to be chosen for its two drummers in the end. And the two best drummers each are to be rewarded with a toast, a souvenir and the little "master drummer".

The Xinglangtiejiu dance is performed at night to add festive joy. When night falls festival celebrators, men and women, old and young, begin to joyfully dance it on a ground lit by lanterns and torches. The dance consists of ten component dances, which are given in the order: the Monkey–Drum Dance, the Cane Crutch Dance, the Hunting Dance, the Mountain-Cutting Dance, the Pumpkin Dance, the Tea-Picking Dance, the Bumper Harvest Dance, the Ox Horn Dance, the Lusheng Dance and the Figured Umbrella Dance. These dances are characterized by boldness, lively rhythm, rich life flavor and distinctive Yao flavor.

The rocket set off at the festival is a short iron tube filled with gunpowder and fixed with a fuse. Dozens, even hundreds, of rockets are lined on the ground, with the same distance in between. Especially-chosen people light them, matching one another for speed.

The antiphonal singing is usually done after the dancing. Young people first sing "interesting songs" and then go, in male-female pairs, to secluded places to sing love songs. Many of the singers try to find their marital partners through the antiphonal singing. Middle-aged and old people sing "tipplers' songs", and they drink and shout after they sing a song. The entertainment is usually not stopped until midnight.

The "joking in drinking" is an amusement popular among the Yao people in Du'an County of Guangxi when they celebrate the festival. In this amusement, each pair of festival celebrators, while drinking, sing songs or tell funny stories containing metaphorically-used words which are intended to satirize each other, It always evokes hearty laughter, hence the name of the amusement.

31. 赶鸟节

赶鸟节是瑶族民间节日，每年农历二月初一举行。节日一到，瑶家老人就忙着用糯米舂粑粑，制成铜钱大小的"鸟仔粑"，用竹子穿起来插在田间地头或堂屋边、神坛旁，让邻家小孩随意取食。人们以此来表示是鸟儿吃了"鸟仔粑"，它们的嘴巴自然会被粘住，也就不会糟蹋粮食了。到了晚上，人们走亲访友，品尝着"鸟仔粑"，祝愿来年好收成。

各村寨的瑶族青年则在节日当天穿上鲜艳的民族服装，汇聚到白头山，三五成群地展开情歌对唱或猜字谜游戏。直到月儿升空，大伙儿才依依惜别。

关于赶鸟节的由来，湖南江华一带广泛流传着这样一个民间传说：很久以前，江华山区鸟鹊成灾，糟蹋山里人的庄稼，害得他们没有收成，只能以野菜为生。这样一来，官府的税收也断了。为了保证税收，皇帝诏告天下，寻求对付鸟患的良策，并承诺赏给除鸟患者九架山头，免九年税收。

耕山人想到了盘云寨的盘英姑。这位姑娘是位唱歌好手。只要她一开口唱歌，鸟雀们就会停止鸣叫，盘桓在她左右倾听歌声，久久不愿离去。这方法果然奏效。大家跟盘英姑学会唱歌后，商定在来年播种之前把鸟儿们引开。到了正月最后一天，大伙儿用歌声把鸟雀吸引到了白头山上。鸟雀们在山上一呆就是半年,等它们回过神来飞回山林时,那年的庄稼早已被耕山人收割回家了。没想到山主向朝廷邀功,说是自己养的画眉把鸟雀吸引到了白头山,庄稼才丰收的。皇帝于是赏赐了他九架山,免掉他九年的税。

耕山人得到消息后非常生气,向皇上状告山主。皇帝派出一位大臣前来查案。到了正月最后一天,耕山人约好都呆在家里围着火塘喝自己的茶。山主提着画眉笼子上了白头山,鸟儿们也跟着飞往白头山,但没听见昔日醉人的歌声,于是就转头飞回林中。大臣明白了真相,怒斥山主。第二天,耕山人欢天喜地地聚到白头山,山上一片欢歌笑语,鸟儿们听见动人的歌声,纷纷跟着飞上了山头,在那里一醉又是半年,耕山人当年又获得了丰收。

从那以后,江华地区的瑶族人民就把每年的二月初一定为"赶鸟节"。

31. Bird-Dispelling Day

The Bird-Dispelling Day, a folk festival of the Yao nationality, is observed on the 1st of the 2nd lunar month. Upon the arrival of the festival, the old people of a Yao family are busy pestling glutinous rice to make copper-sized cakes known as Cake for Birds, stringing the cakes with bamboo slips, and planting the slips in the fields, outside the central room of the house, or near an altar so that children from the neighbouring families can take and eat them as they wish. They do so to mean that birds' bill would be stopped up from rnining their crops, as the Yaos imagine the children, who eat the cakes, to be birds. On the evening of that day people visit their relatives and friends, tasting the cake and wishing a bumper harvest in the year to come.

In their colourful national clothing, the Yao youth of each village converge on Mt. Baitou (white-headed), where groups of them sing love antiphons and guess riddles. Not until the moon rises do they part reluctantly.

As to the origin of the festival, a popular folk legend in Jianghua, Hunan Province, goes that in the hilly area of Jianghua birds used to cause disasters, ruining people's crops, so they had poor harvests and had to feed on wild herbs. As a result, the revenues of the authorities were cut off as well. To ensure the taxes, the then emperor issued an edict seeking a good way to counter the disasters caused by birds. He also promised that whoever got rid of the problem would be rewarded with nine hills and exempted from taxation for nine years.

People living in the mountain thought of Lady Panying, a good singer in the Panyun village. Whenever she sang, birds would stop chirping to linger around her and listen to her songs, unwilling to leave. It did work. After learning how to sing from Lady Panying, people decided on leading birds away before sowing in the following year. On the last of the 1st lunar month, they sang and attracted birds to Mt. Baitou. The birds stayed there for half a year. Before they became sober and flew back to the woods, people had already reaped their harvest. Unexpectedly, the landlord in the mountain, desirous to take credit for the people's success, reported to the court that it was his own thrush that led the birds to Mt. Baitou and saved the crops. Thus the emperor rewarded him with nine hills and exempted him from taxation for nine years.

Being furious with the news, people living in the mountain lodged a complaint against the landlord. The emperor sent a minister to investigate the case. On the last of the 1st lunar month, people a- greed to stay at home and sit around their stove drinking tea. The landlord took the thrush cage with him to Mt. Baitou, towards which birds flew too. Failing to hear the old intoxicating songs, they re- turned to the woods. Having known the truth, in a fit of anger the minister scolded the landlord. The next day people were elated to gather in Mt. Baitou, where they sang and laughed. Birds flew there too as they heard the sweet songs. Being intoxicated, they stayed there for half a year again. Thus people had a good harvest that year.

From then on the Yao people in the region of Jianghua made the 1st day of the 2nd lunar month as the Bird-Dispelling Day.

32. 依饭节

依饭节是广西仫佬族人民的隆重节日，于每年十月择一吉日，以同姓家族为单位举行庆祝活动。仫佬语的"依饭"意为祭祖，据考这一节日来自古时候仫佬族人祭祀祖先的习俗。

节日前夕全村寨都要清扫干净，各家各户都要杀猪、杀鸡、杀鹅、包粽粑。村寨里集体准备的节日文娱活动有舞狮子、耍龙灯、唱采调、走坡、室内歌舞等，其中最具民族特色的是室内歌舞和走坡等几个项目。

室内歌舞活动一般轮流安排在同房族各家的堂屋里举行，人们在堂屋的墙上用彩带挂满最长最丰满的糯米稻谷穗，堂屋中央放一张大桌，桌上放满用芋头和红薯等物品制做的大小不等的黄牛和水牛的模型，用猪獠牙插上当牛角，用麻丝等做成牛尾巴，表示六畜兴旺。桌上还有一大盘五色糯米团，糯米团的周围摆放着甜酒、芝麻、花生、黄豆、胡椒、沙姜、八角等十二种物品，以表示连年五谷丰登。还有猪心、猪蹄、猪肝、鸡、鸭、鱼、蛋等十二种祭品，以祭祀祖先。请来的两位表演者首先表演。他们当中一位穿红色法衣和草鞋，专做请神动作；另一位穿便衣，专门唱经书，请三十六位神，每请到一位神就要换一种唱词。表演者在演唱时，做请神动作者用金竹鞭赶桌上摆放着的"牛群"，有时托着五色糯米盘围绕桌子跳。同房族的兄弟姐妹和亲戚朋友则在周围敲锣打鼓观看、唱歌、跳舞。表演者每唱一句,周围的人就接着喊"呵——呼"声附和。这种歌舞活动从头天早晨开始,到次日天明时才结束。歌舞结束后,就把黄牛、水牛模型和糯米稻谷穗等分给各家。

走坡又叫坡会,其内容主要为男女青年进行社交活动。节日那天,他们起得很早,吃过早饭后就穿着节日服装,带着雨伞和粽粑,结队到野外指定地点去对歌。对歌时自动分成男女两阵,两阵之间不论事先是否相识都可以互相邀请对歌,一般不能拒绝邀请。在邀请对方之前要吹一声口哨,当对方挥着手巾表示同意后就互相站到适宜的地点开始对歌。刚开始时是集体对唱。在集体对唱中青年男女都在互相寻觅心目中理想的对象。当大家都找妥后,就转为成双成对地对唱。如双方在对唱中情意相投,也可约定时间地点再次对唱。仫佬族的许多青年男女都是通过对歌加深了互相了解和认识,进而由唱歌对手转变为情人的。

对歌是仫佬族人民最喜欢的娱乐活动,每个村寨都有好歌手。仫佬族人民的对歌形式主要有三种:其一是"随口答",这是青年男女们表达衷情的对歌形式,没有固定的歌词,一般都是根据对唱时的内容来随唱随编,十分灵活;其二是"古条","古条"是有脚本的历史歌谣,容易流传,中老年人最喜欢唱;其三是"烂口风",这是一种讽刺歌,一般都是在互相取笑娱乐,嘲讽逗趣时才唱。

仫佬族人民的唱歌兴趣非常浓厚,在依饭节期间,他们都要唱到夜半更深,兴尽趣足,才各自归家。

32 . Yifan Festival

The Yifan Festival is one of the grand festivals of the Mulao people in the Guangxi Zhuang Autonomous Region. It is observed by people of the same clan on any supposedly auspicious day of October. Yifan means "offering sacrifices to ancestors" in the Mulao language and the festival, according to surveys, originated from the ancient Mulaos' custom of worshipping their ancestors.

Towards the festival all families are busy cleaning their houses, slaughtering pigs, chickens and geese, and making zongba cakes (a cake made of glutinous rice flour). Villagers offer varied entertainments to mark the festival, such as the Lion Dance, the Dragon Dance, caidiao singing (a local opera of Guangxi), the Field Party (locally known as zoupo), and indoor singing and dancing. Of them, indoor singing and dancing, and the Field Party are of the most distinctive Mulao flavor.

The indoor singing and dancing is usually performed, in turn, in the central rooms of the houses of the Mulao families of the same clan. The walls of the room are decked with substantial glutinous rice ears which are tied with red ribbons; on a big table at the center of the room stand figures of oxen with bodies made of taros or sweet potatoes, horns made of pigs' sharp protruding teeth, and tails made of linen tassels, which are a symbol of thriving domestic animals; also on the table is a big plate of colored glutinous rice balls surrounded by 12 kinds of things-rice wine, sesame seeds, peanuts, soybean seeds, pepper, ginger, aniseeds and so on, which are a symbol of successive abundant harvests of food crops; still on the table are 12 sacrifices to their ancestors-pigs' hearts, pigs' trotters, pigs' livers, chickens, ducks, fish, eggs and the like. Two invited good performers perform first. One of them, wearing a red religious garment and a pair of straw sandals, dances in varied movements supposed to call on the 36 gods to come and the other, dressed in ordinary clothes, chants scriptures, also supposed to call on the gods. The scripture-chanter renews scripture words when each god is supposed to have arrived. While he chants, the dancer pretends to drive the imaginary oxen, with a bamboo whip one moment and, holding up the plate, dances around the table the next. Meanwhile, the spectators, crowded in a ring around the central scene, shout "Oh – Hu", to punctuate each chanted verse of scripture, striking gongs, beating drums, and dancing. The entertainment usually goes round the clock. At the end of the performance, the things on the table are to be distributed to the spectators.

The Field Party, also known as Field Gathering, provides good opportunity for the young to communicate. The young men and girls get up early on the festive morning and, after breakfast, go to an appointed site outdoors for antiphonal singing. All are in gala dress, and take along umbrellas and zongba cakes. There at the site, they divide themselves into two groups based on sex, and each group is free to invite the other to sing no matter whether they are acquaintances. The group, which is invited, should not reject the invitation. A whistle sound is a signal for invitation while waves of a handkerchief are a signal for agreement. When they do group antiphonal singing, which is to come first, every singer observes keenly trying to find a desirable partner from among the opposite-sex singers. When each has found one, they would do the antiphonal singing in pairs. If a pair find each other congenial, the two would do antiphonal singing separately at an agreed place and time. Many of young Mulaos, through the antiphonal singing, make the acquaintance of opposite-sex friends, who might become marital partners later.

Antiphonal singing is the entertainment the Mulao people favor most, and every village has outstanding singers of its own. The songs of the singing are of three kinds based on content. The first kind covers songs, whose words are impromptu-composed according to how the singing is going; and this kind of song is good for the young to express their love. The second covers historical songs with ready words; and this kind of song is easy to circulate and favored by middle-aged and old people. The third covers satirical songs, which are usually sung for amusement or jeer.

The Mulao people take keen interest in singing. During the Yi-fan Festival, they will not stop singing until their interest is satisfied late at night.

33.赶　年

　　赶年是分布在湖北、湖南、四川交界处的土家族人民的传统节日。各地节期不一,但大都在腊月二十八、九日,比汉族的春节提前一、两天,故名赶年。

　　这个节日最早可以追溯到几百年前的明朝统治。1554年,土家士兵与其他兄弟民族的士兵一道被派往沿海地区抗击倭寇来犯。旨令来时,适逢春节将至,为了按期抵达目的地,大伙儿决定提前过年。土家士兵在后来的战斗中大获全胜,土家人从此提前过年以示纪念。

　　节日前十五天,土家各户就开始准备年货。人们贴对联、杀年猪、推豆腐、蒸年糕、灌香肠并采购新衣、新鞋和灯笼、爆竹以及糕点、墨鱼、海带等。

　　除夕夜,家家户户都燃根长木头,一家人就在火堆旁围坐到深夜。有的地方有"守田埂"的习俗,即全家通宵围火而坐,以示对土地的热爱。待到雄鸡叫鸣时,土家人争相打开房门燃放爆竹,这叫"迎新年",意在迎接幸福和好运。

　　节日的特色菜是砣子肉和合菜——肉与蔬菜混熬而成,这种节日饮食也是为了纪念那些年前出征的土家士兵。那时,宴席准备得很匆忙,人们来不及将肉切细,只好蒸大砣的砣子肉,并把肉和蔬菜同锅煮食。后来竟沿袭成俗并代代相传。节日的第二天，人们不再吃蒸饭而是吃煮饭，不吃猪肉而是吃鸡肉。据说他们的祖先在出征前将猪肉都吃光了，以至于返乡后的庆功宴上，只有用鸡肉凑合。

土家人以跳摆手舞著称。摆手舞在土家语中叫"舍巴日"，起源于古时人们为求粮食丰收而设的祭祀土地的仪式。土家的每个村寨都设有摆手场，领舞者多为土家的"土先生"——从事宗教活动的人。摆手歌的歌词在民间口头流传并基本保持着稳定，其主题涉及人类的起源、民族的迁移、生产和社会生活的各方面。摆手舞的伴奏乐器主要有牛角、锣鼓和唢呐。跳舞时，舞蹈者动作一致，但参与人数不限。有时，几个村子的人聚在一起，参与者逾万人。

33. Gannian Festival

Gannian, which means that its celebration is held in advance of New Year, is traditionally observed by the Tujia people who live on the borders of Hubei, Hunan and Sichuan provinces. Though varying in time and place, it falls on the 28th or 29th of the 12th lunar month, one or two days before the Lunar New Year. Hence the name Gannian.

The festival dates back to the Ming Dynasty several centuries ago. In 1554, Tujia soldiers, together with those from other nationalities, were sent to fight against Japanese pirates pillaging the coastal areas of China. The order came when the Lunar New Year was drawing near. In order to reach the front in time, the Tujia people decided to celebrate the Lunar New Year in advance. Later the Tujia soldiers won the battles against the invaders. In memory of the victory, people made it a rule to celebrate the Lunar New Year one or two days ahead of time.

Fifteen days before the festival, Tujia families begin their preparations. They put up couplets and slaughter pigs, make bean curd, glutinous rice cake and sausages, and shop for new clothes, shoes, lanterns, fire crackers, cakes, cuttlefish, kelp and so forth.

On the eve of the festival, each family makes a fire by burning a long piece of firewood. Around the fire the whole family sit late into night. In some places, family members stay up all night to observe the custom of field-ridge guarding, which shows their love of the land. When roosters crow at dawn, the Tujias vie with one another in opening their doors and setting off firecrackers to welcome the new year and to bring in happiness and good fortune.

Large pieces of steamed meat and vegetables mixed with meat are specialties served at the festival. This is said to honor the Tujia soldiers who went to the front right before the Lunar New Year. At that time, the feast was given in such a hurry that people could hardly cut the meat into small pieces. As a result, they steamed it in large pieces and stewed vegetables with meat, which came to be a tradition handed down from generation to generation. The Tujia people, however, eat cooked rice and chicken instead of steamed rice and steamed pork on the 2nd day of the festival. It is said that their ancestors ate up all the pork before they set out to the front, so they made do with chicken at the victory feast after they returned home.

The Tujia Chinese are well-known for their hand dance which is in the Tujia language Shebari. The dance originated from people's sacrificing to the land god to pray for bumper harvests. There is a hand dance fair in every village. The leading dancer is usually a Tujia religious man. Words of the hand dance songs are handed down orally and remain basically unchanged with subject matters covering the origin of human beings, migration of the nationality, production, social life and so forth. The dance is often accompanied by the musical instruments of ox horns, gongs, drums, and suona horns (a sort of woodwind instrument). The movements of the dancers are identical, but the number is not limited. sometimes the number of dancers from several villages is over 10 000.

34. 三月三

　　三月三是海南省黎族人民的传统节日,也是黎族青年的谈情说爱日。据说这个节日的由来还有一段美好的传说故事。那是在很久很久以前,七指岭地区干旱,河水干涸,禾苗枯萎,人们对此一筹莫展,无可奈何地度日盼雨。一天夜里,有个叫白银的聪明小伙子做了一个梦,梦见一位美丽的姑娘对他说:要想摆脱旱灾,必须上五指山的顶峰去吹鼻箫,诱捕百灵鸟,捉到后天就会下雨。第二天早晨,白银把这件事告诉了村寨里的人,就去登五指山,上了山顶就吹起悠扬悦耳的鼻箫,一直吹了三天三夜,才见一只百灵鸟从幽谷中飞来停在身边。白银高兴地伸手去捉,百灵鸟已展翅飞了。白银就去追捕,他跑得快百灵鸟也飞得快,他跑得慢百灵鸟也飞得慢。白银追赶了一座山又一座山,最后竟不见百灵鸟。但他仍信心十足地四处寻找,决心一定要捉到它才下山。正当他继续寻找时,突然听到身后有脚步声,转身一看,是一位美丽的黎族姑娘向他走来,颈上挂着银项圈,身穿绣花裙,她那张白皙俏丽的瓜子脸上洋溢着和颜悦色的笑容,快活地启齿问白银来这里做什么事。白银把来意告诉了她。姑娘听后就和白银一同回到了黎家村寨。姑娘白天和白银一道去耕作,夜间同大家一起唱歌跳舞,吹箫弹琴,不几日连降喜雨,干旱消除,黎家村寨又充满了勃发生机,喜气洋洋的景象。可是管辖十八寨的寨主不允许姑娘唱歌、跳舞、弹琴,姑娘不予理睬,就被寨主抓去了。白银冒着危险救出了姑娘,一同逃到五指山,躲在石洞里,寨主和家丁找到后用火烧石洞,熊熊大火快要烧到他们时,突然石裂山崩,把寨主和家丁都压死了,姑娘和白银却变成了一对美丽的百灵鸟,展翅盘旋在黎寨的上空,却回不了黎寨。乡亲们闻讯赶来送别他们,尽情唱歌跳舞,祝贺他们美满幸福。这一天是农历三月初三,从此黎族人民在每年的三月初三就向他们祝福,并不断延续,最终形成为他们的传统节日。

为了庆祝三月三,黎族人民要提前半个月做准备,男子上山打猎,把猎物腌好封存,妇女在家酿酒舂米,备办节日食品;青年男女备办美丽的服饰和定情礼物。

过节那天人们先聚在一起喝"团圆酒",预祝山地旱稻和狩猎双丰收。然后,老人们自带腌好的野味和糯米酒,到村寨里深孚众望的老人家里去,席地围坐在芭蕉叶和木瓜叶上一同饮酒。其他人则去参加各种娱乐活动。主要的娱乐活动有男女对歌、跳竹竿、跳钱铃双刀舞等。

参加对歌的姑娘们戴着闪闪发亮的项圈、手镯和脚环;与他们对歌的小伙子们穿着漂亮的新衣。对歌时按男女分组,由一对、两对或三对对歌,表达朴实、真挚的感情。如果对歌中双方的情感变得融恰,对歌之后便互相赠送礼物,播下情谊种子。

跳竹竿是一项很受欢迎的娱乐活动,表演者分成两组,一组握竹竿,另一组跳越竹竿。表演前,在地上平行摆好两根木棍,相间数尺,木棍上横放若干根长竹竿,表演时木棍外侧蹲着的人双手握住两根竹竿的顶端，两人同时分合击拍。跳竿者随着或慢或快的节奏，在竹竿分合的间隙中不停地跳跃、转身，做一些优美的动作。跳竹竿气势恢弘磅礴，场面欢快热烈，也是对表演者机智、灵巧和体力的检验。年轻人最喜欢参加这种表演活动，未婚的男女青年则常常通过这一活动来物色自己的伴侣。

钱铃双刀舞也很受欢迎。"钱铃"是用一根铁条将数十个有孔的金属片串起来，挂在一根短木棒上做成的。表演时两名男子都穿黎族对襟无领上衣，颈戴项圈，头裹红巾。其中一人手执双刀，另一人手握钱铃，执双刀者伴刺对方身体各部位，握钱铃者奋力挡、架、搏、击，形式上为双方搏斗，实际上是一种动作非常刚劲、勇猛、矫健、潇洒、优美的舞蹈。随着黎族人民生活的不断改善，三月三的节日气氛会越来越浓，娱乐活动日益丰富多彩。

34. Double Third Day

The Double Third Day is observed, as one of the traditional festivals, by the Li people in Hainan Province. It lends the young people golden opportunities to talk love. The birth of the festival hangs a beautiful legend.

Long long ago, the Qizhi Ridge area in Hainan Province was once hit by a drought so terrible that the rivers dried up and the seedlings of cereal crops withered, and the villagers could do nothing but wait for rain. One night a young man, named Bai Yin, dreamed of a beautiful girl; and she told him that there would be rain if only a lark was trapped and caught by someone who played the bixiao (a bamboo flute) atop the Wuzhi Mountain in the province. The next morning, after he told his fellow villagers about his dream, Bai Yin came up to the mountain's peak. There be kept playing the bixiao, producing melodious strains. A lark really flew over from a deep and secluded valley, and perched beside him after he had played the instrument for three days and nights on end. The young man, quite elated, tiptoed forward, trying to catch the bird when it took wing and flew off. Then Bai Yin ran after it, but the faster he ran, the quicker it flew. It so happened that the bird got out of sight after he had chased past several ridges. Bai Yin was determined that he would not leave the mountain until he caught it. He was searching high and low when someone's footsteps from behind reached his ears.

The young man turned round to see a beautiful Li girl walking to him. Wearing a silver neckband, an embroidered skirt, and a pleasant smile on her fair oval face, she asked Bai Yin why he was there. Having learned the reason, the girl followed him back to his home village. There she farmed with him in the daytime, and at night joined the villagers in singing, dancing, and playing the flute or stringed musical instruments. A few days later, it rained for days in succession, which put an end to the long dry spell and restored the Li villages to their farmer vitality and jubilation. Unfortunately the brigand chief, who was in control of the 18 villages in the area, forbade her to sing, dance and play musical instruments any more, and had her taken away later due to her disobedience. Bai Yin, in spite of dangers, rescued her from the brigand chief's grip. Then, they both fled into the Wuzhi Mountain and hid in a cave there. The brigand chief came in pursuit and ordered his retainers to set fire to the cave. The raging flames were about to lick them when the mountain's rocks flew booming, which stroke the chief brigand and his retainers all to death. At the same moment, the girl and the young man turned into a pair of lovely larks, which wheeled in the air over the village before departure of it. At the news the villagers gathered in haste, singing and dancing, to see them off and extend congratulations on their happy union. This story happened on the third day of the third lunar month. From then on the Li people, therefore, gave the couple their blessings on the day every year; hence the present Double Third Day.

The Li people often make preparations for the celebration of the festival half a month in advance: Men hunt wild animals and preserve the game in salt; women make wine, husk rice and prepare other foods; and young people busy themselves with buying beautiful clothes and keepsakes.

On the festive day, all members of a family first gather to drink "reunion wine" and express wishes for bumper harvests of both upland rice and game. Then all the elders of village call on the most venerable old man in the village and they sit on palm leaves or papaya leaves in his house, drinking glutinous rice wine and eating preserved game, both brought there by the callers; other people take part in different entertainments, mainly the antiphonal singing, the bamboo pole skipping and the coin-sword dance.

The girls who are going to do antiphonal singing wear bright neckbands, bracelets and ankle bangles, while their partners of lads are dressed in attractive new clothes. Grouped on the basis of sex, the singers may do the singing one vs. one, two vs. two or three vs. three. Some pairs of the singers, who have found themselves in harmonious relations through the singing, present each other gifts, which are good promoters of friendship.

The bamboo pole skipping is one of the popular entertainments. For the performance, a big rectangular frame is set up, with two wooden poles placed vertically and several feet apart on the ground, and a number of longer bamboo poles placed horizontally on the wooden poles. The performers are divided into two groups, one consisting of bamboo-pole holders, and the other of skippers. At the beginning of the performance, the bamboo-pole holders squat outside either of the two wooden poles and each pair of them, who are face to face, hold the two ends of two bamboo poles. Then each pair move their bamboo poles apart and close alternately to beat time, while each of the skippers tries to skip into the room between two bamboo poles the moment the poles move apart, presenting graceful movements. The performance is often a scene of magnanimousness, and a trial of intelligence, deftness and strength. And it is favored by young people, especially unmarried ones, as they wish to find their marital partners through the performance.

The coin-sword dance is also favored by the holidaymakers. The dancers are two men, both wearing collarless jackets in the Li style, neckbands and red head scarves; one of them holds two swords, one in each hand, and the other holds a short wooden stick, which is fixed with dozens of coin-sized metal pieces strung with an iron wire. While dancing, the one with swords feigns to kill the other and the latter tries different means to ward off the feint attacks with his wooden stick. The dancers present vigorous, bold and graceful movements though they seem to be fighting with weapons.

With their living standard rising, the Li people will offer more and more colorful entertainments, which make the traditional festival increasingly joyful.

35. 丰收节

　　丰收节是台湾省高山族人民的年节,节期四天,在每年的七月末至八月初,有的地方则在十月份,具体时间由各部落的头人决定。人们在节日里祭祀祖先神灵,祈求来年再获丰收,故名丰收节。

　　丰收节前两天,部落头人要通知各家作庆祝节日的准备。男子打猎、捕鱼、杀猪、宰羊,砍柴准备节日生篝火;妇女在家做新衣、酿米酒;家家门前挂一束名叫"司快司"的野草。

　　除夕之夜,男子们上山打猎,妇女们到广场去跳舞或参加其他活动。初一黎明时分,男子们钻木取火点燃"兰巴子"草,约燃烧半小时后让其熄灭,接着再次钻木取火来供妇女们煮糯米饭,蒸糯米糕、烧菜。早餐后妇女们要将菜放在祭篮里带到集中地点去,由五位女巫主持祭祀祖先神灵。男人们则带着打猎用具在另外的地方举行打猎的祭祀仪式。初二妇女们继续集中祭祖先神灵,男子们上山打猎。如有所获,要把猎物抬到部落里主管历法的人家里去,再举行一次用弓箭射兽头的集体活动,最后由部落头人将肉平均分给各家一份。初三举行凿齿仪式,凡是年满八岁至十三岁的男女孩子都要凿去上腭两个虎牙的齿冠部分。凿完齿后把孩子们集中在一起,不能回家,由家里人送饭,直到节日结束时为止。他们集中时白天休息,晚上可到广场去观看跳舞并参加文娱活动。

在丰收节日里各部落都要举行唱酒会。唱酒会仪式一般在日落西山时开始,首先由身份较高的人端着斟满酒的酒杯,用手指沾酒向天、地、左、右弹酒,以祭天、地、神和祖先,祈求丰收,然后大家一齐举杯饮酒、唱歌、跳舞。在鼻箫、弓琴、嘴琴等乐器伴奏中,唱着一首又一首优美动听的民族歌曲,跳起高山族人民的节日舞蹈,其中最为优美动人的是高山族舞蹈——拉手舞。跳舞时参加人数不限,少的五、六人至十余人也可,多的上百人。跳舞时男女相间排成长列,手拉着手。列首的人能歌善舞,众人随其领歌领舞,一齐欢乐地歌舞起来。

节日期间,日月潭附近的杵歌舞也别具一格。杵歌舞只限妇女参加,表演时一队妇女手握长杵,环绕一块大盘石有节奏地敲击盘石,意寓在石臼中舂米的劳动节奏,并伴以悦耳的歌声,使场面欢快,充满兴致。

高山族中雅美人的节日舞蹈只限于少女参加,其中以摆发舞最富民族特色。跳舞时其长发随着脚步的前进而有节奏地上下摆动,开始较慢,其后越摆越快,并屈腰使长发触地。如此持续上下摆动,直到精疲力尽。

高山族的卑南人在丰收节还要举行编花冠赛、搭棚屋赛、烤肉赛、蒸饭赛和舂米赛。姑娘们在比赛前挑选各色花草,力争在最短的时间内编成美丽芬芳的花冠。搭棚屋比赛则是青年男子们的活动项目,他们削篾条当绳子捆扎竹屋架,在规定的时间内搭成一间小棚屋,最后由裁判员检查评分,评出最结实而又美观的小棚屋。参加烤肉比赛的男女青年们从生火开始,把肉切成薄片穿在竹签上用火翻烤。参加蒸饭的也多是年轻人。他们把嫩刺竹锯成两头带节的竹筒,将一端打个洞装进米和水,用甘蔗或蔗叶堵塞洞口放在火上烧烤。参加舂米比赛的也多是青年男女,他们自带杵臼和竹箩到赛场,舂相同数量的谷子,号令一下比赛开始。评分标准主要是脱壳率和损耗率等二项指标的综合得分。

35 . Bumper Harvest Festival

It is the New Year of the Gaoshan people in Taiwan Province of China. The festival lasts four days from the end of July to the beginning of August, or in October in some regions of the province; and the exact time is decided by the chief of a tribe. Its celebration is featured by offering sacrifices to ancestors and gods for more bumper harvests, hence the name of the festival.

A tribe's chief would remind all the households to make festive preparations a couple of days before the festival: Men hunt, fish, slaughter pigs and sheep, and cut firewood for festive bonfires; women sew clothes and make rice wine; every household hangs on its front door a bundle of wild grass known as sikuaisi in the Gaoshan language.

On the festival's eve, men hunt in the mountains while women dance or engage in other entertainments on public grounds. At dawn of the first day of the festival, men drill wood to make fire and, with the fire, light a stack of hay known as lanbazi in the Gaoshan language. They stamp out the burning hay after it has burned about half an hour. Then, they make fire again by drilling wood for women to steam glutinous rice and cakes, and make dishes. After breakfast, women take sacrificial dishes, in baskets, to an appointed place to attend a rite for worshipping ancestors and gods, jointly presided over by five witches; in the meantime, men hold a rite to worship the god of hunting in a different place, each of them bringing along hunting gear. On the second day of the festival, women continue their previous rite for worshipping ancestors and gods while men hunt in the mountains. The hunters should take the hunted animal, if they are lucky enough to have one, to the house of the man who is in charge of the calendar affairs of their tribe. There, they have a game, in which they shoot arrows at the hunted animal's head. After the game, the tribe's chief distributes the animal meat to all the households. On the third day of the festival, they hold a tooth-grinding rite. At the rite all children, aged 8 to 17, have the coronas of their protruding canine teeth ground off. After the rite the children stay together in the daytime and go to public grounds to watch dancing and other entertainments in the evening. They do so until the end of the festival.

During the festival, every tribe is to hold a singing-drinking party. When it begins at dusk, a man from the tribe, with a higher status, dips his finger into wine in a cup and flicks it successively to the sky, the ground, the left and the right. This is an embodiment to worship the Heaven, the Earth, gods and ancestors, and to wish for bumper harvests. After the procedure, celebrators begin to drink, sing and dance. They sing folk songs and dance folk dances to the accompaniment of varied national instruments like bixiao (a local flute), gongqin (a local plucked instrument) and zuiqin (a local wind instrument). Of the dances, the Hand-in-Hand Dance is most graceful. The number of dancers varies from several to about one hundred. They stand in a line, male alternating with female and hand-in-hand. At the head of the line is a particularly good dancer and singer. When he leads off, other performers follow him, dancing and singing joyfully.

The Gaoshan people in the region of Sun-Moon Lake like to present the Pestling Dance during the festival. The dancers are females only. They dance around a big stone, pestling the stone rhythmically as if they were pestling rice. The dancing, accompanied by the melodious singing, makes a scene of great joy.

The Yamei people, a branch of the Gaoshan nationality, like to present dances to mark the festival, but the dancers must be young girls only. Of the dances they offer, the Hair-Swaying Dance has the strongest national flavor. They dance in rhythmical steps while swaying their long hair up and down. When the speed gets quicker and quicker, they bend lower and lower until they are exhausted and their hair touches the ground.

The Beinan people of the Gaoshan nationality like to hold competitions of crown weaving, shed building, meat roasting, rice steaming and rice pestling during the festival. The competitors of crown weaving are usually girls. They, matching each other, try to weave crowns with varied flowers and plants in the shortest time. The competitors of shed building are usually young men. They first split bamboo into slips for tying the framework of the shed and then build sheds with the frameworks, trying to make the solidest and the most exquisite one in the set time. The competitors of meat roasting are young people. They slice meat, string the slices on bamboo needles and roast them on fire, matching each other for best-roasted meat within the set time. The competitors of rice steaming are also young people. They each prepare a bamboo tube, each end of the tube with a joint, and make a hole through one joint. Then they put rice and water into the tube through the hole, stuff the hole with sugarcane or its leaves and roast the tube on fire, trying to steam the best rice within the set time. The competitors in rice pestling are usually young people. They take their own pestles and mortars to a competition ground. When a signal is given, they begin pestling rice of the same quantity all at once. Their comprehensive marks are based on the rates of husked rice and damaged rice.

36. 吾时高节

云南兰坪、丽江、维西、宁蒗等地的普米族人民将春节叫做吾时高节,"吾时高"在普米语中意即"新年"。节日从农历12月的最后一天开始,为期四天。

大年三十,各家都做大扫除、贴对联喜迎新年;还在宅院里撒满松针,在屋顶和门上栽插松枝和腊梅,以示迎接祖先归来与家人共度佳节。除夕夜里,到处爆竹声声,家家忙做年饭。吃年饭前,要在铁三角的顶端放置三片肉、三块粑和三杯酒祭拜灶神。

大年初一,一俟雄鸡报晓,人们就燃起爆竹、鸣起海螺,宣告新年的到来。待全家起床后,家长带上酒、牛奶和松枝等上屋顶祭房头,祈祷新年粮食丰收;之后,年轻人争相去溪边取净水,叫做"新年抢新水"。据说最先抢到新水的人在新年里会幸福如意。

新年一大早,家有十三岁小孩的人家要为孩子举行成人仪式,也即普米人的"穿裤子礼"和"穿裙子礼",因为穿裤子和裙子是普米族成年的标志。女孩的仪式由母亲举行:女孩左手持麻布、麻纱等日用品,右手拿着手镯、耳环、串珠等饰品,双脚分别踩在象征财富和粮食丰收的猪膘和粮袋上。在巫师祭拜完灶神和祖先后,母亲就换下女儿常穿的麻布长衫,给她换上短衣和百褶裙。之后由女孩拜谢在场的亲友并给他们敬酒,亲友们则纷纷祝贺她长大成人。男孩的仪式由舅父主持:他也须站在猪膘和粮袋上,但右手拿的是尖刀,象征勇敢;左手拿的是银元,象征财富。巫师祈祷完毕,舅父就换下外甥的长衫,给他穿上短衣和裤子,并给他系上腰带。男孩随后向灶神和在场的亲友叩头,为他们斟酒,并接受他们的祝贺。

普米人有新年邀路人作客的习俗。邀请到第一位路人的人家喜气洋洋,因为普米人认为客人能带来好运。没邀请到路人的人家在座位上放块石头代替。

节日里有唱歌、跳舞、荡秋千、赛马等活动。节日的最后一天,年轻人上山举行"灭虫"仪式。他们把象征小虫的爆玉米花、炒米花等带上山,倒进大簸箕里;姑娘们则摘下象征大虫的手镯,埋进爆米花里。

36. Wushigao Festival

The Wushigao Festival is the Lunar New Year of the Pumis, who live in the counties of Lanping, Lijiang, Weixi and the Yi Autonomous County of Ninglang in Yunnan Province. Wushigao means New Year in the Pumi language. The festival begins on the last day of the 12th lunar month and lasts 4 days.

On the 1st day of the festival, all households give thorough cleaning to their houses and put up antithetical couplets to usher in the New Year. Also they scatter pine needles in their courtyards, hang pine branches and wintersweet blossoms on roofs and doors, a symbol to welcome their ancestors to join them in festival celebration. On that evening, people set off firecrackers and have reunion dinners. Before dinner, they lay on a trivet 3 pieces of meat, 3 pieces of glutinous rice cake and 3 cups of alcohol to worship the kitchen god.

At the first rooster crow on Lunar New Year's Day, villagers set off firecrackers and blow conches to announce the approach of the New Year. After all rise, the head of a family will climb onto the house roof and offers it sacrifices such as alcohol, milk and pine branches to pray for peace and bumper harvests in the New Year. Afterwards young people rush to a brook for clean water. The custom is known as Rushing for Auspicious Water on New Year's Day. The person who first fetches clean water is supposed to have good luck and happiness in the New Year.

Early that morning, the families with 13-year-old children hold rites to mark their adulthood. This is referred to as Wearing-Trousers Rite in the case of boys and Wearing-Skirt Rite in the case of girls, for the two kinds of wearing apparel are respective markers of men and women. The rite for a girl is directed by her mother. At the rite, the girl straddles on a piece of fat pork representing wealth and a sack of grain symbolizing bumper harvests, with ornaments like bracelets, earrings and beads in her right hand, and daily necessities like gunny cloth and ramie yarns in her left hand. Her mother, after the sorcerer's prayer to ancestors and the kitchen god, helps to change her linen gown into the blouse and pleated skirt. The girl then kowtows and presents a drink to her relatives and friends who are there to congratulate. The rite for a boy is hosted by his uncle. The boy stands the same way as the girl does, but with a dagger symbolic of bravery in his right hand and a silver dollar symbolic of wealth in his left hand. His uncle, after the sorcerer's prayer, helps to change his gown into the coat and trousers, and helps him to wear a waistband. The boy kowtows and presents a drink to his relatives and friends for their congratulations.

The Pumi people also observe the tradition of inviting passers-by home on New Year's Day. The family that manages to invite the first passer-by home will be much honored because the guest is believed to bring with him good luck. The family that fails to have a guest puts a stone in a chair as a symbol.

There are festivities like singing, dancing, swinging and horse racing during the festival. On the last day of the festival, Pumi youths climb up a mountain to perform the ritual of exterminating pests. Pop corns, pop rice and the like symbolic of small insect pests are taken there and dumped into a big winnowing fan. Bracelets symbolic of big insect pests are buried among the pop crops by their wearers, the Pumi girls. All ready, they sit around the winnowing fan and eat up the pop crops over singing, which signifies exterminating the insect pests. When a bracelet turns up while eating, they will touch its wearer's wrist, a sign to kill a big insect pest. This ritual gives voice to the Pumi people's wishes for bountiful food.

37. 怀亲节

　　农历四月十八日,是新疆维吾尔族自治区锡伯族的祖先在二百多年前自辽宁西迁至伊犁的纪念日。为此有人从其时称为"四·一八"节,有人从其事称为"迁移"节,锡伯族人从其方向称为"西迁"节,若按照锡伯语的音译则为"杜因拜专扎坤"节。本文从其意名为"怀亲"节,即锡伯族西迁后怀念故乡缅怀亲人的神圣节日。

　　锡伯族人原来居住在今天的辽宁、吉林、黑龙江和内蒙古东部一带地区。1755–1759 年,清政府在先后平定了准噶尔和大小和卓木的叛乱之后,在伊犁设立了将军衙门统辖新疆。那里虽然有满、汉、蒙古和索伦兵驻守,但清政府仍然感到兵力不足,须增强防守能力。于是在1764年(清乾隆二十九年)决定再从盛京将军管辖的沈阳、辽阳、开原等十七个城镇抽调擅长骑术和打猎的锡伯族官兵1 018人, 连同家属共3 275人,分编成十个队,在满族副将领哈木古朗的带领下,于同年农历四月十八日设盛宴告别了留在东北的父老乡亲。出发前西迁的和留居东北故乡的锡伯族男女老少都聚集在盛京的家庙太平寺,举行了隆重的祭奠祖先的仪式,然后老弱病幼者坐牛车,青壮年人步行。从盛京启程后途经张家口,再沿现在中蒙边境的杭爱山、乌里雅苏台等地西行。他们历尽千辛万苦,越过万水千山,耗时一年零五个月,于1765年农历9月才到达新疆伊犁地区。1766年1月他们又奉调去伊犁河谷的察布查尔。从此他们在那里一面抵御外敌侵扰,保卫祖国边疆,又一面垦荒屯田,兴修水利,营造新的家园,最终使人烟稀少的察布查尔荒原变成了阡陌相连的米粮仓,出现了村落相望的居民点,使荒凉的伊犁河谷呈现出一派繁荣富饶的景象。

但西迁至伊犁的锡伯族人民始终思念故土亲人,于是他们及其后裔就把西迁出发的农历四月十八日作为圣日庆祝,并把这种思乡怀亲的聚会称为"娘娘会"。从此以后,每年的怀亲节这一天,家家都要去大庙举行祭祀活动。聚集在一起吃羊肉、鲜鱼和高粱米饭。然后有的年轻小伙子骑着骏马,年轻妇女和老人则或坐车或步行,三五成群地到野外去游玩、野餐。不过人们一般都去赶庙会,并按村庄和乡镇聚集在一起听艺人们讲述先民西迁的故事,同时举行唱歌、跳舞、赛马、叼羊、射箭、舞龙灯、耍狮子、踩高跷等娱乐体育活动,其中场面最热烈的是射箭、念说和歌舞等活动项目。

射箭比赛是怀亲节重要的活动内容,以村庄或乡镇为单位组队进行团体比赛。节日那天,附近百里内外的各族人民也从四面八方骑马前来观看,赛场上人山人海,热闹非常。箭靶是用马皮和毛毡制成的,靶上粘着蓝、黄、绿、黑、紫、红等六色布圈,靶心红色。也有扎草人当作靶的。比赛使用特制的响箭,箭头用兽骨制成,呈尖圆形,上面钻有四个小孔,当箭一离弦,便发出呼啸震耳的响声。比赛时各队参赛的总人数没有硬性规定,只要人数相等即可。射箭手的年龄也没有限制,他们既要立射,也要骑射,各显其能,射术高强,而观众们则不时爆发出阵阵喝彩声,响彻数里,赛场上始终洋溢着欢乐的气氛。比赛结束后,输了的各队射手们要排着队,敲锣打鼓,吹着苇笛,带上肉、油和大米,前往获胜队的村庄或乡镇去祝贺。当然获胜的村庄或乡镇则要设宴招待,共同庆贺。席间由年长者给获胜队的前三名射手颁发弓、箭、袍、靴等奖品。从前比赛的双方常以牛或羊为彩头,输队被罚出的牛羊要当场屠宰,用大锅清炖,大家共享。

"念说"是一种类似汉族民间"说书"的一项节日活动内容。节日期间往往有数十人围坐在一处听民间艺人讲述各种民间故事。说书人一般具有良好的艺术口才,音调激越昂扬,绘声绘色,富于感染力,能有力地吸引听众。讲述的内容除了锡伯族的传说故事而外,还有一些中国的古典名著,如《三国演义》、《水浒传》、《西游记》、《红楼梦》等。现在生产知识、文学作品、报刊上的一些文章,也成为了说书人的故事内容。

锡伯族人民能歌善舞,在节日里都要演唱曲调优美、情意缠绵、欢快热烈的情歌。开始时先由一人独唱,继而转为男女对唱,最后变为一人领唱,众人合唱。随后人们又在"东布尔"、三弦琴、四胡、满达林、笛子等乐器的伴奏中,随着民歌旋律翩翩起舞。其中的一种贝伦舞的步法与东北的秧歌舞相似,但上身的动作则具有蒙古舞的风格。开始时小伙子们迈着舞步入场,姑娘们则以目传情,笑脸相迎,接受邀请,起身旋转着一同起舞。小伙子们的鸭步,姑娘们的斜肩,都展示着妙趣横生的舞蹈动作,而且加入跳舞的人越来越多,从而一步一步将节日的气氛推向高潮,让舞场内外的人们都一同感受到了怀亲节的欢乐。

37. Nostalgia Festival

The Nostalgia Festival is observed by the Xibo nationality on the 18th of the 4th lunar month because on this day over 200 years ago, the Xibos' ancestors set off to move from Liaoning Province to the Present Yili area of the Xinjiang Uygur Autonomous Region. It is also named the Festival of the 18th of the 4th Lunar Month based on the date, the Movement Festival based on the event, or the West Movement Festival based on the direction as Yili lies to the west of Liaoning. It is, in this article, differently named the Nostalgia Festival based on the immigrants' longing for their native place.

The Xibo people in Yili area have their ancestral home in the eastern parts of Liaoning, Jilin, Heilongjiang and Inner Mongolia. The Qing Dynasty government had the Senior Officer's Yamen established in what is today's Yili City to govern Xinjiang after it had successively put down the rebellions unleashed by some tribes in Xinjiang's Zhunge'er, Great Hezhuomu and Lesser Hezhuomu from 1755 to 1759. Though it posted troops of the Manchus, Hans, Mongolians and Ewenkis in the area, the central government felt the area to be insecure and, therefore, dispatched to the place in 1764 (the 29th year of the reign of Emperor of Qianlong) an army of Xibo men, who were formerly stationed around Liaoning's 17 cities including Shenyang, Liaoyang and Kaiyuan, all in the military area of Shenjing (today's Shenyang City). The army consisted of 1 018 officers and men, all good riders and archers; these men and their family dependants came to the total of 3 275. They left their native place for Yili to its west, on the 18th of the 4th lunar month of that year, in 10 detachments and under the command of Deputy Commander Hamugulang of Shenjing Military Area, who was a Manchu. Before departure, they gave a grand banquet to bid farewell to their kin and kith who were to stay behind and, along with the latter, held a mammoth ceremony to worship their ancestors in their ancestral temple named Taiping in Shenjing. Then, they marched west, with the old, weak, sick and disabled riding ox carts, and sturdy ones going on foot. The marchers first reached Zhangjiakou, then traveled along the Heng'ai Mountains and through the Wuliyasutai area (both bordering Mongolia), and finally arrived in the area around Yili City in the 9th lunar month of 1765. They traversed numerous mountains and rivers, and went through untold hardships during the 5-month-long march. In the first lunar month the next year, they further moved to the Chabucha'er area in the Yili Valley under orders. There, the new comers began to reclaim wasteland to grow food grain, construct new water conservancy works and build their new homeland, while defending the border against foreign attacks. Their hard work turned Chabucha'er from wilderness into a place where fertile fields were crisscrossed with paths and many hamlets were found close from one another, bringing prosperity to the barren Yili Valley as a whole.

The Xibo settlers always longed for their relatives and friends in their native place, despite the new homeland's flourish. So they gathered to observe the 18th of the 4th lunar month as a holy day, and called the gathering "Meeting of the Goddess of Fertility". This custom was handed down from generation to generation. Now on the day all Xibo families in Yili would gather in temples to hold sacrificial activities, and eat mutton, fresh fish and cooked sorghum. After the gathering, young men go out on horseback on an outing, while girls and old people go to the open country, by car or on foot, to sightsee or have picnics. Nearly all the Xibos go to the temple fair that day. At the fair they assemble, by village or by township, to listen to folk entertainers' storytelling about the west movement of their ancestors. Other items are also offered on the day, such as singing, dancing, horse racing, sheep wresting (a game with riders wresting sheep on horseback), archery, dragon dance performing, lion dance performing, walking on stilts, etc. Of them, archery, storytelling, singing and dancing are highlights.

The archery is performed among teams representative of villages or townships. Multinational spectators come on horseback from surrounding places, some of which are about 50 kilometers away, to watch the competition. The arena is a sea of people and a scene of bustling. The target for archery is made of horse hide and felt, with a red bull's eye surrounded by six circles, respectively marked by cloth pieces of blue, yellow, green, black, purple and red. A scarecrow may serve as a target on some occasions. The arrow, while flying ahead, whizzes because its head is made of a beast bone, pointed and round, with four small holes. The competitive teams each should have the same number of archers, though the number is not limited, and the archers may be at different ages. The competitors are required to shoot both from a standing position and on horseback. Every archer shows a superb marksmanship, which usually arouses thunderous cheers from audiences and turns the arena into a scene of great joy. Immediately after the game, all losers should go to the village or township of winners in a procession to congratulate the latter on their success, beating gongs and drums, playing the lusheng (a reed-pipe wind instrument), and bringing along meat, oil and rice as gifts. The winners, in return, give a banquet in entertainment and in congratulation as well. At the banquet, a venerable elder awards the first three winners bows, arrows, robes, boots and other prizes. The winners used to be awarded an ox or a sheep, which the losers had to give as punishment. The animal was to be slaughtered and stewed in a cauldron for all to share then and there. This practice already fell into disuse.

The Xibo storytelling is something like the storytelling popular among the Han folks. During the festival, scores of people are often seen sitting together to listen to folk stories told by a folk entertainer. Most of the story tellers speak eloquently and fluently in a loud and spirited tone, which often attracts big crowds. The stories are mainly based on, in addition to the legend of the Xibos, Chinese classics, such as The Romance of the Three Kingdoms, Water Margin, Record of a Journey to the Western Heaven, A Dream of Red Mansions, and so on. Now they are also based on production knowledge, stories in modern literary works and stories in newspapers.

Most of the Xibos are good singers and dancers. During the

Nostalgia Festival they like to sing love songs in a tone, which is melodious, brimming with tender affection or joyful. It is a usual practice in such singing performance that a solo comes first, antiphonal singing between men and women follows, and a massive chorus led by a singer comes last. At the climax of excitement, some singers suddenly break up and begin to trippingly dance a dance named beilun, to the accompaniment of the dongbu'er (a plucked instrument), sanxian (a three-stringed plucked instrument), sibu (a four-stringed bowed instrument), mandolin, flute, etc. The Beilun Dance is similar to the Yangge Dance popular in northeast China in terms of the foot movements of dancers, but to typical Mongolian dances in terms of the upper body movements of dancers. At the beginning, young men dance to the stage while waving their right hands to invite girls to join them, and the invitees rise to accept the invitation while smiling and casting affectionate eyes on the former. The male dancers' waddling steps and the female dancers' shrugging shoulders are both fascinating. Attracted by the graceful dancing movements, more and more people from audiences join the dancers, which throws both dancers and audiences into great joy.

38.木脑节

　　木脑节是云南省德宏地区景颇族人民的歌舞活动,其中"木脑"意为"大家跳舞"。传统木脑节于每年农历正月十五过后的半个月中的任一双日开始举行,节期一至四天,以娱乐为目的。但现在除举行传统木脑节外,景颇族人民有时也为迎宾送客、男婚女嫁、亲人团聚,庆祝丰收等目的而举行木脑节,形式与传统木脑节大体相同。

　　景颇族人民欢度木脑节源于一个有趣的传说故事:相传在很久以前,"木脑"盛会只在天上举行,是专供天仙们娱乐的一种歌舞活动。有一次太阳为了把木脑盛会办得更有乐趣,就派遣使者来邀请地上的所有动物去参加。动物们接受了邀请后指派所有的鸟类前往参加。鸟儿们在参加木脑活动中也学会了天上流行的那些歌舞,它们返回地上后就推选学得最好的孔雀为头领唱和领舞,向地上的人类和各种动物,表演木脑歌舞。景颇族人民的祖先看到鸟儿们表演的歌舞非常优美动听,就决定景颇族人民也要举办自己的木脑歌舞会。当他们举办了第一次木脑盛会后,景颇族人变得更加聪明、活泼、勤劳、勇敢。于是他们就正式决定在每年的农历正月十五过后择双日举行木脑盛会。久而久之,在沿袭过程中就逐渐演变为定期举行的传统节日。其实木脑节原是景颇族人民的一种群众性祭奠活动。

每逢木脑节，要在大广场的中央竖起十余米高的一根旗杆和两根约十余米高的栗木制成的木脑柱，各距一定距离。木脑柱两侧画着精美的图案，其中右侧木脑柱常画蕨菜，象征团结向前；左侧木脑柱则常画一个由四方形等分的三个三角形，每个三角形各涂一种颜色。在两根木脑柱之间交叉着两把银光闪亮的大刀，象征景颇族人民骁勇强悍的性格。在两根木脑柱旁还各竖立着一块约七八米高的大木板，上面画着各种美丽的图案，象征景颇族人民子孙兴旺发达。另有两块横匾挂在木脑柱和大木板的下部，上横匾画着雄伟的喜马拉雅山，传说那是景颇族人民的发祥地；下横匾画着家畜和农作物，表示他们对美好生活的向往。靠近木脑柱和横匾处筑有两座高台，寓意展望美好而无量的前程。在围绕高台的矮木柱上挂着景颇族人的乐器，其中有直径约1.8米的两面大铜锣，两个高约为2米的大皮鼓。最外层围着开了两道门的竹篱笆，寓意吉祥和胜利。

节日开始那天，景颇族人民都喜气洋洋地梳妆打扮：小伙子们身穿黑色衣裤，头裹缀着红穗的洁白包头布，手执闪光的长刀，犹如整装待发的战士；姑娘们则身穿黑色对襟或左襟短衣，颈戴银项圈，身佩彩珠，腰上围着光彩照人的羊毛花裙，腿缠毛织护腿带，手握各色手帕和花环，宛如孔雀开屏，美丽非常；而老人们通常身背织有民族图案的布制行李袋、食品，肩上扛着装满米酒的竹筒。他们从数百里范围内的山乡成群结队汇集到举行木脑盛会的广场。

附近的其他民族的人也常常参加木脑节。他们进入广场时有各种表演。例如，傣族人一般跳着孔雀舞，阿昌族人敲锣打鼓,独龙族人鸣枪放炮,傈僳族人则弹着三弦琴……由于有各民族的参加助兴使木脑节的活动更加丰富多彩。

木脑节仪式开始时,在笙管、大鼓、铜锣等各种乐器的伴奏声中,一队盛装耀眼的景颇族妇女顶着盛满鸡蛋、糯米粑粑、米酒、红枣等礼物的竹篮,在"哦啦、哦啦……"的喊声中缓步入场,表示热烈欢迎前来参加木脑盛会的各族宾客。接着景颇族的男子们对空鸣放礼炮。来自各地的景颇族人之间开始互相交换礼物,表示友谊,互相敬米酒,象征团结;青年男女们在气势雄壮、震撼广场的欢乐中放声歌唱,翩翩起舞。这种尽兴狂欢的歌舞活动,往往从白天直达深夜,又从深夜欢乐到天明,以至持续数日。直到节期最后一天为止。

在木脑节日期间,景颇族人民最喜欢的活动是木脑舞。木脑舞由两位技艺娴熟而又德高望众的老人领头。老人头戴美丽的孔雀羽帽,身穿宽大的汉族龙袍,手挥景颇族长刀。起舞时数以万计的人都踏着整齐刚健的舞步进场。在歌舞场上,手持银光闪亮的礼刀的男子与女子配成舞伴,以螺形进退的舞步在广场上表演迎宾舞,向坐在广场四周的来宾们敬礼致谢。接着姑娘们挥舞着手绢和纱巾,将竹筒盛着的米酒献给宾客,表示敬重和祝愿。姑娘们那花色鲜艳的筒裙在舞场上飘曳,那颈上和胸前佩戴的银泡、银毫、银牌、银链等饰品丁当作响,银光耀眼,使木脑舞显得更加有声有色,令人难忘。

在木脑舞跳得最热烈的时候,参加木脑节庆祝活动的各族人民群众也兴高采烈地加入,与景颇族人同歌共舞,但必须有景颇族人领歌领舞。人们在广场上尽情地边歌边舞,用优美而又有力的舞蹈动作抒发欢乐的心情,用歌声追忆景颇族先民们创建家园的历史,用歌舞描绘幸福的新生活,企盼更加美好的未来。

38 . Munao Festival

The Munao Festival, in which munao means " all people dance", is a song-and-dance festival held by the Jingpo people living in the Dehong Dai and Jingpo Autonomous Prefecture, Yunnan Province. The traditional Munao Festival starts on any of the even-numbered days in the second half of the first lunar month, and lasts one to four days for recreation. Nowadays, however, the festival is sometimes held also for other purposes, such as welcoming or seeing off guests, wedding, reunion of family members, celebration of good crops, and what not. But all are nearly the same as the traditional one in form.

It is said that the Munao Festival is linked to an interesting legend. Long long ago, according to the legend, the festival was merely held in Heaven to provide amusements to the goddesses. To make the festival more joyful and attractive, the sun sent down an agent to invite all animals on earth to attend the festival in Heaven; on the invitation the earth sent all of its birds to go there. Back on earth, the birds, with the peacocks as leaders, performed the songs and dances they had learned at the festival in Heaven for human beings and other animals. Attracted by the birds' sweet songs and graceful dances, the Jingpos held their own Munao Festival. And their first try turned out to be a success, for those who had attended the festival became more intelligent, vivacious, hardworking and courageous. Encouraged very much, they decided to hold the festival regularly on one of the even-numbered days in the second half of the first lunar month. This is thought to be the origin of the present traditional Munao Festival. But more reasonably, the festival is derived from the Jingpo people's massive sacrificial service in ancient times.

For the festival, a group of facilities are to be built: A flagpost and two chestnut posts, locally known as Munao posts, are erectly fixed in the center of a big ground, with a certain space in between, each over 10 meters high; each of the Munao posts is beautifully decorated with the patterns of pteridophyte plants on its right face, a symbol of the Jingpos advancing in a close rank, and with the patterns of three triangles derived from an equal division of a quadrilateral and painted different colors; between the Munao posts are two glittering long swords fixed in the shape of a cross, a symbol of the Jingpo people's valiantness; beside either of the Munao posts stands erect a wood plank in line with the posts, about 8 meters high, drawn with varied beautiful patterns symbolizing the Jingpo people's flourishing population; fixed on the lower parts of the Munao posts and the planks are two horizontal wood boards, the upper one drawn with the pattern of the Himalayas said to be the native place of the Jingpo nationality, and the lower one bearing the patterns of domestic animals and crops symbolizing the Jingpos' longing for a happy life; just before the horizontal wood boards stand two platforms, which mean that the Jingpos stand on high places looking forward to a bright future; fixed around the platforms are wood sticks hung with musical instruments including two bronze gongs, 1.8m in diameter, and two oxhide-headed drums about 2 meters high. Running round all these facilities is a bamboo fence with two doors, a symbol of auspiciousness and success.

On the day when the festival begins, joyous celebrators are in gala dress. The young fellows of them wear black jackets, black trousers, and white turbans decorated with red tassels, and have glittering swords in hands, who look well like soldiers ready to start out. The girls of them wear black jackets with buttons down the front or the left, silver necklaces, strings of colorful beads, beautifully patterned woolen aprons and woolen puttees, and have colorful handkerchiefs and garlands in hands, which make them as beautiful as peacocks spreading their tails. The old people of them bring along cloth luggage bags embroidered with the Jingpo-style patterns, food and rice wine contained in bamboo tubes. All of them come to a big ground for the festival, some from mountainous areas several hundred li (two li makes one kilometer) away.

People of other nationalities living in the neighboring areas often join the Jingpos in celebration. Getting into the ground, they offer their own performances. For example, the Dai people dance the Peacock Dance, the Achang people strike gongs and beat drums, the Dulong people fire gunshots, and the Lisu people play the sanxian (a three-stringed plucked instrument)... These people always add attractions to the festival.

The formal festival celebration begins with a ceremony. At its beginning, a team of well-dressed girls slowly walk to the center of the ground to the music of the Sheng (a reed pipe wind instrument), oxhide-headed drums, bronze gongs and other instruments while they keep shouting "O–La–" to welcome all participants, each carrying on her head a bamboo basket containing eggs, glutinous rice cakes, rice wine and red dates; then some Jingpo men fire salvoes into the air; still then the Jingpos exchange among themselves gifts symbolizing friendship and present each other rice wine symbolizing unity. Soon afterwards, young men and girls begin to sing loud and dance lightly to thunderous cheers and sounds of musical instruments. The revelries may last one day and one night, or days and nights, or even till the end of the festival.

Of all the items offered at the festival the Jingpo people like the Munao Dance best, which is a massive group dance. Two prestigious elders lead the dancing, who wear hats adorned with colorful peacock feathers and the Han-style robes embroidered with the patterns of dragons, and have the Jingpo-style swords in hands. When the dancing begins, tens of thousands of other dancers vigorously walk into the arena, with men and girls pairing off. Then the paired-off men and girls dance in forward movements and backward movements along a winding line, each man holding a ceremonial sword, an expression of welcoming guests. Still then the girls, waving silk scarves, present rice wine in bamboo tubes to the guests, an expression of their respect and good wishes for the latter; their decorative silver trinkets keep jingling and glittering, which makes the dancing more attractive and unforgettable. At the climax, the guests of other nationalities usually cannot control themselves from joining the Jingpos, but they have to be led by the latter in singing and dancing.

The celebrators all sing and dance to their heart's content. Through the performances, they express their happy feelings, review the history of how their ancestors built their homeland, depict their new life and envisage their bright future.

39. 扩塔节

扩塔节是云南省临沧、澜沧、耿马、孟连等地区的拉祜族人民的新年节,因此又称"过年"和"春节"。

扩塔节是拉祜族人民众多节日中最隆重的一个传统节日,在农历正月初一至十五举行。但实际上节日期间只有九天,其余几天可从事生产及其他活动。

拉祜族人民十分重视过扩塔节。在每年的入秋后,各家都开始着手准备过节所必需的物品。妇女们在家制做各种华丽的民族服饰;成年男子们上山打猎,准备山珍野味;青年男女们制做芦笙、口弦、荷包;儿童们做陀螺,搓麻线。从腊月二十六日清晨起开始清扫室内外卫生,杀猪烧肉,并在村寨范围内栽种松柏树,挂上芭蕉等物作为祭品,以祭祀天神和地神,祈求来年五谷丰登,丰衣足食。

到了除夕之夜,家家户户都要舂米做糯米粑粑,然后全家人在吃年夜饭时共食。饭后人们要给家畜喂年饭,还要把糯米粑粑放一点在犁、锄、砍刀等农具上,以感谢它们在过去的一年中和主人合作得很好,种好了庄稼,做出了贡献。过去有些地区的拉祜族人民在太阳未下山之前要面向日落处迎接祖先的灵魂回来一同过年,晚上要先给祖先们敬献饭菜酒等祭品,仪式结束后全家人再吃晚饭。有的地区的拉祜族则在黄昏时鸣火枪二响,请父母亡灵回家过年。当晚老年男女们要到寺庙里去守岁,通宵不眠。

从初一开始的扩塔节活动分为三个阶段。第一阶段从正月初一到初四,称为大年。初一凌晨雄鸡啼鸣时,各村寨的青年男女们就在火枪火炮声中奔向山泉去抢"新水"。他们认为"新水"是纯洁、幸福的象征,首先抢到"新水"的人家,当年的水稻将会早成熟,获得好收成;第一个抢到"新水"的人会消灾免祸,得到幸福。取回家的"新水"要先献佛敬祖,然后作为家里老人的洗脸水,老人则要向年轻人颂词祝福。

在初一清晨,如人们听到村外传来火枪声,全村男女老幼都要到村口去迎接在外打猎或干活儿归来的村里人。由村里的老人向他们敬酒、撒米、祝贺他们新年快乐,吉祥如意。

早餐后,老人们要带糯米粑粑去寨主家拜年,随后各家各户开始互相拜年、祝福。拜完年后人们又聚集到村寨里的广场,举行各种娱乐活动,其中有芦笙舞、丢荷包、打陀螺、荡秋千等。

在初一这天,拉祜族人要给狗喂好饭菜。传说拉祜族人居住的地方原来没有水稻,狗就漂洋过海到产水稻的地方去,上岸后立即到人家的晒谷场里打滚,全身粘上谷子后又渡海返回。人们就把狗尾巴上仅存的那些谷子用来播种,从此才有了大米饭吃。人们为了感谢狗的功德,就在每年的正月初一这天给狗好饭菜吃。

初二上午,人们带着糯米粑粑、酒、肉等礼物走村串寨,互相拜年。从下午开始举行盛大的歌舞活动,老人们吹葫芦笙,小伙子们弹小三弦琴,其他的中青年男人们合着节拍跳三跺脚舞。姑娘们则吹着用竹片做的口哨,互相手搭着肩一排排地参加跳舞。姑娘们的口哨上坠着鲜红色的绒线穗子,随着姑娘们在场上的舞姿有节奏地摆动,婉如一串串跳动着的火焰闪闪烁烁、忽隐忽现。

在初三这天,有的拉祜族村寨还要吃团圆饭。届时各自带着饭菜和酒肉到事先约定的人家去聚餐,按男女分桌而坐,女的在右桌,男的左桌。开饭前要首先祭祀神灵,仪式结束后才开始吃饭喝酒。到傍晚离散前,要把吃剩的遗弃物收拾干净,再用火在寨外烧尽,以保持寨内清洁干净。

在初一到初四的四天里,拉祜族人民都在尽兴地唱歌、跳舞和参加各种娱乐活动,其中的"斑鸠拣谷子"舞是主要的传统舞蹈。这是因为他们那里丰收年的斑鸠特别多,斑鸠就成了丰收的象征,也就认为斑鸠给他们带来了好运,所以在扩塔节这个重要的节日期间自然就要跳"斑鸠拣谷子"舞。这个舞蹈的表现形式是三只斑鸠飞到晒谷场拣谷子,其中两只小斑鸠一边嬉闹一边争抢觅食,老斑鸠就教训小斑鸠,要它们团结友爱,互相谦让,关心他人。最后两只小斑鸠和好如初,吃饱后一同飞走了。

第二阶段的过年在初八初九两天,又称为"小年"。这是因为拉祜族人爱好打猎,若是有人外出打猎未能及时赶回家过大年,就用这两天给他们补上。过小年的娱乐活动主要是各村寨都荡秋千。据说这种娱乐活动来源于一个传说故事。按照拉祜族人的传统习惯,在临近过年时各村寨都要搭一个木架,把肥猪吊在木架上屠宰。那些肥猪不服气,死后它们的灵魂就到厄莎天神那里去告了状,请求厄莎天神为它们报仇,把那些吃了它们肉的人也吊一次予以惩罚。厄莎天神受理了这一案件后作出如下判决:过大年前人可以吊宰肥猪,但过小年时人也必须以同样的方式将自己吊起来,以表示认罪。人们听到了这一判决后非常惧怕,但最后想出了一个对策,即在平地上竖起一个木架,在横梁上系两根绳子,吊下来后再拴上坐板,过小年时村寨里的男女老幼都坐在坐板上悬空来回摆荡,以表示自己把自己吊在木架上了。这便是他们过小年时人人都要荡秋千的来源。

第三个阶段的过年在正月十三至十五日,其活动内容还是唱歌、跳舞、荡秋千及其他各种娱乐活动。拉祜族人民在这个重要节日的最后三天中仍然继续尽兴娱乐,欢欢喜喜过完新年。

39. Kuota Festival

The Kuota Festival is observed by the Lahu people who live in Lincang, Lancang, Gengma and Menglian counties, Yunnan Province. It is their New Year Holiday, also known as the Spring Festival.

The Kuota Festival is the most important one of the numerous festivals celebrated by the Lahus. It lasts from the 1st to the 15th of the first lunar month, but it is disconnected with six days of intervals, during which people may do business other than celebration.

The Lahu people attach so great importance to the festival that they set about preparing festival necessities early when autumn sits in: Women make gorgeous national costumes of different kinds at home; adult men shoot wild game; young people make the lusheng (a reed-pipe wind instrument), whistles and pouches; children make toy tops and twist flaxen threads. On the early morning of the 26th of the 12th lunar month, the Lahu people begin to clean their houses, both inside and outside, slaughter hogs, roast pork, and plant pines and cypresses around their houses, and hang the trees with some bananas as sacrificial offerings to the god of Heaven and the god of the earth, an expression of wishing for a bumper grain harvest and a well-to-do life in the new year.

On the New Year's Eve, every household pounds glutinous rice with mortar and pestle to make cakes, and eat them later at the family reunion dinner. After the dinner, they feed their domestic animals with good food supposed to be a New Year meal and put some shreds of glutinous rice cakes on their ploughs, hoes, hacks and other farm implements in thanks to them for their close cooperation with their owners in farming in the past year. In old days, the Lahus in some regions would, facing the sunset direction at sunset, call on their ancestors' spirit to have the New Year holiday with them; at the family reunion dinner they would offer sacrificial dishes and wine to their ancestors before they themselves had any; in some other regions they would fire two gunshots to call on their ancestors for the holiday at dusk, and all would stay through the night in a nearby temple. Such traditional customs, however, are no longer followed nowadays.

The festivities begin on the first day of the first lunar month and cover three periods. The first period, from the first to the 4th, is known as the Major New Year Holiday. Hearing the first crow of a cock at the first daybreak, young villagers, men and women, hurry to mountain springs to fetch fresh water amid gunshots. The fresh water, symbolizing purity and happiness, is thought to bring a good and earlier harvest of rice to the household that first gets it, and ward calamities off and bring happiness to the one who first gets it home. The fresh water home should be offered first to ancestors and Buddha as sacrifice, and then to the elders of the family as washwater. And the elders say words of good wishes while accepting the water.

On hearing the gunshots at the daybreak of the day, all of a village go to the entrance to the village to greet those who are back home from hunting or other routine outside. On this occasion, the venerable old villagers offer wine to and scatter grains of rice on the greeted, an expression of wishing them a happy New Year and good luck.

After breakfast old people of a village, bringing along glutinous rice cakes as gifts, pay New Year calls to the village's chief. Then other villagers of the village call on each other for New Year greetings. Still then they crowd a square and offer various entertainments, such as dancing the Lusheng Dance, tossing pouches, whipping tops, playing on swings and so on.

This day sees another custom-the Lahus feed their dogs with nice food, which hangs a legend. Long long ago, the legend goes, there was no rice growing in the Lahu-inhabited region. A dog swam across a sea and got to a rice-growing area. Once ashore, it rolled on a sunning ground, which had many grains of rice stuck on its wet skin. Then the dog swam back and, when it got ashore, only a few grains remained on its tail because of long swimming. Relying on the leftover grains, the Lahus began to grow rice in their home region. Hence, they follow the custom every year in thanks to the dog for its great meritorious service.

On the second day morning, villagers go from village to village to wish one another a Happy New Year, bringing along glutinous rice cakes, wine, meat and other gifts. This day's afternoon sees spectacular festivities: Some old men play the lusheng; some young men play the sanxian (a three-stringed plucked instrument); some middle-aged and young men perform a tap dance to music; some girls dance while they play the whistle (made of thin bamboo strips), standing in lines with hands put on each other's shoulders. Each of the whistles is attached with a bright red tassel, which moves up and down along with the rhythmical dance movements to offer a glittering and moving flame.

On the third day, the Lahus in some villages follow the custom of eating a village reunion dinner. The custom has it that all of a village, bringing along meat and wine, gather for the dinner at the appointed household and time. There they sit at different tables according to sex, females at the right ones and males at the left ones. Before they begin to have food and wine, they hold a ceremony to worship gods. Towards the close of the dinner at dusk, they collect all leftovers and burn them far outside the village as to keep the village clean.

The Lahu villages are bustling with some more entertainments in the first period of the festival, one of which is the dance called "Turtle-Doves Picking-Up Grains". This dance is performed because the birds are extraordinarily numerous in the region in bumper harvest years and the birds, therefore, are thought to have brought the locals good luck. The dancing presents the scene: Three turtle-doves, two young ones and a mother one, fly onto a sunning ground for grains, and the young ones merrily scramble with each other for food. At the sight, the mother turtle-dove teaches them to be friendly, be modest and show concern for each other. Finally taking the teaching, the young turtle-doves get harmonious as before, eat their fill and fly away with their mother.

The second period, from the 8th to the 9th of the month, is referred to as the Minor New Year Holiday. This holiday is made for those who have missed the Major New Year Holiday because of hunting in mountains. To play on swings is one of the main entertainments held in this period. The game has a legendary story behind. According to the legend, the Lahus of every village used to hang a hog from a wood stand and kill it towards the Kuota Festival for a dinner. Resentful, all the slaughtered hogs' spirits accused the slaughters before the heavenly god named Esha, and begged the god to revenge them by hanging the slaughters the same way. The god accepted the case and made the verdict that the Lahus were allowed to hang and slaughter hogs towards their Major New Year Holiday, but the slaughters must have themselves hung for a little while in the Minor New Year Holiday the way the hogs were, as an expression of admitting their guilt. Frightened very much, the Lahus thought hard and worked out a countermove: They erected two wood posts on the ground, some distance apart, fixed a horizontal bar atop the posts, tied two ropes apart to the bar and fixed a horizontal plank at the ropes' ends, forming what's today's swings. Then all villagers, male and female, old and young, sat on the plank in turn and had themselves move to and fro. This was something like hanging the hogs, and was thought to be the origin of playing on swings by the Lahus.

The third period lasts from the 13th to the 15th of the month. It likewise sees different entertainments, such as singing, dancing, playing on swings and others. The merry-making keeps the holiday-makers excited and happy till the end of the festival.

40．纳顿会

　　纳顿会又称七月会、庆丰收会，是居住在青海省民和县官亭、中川、甘沟等地的土族人民的传统节日。

　　土族系蒙古族的一个分支，他们自称白蒙古族，1949年新中国成立后改称为土族。"纳顿"在蒙古语中意为"戏耍"、"浪庙会"，纳顿会相当于蒙古族的传统节日"那达慕"大会，于每年庄稼成熟时的农历七月中旬至九月中旬举行。纳顿会的规模大小视当年的农业收成好坏而定。通常是在丰收年要举行大规模的纳顿会，若遇上灾年或歉收年份也可不举办。

　　纳顿会以村庄为单位次第举行，每村会期一天。在会期前，要在会场的正北或正西方向搭一顶帐篷，备好锣鼓、假面具和服饰。会期日早晨，每家都要带一对大蒸饼和烟、酒、糖果，到会场后交给负责管理这些物品的人。纳顿会结束时管理人员要把蒸饼等物分发给与会的人们。

　　纳顿会开始时，由本村推举出数十人至数百人老人和中青年人组成一支队伍，称为"会手"，按辈份和年龄列队。其中老人们身穿长袍，手执彩旗、扇子、笛子和木制兵器等在前面领队，其后面有锣鼓手跟随；中青年人装束十分华丽，也手拿彩旗和柳条尾随。这支队伍按照锣鼓的节拍纵情地翩翩起舞，边舞边走边呼"大好"，到距村庄外数百米的固定地点去迎接时更是热闹非常,锣鼓喧天,器乐齐鸣,各自起舞,来回旋转三次,并不断高呼"大好"、"大呀好"。然后由东道村庄德高望众的几位老人向外村的"会手"们敬酒,表示欢迎。敬完酒后双方会合在一起互相握手,祝贺五谷丰登,人畜两旺,一同欢呼"大好",这时更加用力敲响锣鼓,以示彼此同乐。之后东道村"会手"向两旁让开一条路,待外村"会手"走完后跟着一同进入会场,开始表演节目。演员们戴着假面具扮成老人、妇女、儿童,以及扮演关公、张飞等历史人物,在锣鼓及乐器伴奏下边舞边唱。

通常表演的第一个节目是"庄稼其"舞蹈。表演者身着庄稼人的地道服装,其内容充满着浓厚的土族农村生活气息,展现了民族风情。

其次是表演极具神话色彩的舞蹈"杀虎将"。这是一个再现土族祖先在远古时代从事游牧业生产的情景,杀虎将意寓土族祖先的化身,他又集中体现了土族人民前赴后继,世世代代与大自然不懈斗争的英勇精神。

最后表演安昭舞,使整个场面自始至终都洋溢着欢快至极的愉悦气氛。

纳顿会的挨村游乐活动都是首先从中川乡的宋家村开始,逐村串游庆贺,每村一天,直至游完中川、官亭、甘沟等乡的所有土族村庄时才结束。

关于纳顿会的来历,在土族民间有这样一种说法:从前在土族居住的中川地区很少下雨降雪,旱灾不断,严重时秋后颗粒无收,人们生活非常艰苦。为了祈求风调雨顺、五谷丰登、六畜兴旺,他们请巫师把道教符文画在柏木牌子上,在村口筑雷台,又在三岔路口埋下画有符文的木牌子、狗头和五色粮食等物品。在上面堆满石头,插上柳条、矛和弓箭等,称为俄堡。家家户户都要用木斗装着五色粮食和铜钱、棉花、羊毛、茶叶、布匹等作为供品在巫师的主持下去祭奠那些牌子、雷台和俄堡,全家老幼早晚都要去跪拜,祈求它们保佑丰收。但不论人们怎样虔诚地祈祷,年事始终未见好转,生存环境无丝毫改善。正在人们一筹莫展之际,有人从四川灌县二郎庙请来了二郎神的木雕像,并说明他是修建世界著名水利工程都江堰的水利专家李冰之子李二郎的化身,能改天换地、呼风唤雨、消除旱灾。人们知道后非常高兴,于是当地土族居民立庙供奉李二郎神像,祈求他保佑人们能获得好收成。果然该村当年风调雨顺,获得了丰收,乐得人们满心欢喜。村民们用八抬大轿把二郎神像抬到其他一些村庄,一路上锣鼓喧天,鞭炮轰鸣,载歌载舞。沿途村民都伏地跪拜,供茶祭酒,备鸡羊献祭,以谢二郎神的赈济之恩。欢欣不已的人们就这样一个村庄接一个村庄的庆贺,从七月中旬一直到九月中旬才庆贺完毕。这便是纳顿会的开始。

但据考,土族人民举行纳顿会的历史很悠久,比上述传说要早得多。

40. Nadun Festival

The Nadun Festival, also known as the Seventh Lunar Month Festival and the Bumper Harvest Festival, is a traditional festival observed by the Tu nationality inhabiting the townships of Guanting, Zhongchuan and Gangou in Minhe County, Qinghai Province.

The Tu people used to call themselves white Mongolians as they belong to a branch of the Mongolians, and began to have their present name after the founding of new China in 1949. Nadun, a Mongolian term, means making merry or strolling around a temple fair. The Nadun Festival, something like the Nadamu Festival of the Mongolians, is held somewhere from the middle of the 7th lunar month to the middle of the 9th lunar month.

The scale of the festive celebration depends on a village's farm harvest situation, usually a grand celebration in a bumper harvest year and probably no celebration in a bad harvest year.

The Tu villages, one by one, organize their own one-day festive celebrations. Before the festival arrives, villagers of a village pitch a tent at the site due north or due west on a ground, and get ready gongs, drums, masks and costumes, all to be used in later festivities. Early on the festive morning, every household hands in, to a man in charge, two big steamed cakes, some cigarettes, wine and sweets, which are to be distributed to festival celebrators by the man in charge towards the close of the celebration.

After the celebration begins dozens, or even hundreds, of villagers of a village, who are picked out as "celebration performers", stand in a procession according to the order of clan seniority and age. In the front section of the procession are elders who are dressed in long gowns and holding colorful pennants, fans, flutes or wooden weapons; after them are gongmen and drummers; and in the rear section are middle-aged and young men who are dressed in gorgeous costumes and holding colorful pennants or willow twigs.

Dancing joyfully to the beats of gongs and drums and repeatedly shouting "very good", the processionists march on towards an appointed site near the village to greet the "celebration performers" from a neighboring village, who come to join in celebration. When they meet, the two groups begin to dance in whirling movements and shout "Very good! Very—good!" to the deafening sounds of gongs, drums and other musical instruments. Then several respectable and prestigious elders from the host village propose toasts to the guests, an expression of welcome. This procedure is followed by warm hand shaking, congratulation on good harvests and flourish of both men and livestock, more cheers, and more resonant sounds of drums and gongs. Still then, the "performers" of both sides walk in a procession, the guests in the front, towards the celebration ground, where they are to give performances. All along the way, they sing and dance to the accompaniment of gongs, drums and other musical instruments, wearing masks of old men, women, children or historical figures like Guan Yu and Zhang Fei, two generals in Shu Kingdom of the Three Kingdoms (220–265).

The first item performed is usually the Crop Dance. And it vividly reflects the customs and rural life of the Tu nationality, with dancers disguised as farmers.

The second item is a mythological-flavored dance named "Tiger-killing Warriors". And it mirrors how the Tu people's ancestors in ancient times led a nomadic life of raising livestock. The warriors are the incarnation of the Tus' ancestors, and the embodiment of the Tus' courage, on which the Tus have made unremitting efforts to struggle with nature from generation to generation.

The last item is the Anzhao Dance, which always brings a hilarious atmosphere.

The Nadun Festival celebration always begins in Songjia Village of Zhongchuan Township, then it spreads through other Tu villages in the townships of Zhongchuan, Guanting and Ganguo, one day for each village.

The festival's origin hangs a story popular among the locals. According to the story, the area of the present Zhongchuan Township was frequently hit by droughts a long time ago. The serious ones often brought autumn crops to total failure, and reduced the villagers to misery. To pray for favorable weather, good harvests and thriving domestic animals, the villagers of a village requested a sorcerer to do magical practice. The latter prepared a cypress wood plate drawn with Taoist magic figures and inscribed with Taoist spells, had a platform named Lei constructed at the entrance to the village and a mount named E set up at a fork in a road; inside the mount were the wood plate, a dog's head and five kinds of grain; outside the mount were piled-up rocks and inserted willow twigs, spears, bows and arrows. Under the auspices of the sorcerer, the villagers kowtowed once in the morning and once in the evening to the cypress wood plate, the Lei Platform and the E Mound for good crops, offering the sacrifices of copper coins, cotton, wool, tea, cloth, and five kinds of grain. Yet they never had any better harvests and living conditions no matter how devoutly the villagers prayed. They were at their wit's end when someone respectfully brought to the village the wooden statue of the Erlang God from the Erlang Temple in Sichuan's Guanxian County, and explained that the god was the incarnation of Li Erlang and was able to change the world, summon wind and rain, and ward off droughts since he was the son of Li Bing, who had directed the construction of the world-famous irrigation works Dujiangyan Weir located at the same place as the Erlang Temple. Then the elated villagers enshrined the statue in a temple they built to pray for bumper harvests. As expected, they had good fortune that year. The villagers, even more elated, carried the statue in a big sedan chair and toured the nearby villages, to the deafening sounds of gongs, drums and fire crackers all the way, while the villagers from other villages kowtowed to welcome it, laying out along the road the sacrifices of wine, chickens and sheep in the hope of obtaining their own good harvests. This is the supposed birth of the Nadun Festival.

It is a legendary story after all. The festival actually had come into being much earlier.

41. 花炮节

　　花炮节是侗族人民的传统节日。由于侗族人民生活在贵州、湖南、广西毗邻的广大地区，因此举行花炮节的日期便因地而异，如广西程阳地区在农历正月初三，光辉地区在正月十五，梅林地区在二月初二，斗江地区在二月十五，三江地区在三月初三，林溪地区在十月二十六日。本文介绍的是三江地区三月初三的花炮节，节期一天。

　　三江地区的花炮节具有悠久历史，也源于一个美好的民间传说故事。据说在很久很久以前，有位聪明、美丽、善良的侗族姑娘在河边玩水，忽然看见一条水蛇在追逐一条小花鱼，小花鱼无处可藏就游到了姑娘的跟前，水蛇也紧跟着追了过来，张开血红的大嘴，吐出长长的舌头，正要一口吃掉小花鱼时，眼明手快的侗族姑娘迅速挥起玩水的竹竿，奋力猛击水蛇的头部和脖子，打死了水蛇，救了小花鱼。过了几天，这位姑娘又到河边去洗衣服，看见一位妩媚婀娜的小姑娘站在水面上向空中抛撒鲜花玩耍。当她看见了侗族姑娘后就上前对她说："我叫小花，是龙王的小女儿，谢谢你打死水蛇救了我。"从此小花和侗族姑娘成了好朋友，并经常到侗族村寨去抛撒鲜花娱乐。龙王知道后就把小花关了起来，不许她与人间往来。心地善良的侗族人民非常同情和思念小花，就在每年三月初三,即小花初次来侗族村寨抛撒鲜花的那天去河边散花,以示和龙女小花一同娱乐。在年复一年的撒鲜花过程中,逐渐形成了侗族人民的节日。后来三江地区的经济有了很大发展,形成商品集散地,那些有远见卓识的商贾们为了招徕四方宾客,促进本埠经济发展,就给撒花节增加了放花炮的新内容,而且使场面十分壮观热烈,观赏放花炮的客商和游人数以万计。久而久之,人们就把三月初三的撒花节改称为"花炮节",并流传至今。

在花炮节的前几天,从远处前来观赏放花炮的客商就络绎不绝地来到三江及附近地区,他们也带来了木器、竹器和其他用于交换的土特产品。三江地区的壮族、苗族、瑶族、汉族及其他民族的人们也穿戴一新。带着各种手工织品或其他产品前往参加物资交流和观赏放花炮。

参加花炮节的侗族人民都穿戴着节日的盛装,打扮一新。姑娘们身穿侗布缝制的六层镶花边衣裳,束着花围腰,挽着高高的发髻,佩戴耳环、项链、手镯等银质饰物;小伙子们穿着白内衣,九扣蓝靛服和塑胶鞋。他们成群结队地从四面八方汇聚到举行花炮节庆祝活动的广场。

花炮节的主要活动项目是放花炮和抢花炮。花炮是由专业工匠制做的一个长约10厘米,口径比茶杯小的铁筒,内装火药,铁筒外用铁丝绕成约茶杯口径大小的铁环,铁环外用各色丝线捆扎好,再把铁环套在花炮上。放花炮前要把花炮放在铁炮口上,然后点燃铁炮,以铁炮的巨大冲力将花炮射上高空。当铁环降落时,各花炮队的队员们一齐冲向降落地点,奋力争抢铁环。放花炮要放三炮,头炮象征人财两旺,二炮象征幸福安康,三炮象征吉祥如意。

抢花炮的人必须是花炮队员。花炮队以村寨为单位组队,参加的总队数不限,但各队的人数必须相等,一般每队人数为十到二十人。队员必须穿较短的白衣黑裤,腿扎绑带。队员抢花炮时必须遵守规则,按规定可以互相挤、抢、护、传、拦,但不准打、踢、拳击,禁止带利器。如队员违犯规则,即取消全队抢花炮的资格。

放花炮一般在节日上午十点过后举行。放花炮前要举行仪式:首先由老人们抬着装上花炮、镜屏和彩礼(包括红鸡蛋、糯米粑粑、米酒和猪肉等)的花篮,在芦笙队簇拥下跟在舞狮队后面,随后的是几十个青少年,他们都手举挂着四五千枚小鞭炮的长竹杆,跟着仪仗队边游行边放鞭炮。仪仗队沿街游行或绕村寨一周,然后到预定的放花炮场。花炮场是直径约一百米的圆形广场,抢花炮的队员们站在圆周外的起跑线上。接着举行第二项仪式,由男青年组成一个仪仗队,他们都穿青衣、白裤,扎绑腿带,腋下拎着绣花荷包和盛着火药的葫芦,头帕上插着带叶的树枝,胸前挂着银链。他们在场内首先鸣放一阵粉枪,预示放花炮即将开始;接着鸣放小鞭炮,提醒各队作好抢花炮的准备;待各队队员都各就各位时,仪仗队开始点燃放在广场中央的铁炮。当一声震耳欲聋的巨响过后,各色彩线拥扎着的铁环从空中缓缓坠落下来,这时抢花炮的队员们如离弦之箭,一齐向铁环坠落地点猛冲过去争抢。同队的队员们既要勇敢地争抢,又要掩护抢到铁环的队友。若有一人抢到铁环,其余各队的队员都一同冲上去争夺。这种互相争夺往往要反复重演,持续较长时间,直到最后一位勇敢而又幸运的队员突破重围,双手高举铁环跑到了指挥台上,才算获胜,结束争抢。这时全场爆发出排山倒海般的掌声、欢呼声和器乐声。当指挥台验明铁环,宣布抢到第一炮铁环的优胜者姓名时,广场上再次爆发出热烈的欢呼声。接着开始放第二炮和第三炮,每一炮都重演一场激烈的争抢和雷鸣般的欢呼,从而使花炮场上出现一个又一个欢乐的高潮。当第三炮的争抢结束后,老人们要向三位优胜者颁发镜屏和彩礼。三位优胜者回队后和队友们一起扛起花炮,像胜利归来的英雄一样迈着健步,开始举行放花炮结束仪式。按照花炮节的传统习惯,优胜者要制做一个新的花炮铁环,并于第二年举行花炮节的当天送到现场,称为"还炮"。

　　放花炮结束后还要举行各种游艺活动,其中有精彩的侗戏、演彩调、赛芦笙、打球、打靶、射箭比赛、品评猎枪、斗鸟和多耶。最具侗族情调的当数"斗鸟"和"多耶"。

　　斗鸟的声势很浩大,有成千上万的人参加和观看。他们提着鸟笼自由组合在一起,大约十人左右为一组,使整个草坪顿时成为了斗鸟的拼搏场。他们斗鸟首先隔着鸟笼相斗,如果两只鸟势均力敌,不分胜负,就将两个鸟笼门相对,然后立即打开笼门,让两只鸟在一起搏斗。这时两只鸟便在两个鸟笼里来回展开争夺雌雄的决斗。结果输了的那只鸟在笼里垂尾打转,"咯咯"地沉鸣呼救;而获胜者则更加趾高气扬,翘尾紧迫不舍,"咕咕"地高叫威逼。百战百胜的鸟被称为鸟王,其身价可值一头水牛犊。

　　"多耶"是节日当天夜间青年男女们表演的一种侗族民歌。在侗语中,"多"意为"歌舞","耶"为"团歌"。按传统习惯,表演多耶时女队唱男队答。每一组里女队唱三首歌,男队也答三首歌。女队唱时手拉手围成一个圆圈,其唱法是合唱一句重复一句,然后两声部合唱,唱一句舞一步;男队唱时手攀肩成一圈,边唱边舞,领唱者唱一句,其他人一齐重复末尾三个字。但男队唱的歌词要求回答女队歌词的意思,并步女队的歌韵。因此要求男队领唱者必须具有敏捷的组词与歌唱的才智,否则不堪担当领唱者。

由于三江地区的花炮节富有经济因素,因此每年的花炮节又是一个规模较大的商品交易会,到处都是琳琅满目的当地刺绣品、工艺品、农副产品。侗族人民在通过花炮节愉悦身心的同时,又带动了经济发展,因而使花炮节长期以来一直受到人们的厚爱,使花炮节办得一年比一年好。

41. Fireworks Festival

The Fireworks Festival is a traditional festival observed by the Dong people who are distributed over different parts of Guizhou, Yunnan and Guangxi. Because of the wide distribution, the Dongs celebrate the festival on different days. Take the Dongs in the Guangxi Zhuang Autonomous Region for instance. Those living in the Chengyang and Guanghui areas respectively celebrate the festival on the 3rd, and the 15th of the first lunar month, those in the Meilin and Doujiang areas respectively do it on the 2nd and the 15th of the second lunar month, those in its Sanjiang County do it on the 3rd of the 3rd lunar month, and those in the Linxi area do it on the 26th of the 10th lunar month. The following is on the celebration by the Dong people in Sanjiang County.

The festival there has a long history and hangs a wonderful folk story. Long long ago, the story goes, a clever, beautiful and kind-hearted Dong girl played with water on a riverside when she saw a snake chasing a little variegated fish. Unable to find a shelter to hide, the fish swam to the girl for help; the snake followed the prey in hot pursuit, with its forked tongue moving outside its open mouth. It was about to catch the fish when the girl nimbly killed the snake with the bamboo pole which she had played water with. A few days later the Dong girl, when she came to the riverside to wash clothes, saw a little charming girl standing on the river and tossing flowers for pleasure. The charming girl came over to the Dong girl when she saw the latter, and said, "I'm the Dragon King's daughter named Little Flower. Thank you for saving my life." Later, Little Flower became a good friend of the Dong girl and often went to the latter's village to toss flowers for pleasure. Having learned this, the Dragon King shut up his daughter to keep her from outside. From then, the Dong villagers went to the riverside to toss fresh flowers on the 3rd of the 3rd lunar month every year, on which Little Flower had first come to their village to toss fresh flowers, to express their sympathy with and memory of her. Through years, the practice evolved into a festival. Later on, Sanjiang County saw great growth of economy and the county seat became a distribution center for goods. So some far-sighted businessmen initiated a grand fireworks display at the festival, intending to draw customers far and wide. The strategy turned out so successful that tens of thousands of businessmen and tourists went there to watch the fireworks display. Some years later, the festival was named Fireworks Festival.

Several days before the Fireworks Festival streams of businessmen from afar come to Sanjiang County's seat, bringing along bamboo articles, wood articles and other special native products for interflow. Meanwhile, the Zhuangs, Miaos, Yaos, Hans and other peoples in Sanjiang also come to the city either to conduct interflow of commodities or to watch the fireworks display, all clad in their holiday best, bringing various arts and crafts or other goods.

On the festive day, the Dong people come in groups from all directions to a square in the city, where entertainments are to be given for celebration. The girls of them wear costumes trimmed with six layers of lace and made of home-made cloth, have on spotted aprons, wear topknots and adorn themselves with earrings, necklaces and bracelets, which are all made of silver. The young men of them wear white shirts inside, 9-buttoned indigo-blue jackets outside and rubber-soled shoes.

The major items on the festive programme are letting off fireworks and scrambling for fireworks' rings. A firework, made by craftsmen, consists of three parts: an iron tube about 10 centimeters long, with the caliber of an ordinary tea cup, and filled with gunpowder; an iron ring bigger than the tube in diameter and wrapped with multicolored silk threads; an iron launcher. Before it is let off, the tube is first coiled by and tied to the ring, and then tied to the launcher. When the fireworks is lit, the tube with the ring shoots into the air on the powerful thrust. At the moment the ring falls down to the ground, crowds rush to scramble for it. The custom has it that three fireworks are to be let off, respectively symbolizing abundant wealth, good health of men and good luck of men.

The ring scramblers must be the members of competitive teams representative of different villages. The teams are not limited in number, but their members must be equal in number, usually ranging from 10 to 20. All the members must wear white jackets and black trousers, and have their legs tightly wrapped with puttees. They shall abide by the rules for the game, which stipulate that they are permitted to squeeze each other to scramble for the ring, shield the ring, pass on the ring and block opponents from the ring, but not permitted to beat or kick opponents and carry any sharp weapons. Any rule breaker causes disqualification of his team from the contest.

The fireworks display, usually given after 10 o'clock on the festive morning, is preceded by two ceremonies. The first one is actually a parade. At its head are dancers performing the Lion Dance to the accompaniment of the lusheng (a reed-pipe wind instrument); following them are some old men who carry on their shoulders a big festooned basket containing fireworks, screen-like mirrors and gifts of red eggs, glutinous rice cakes, rice wine and pork; then come scores of young men who keep letting off long strings of firecrackers hung from long bamboo poles. The parade goes through villages and finally comes to a ground for the fireworks display. The ground is usually round, and about 100 meters in diameter. All the members of the competitive teams stand along a starting line outside the circular line around the ground. Then comes the second ceremony. First appear a team of young honor guards, who wear black jackets and white trousers, have their legs wrapped with puttees, carry under their arms some embroidered pouches and gourds containing gunpowder, have their turbans decorated with twigs, and hang silver chains from their necks. They first fire gunshots to announce that the fireworks display is about to begin, and then let off firecrackers to put the competitive teams in readiness. Still then, the honor guards let off the first fireworks at the center of the ground. Immediately after a deafening boom of explosion, the iron ring of the fireworks falls from the air. At the moment, all scramblers dart forward, like an arrow discharged from the bowstring, to scramble for it. When one scrambler has the ring in hand, his fellow scramblers must struggle hard to shield it and his opponents try every means to take it over. The scrambling usually lasts long, probably with changes of the ring holder in between, until a lucky fellow struggle out of tight encirclements and, holding the ring high, comes running to the command platform. The moment when the victor gets there, all spectators burst into thunderous applause and cheers accompanied by musical sounds. When the judge on the command platform confirms and announces the victor, spectators clap and cheer again. Then comes the letting-off of the second fireworks and, some time later, the third. Either arouses the same excitement. When the third victor is announced, some venerable elders award the three victors each with a screen-like mirror and the gifts of red eggs, glutinous rice cakes, rice wine and pork. Then the victors, carrying the launchers together with other members of their own teams, walk on in processions with vigorous strides like heroes, as a closing ceremony. The custom has it that winning teams each must coil a new ring for the next festival, and bring it to the same ground on the same day the next year. This is called "returning fireworks".

Following the fireworks display are some other entertainments. They include Dong opera singing, caidiao (a local opera in Guangxi) singing, lusheng (a wind instrument) playing contest, ball playing, archery, shooting contest, hunting-rifle evaluating, birdfight and duoye singing (folk-song singing). Of them, the last two items are Dong-flavored most.

The birdfight often draws tens of thousands of spectators, presenting a spectacular scene. About ten participants gather on a grassy lot, each holding a cage with a bird in. First, the birds are paired off to fight, each in its own cage. If the victor bangs in the balance, the cages will be moved to set their two doors open to each other. Then the two birds are locked in fierce fighting, in this cage one moment and in the other the next. The defeated bird, with its tail drooping, keeps moving about and chattering in its cage as if begging for help, while the winning bird, very cocky, with its tail raised, keeps cocking and chasing its opponent. The winning bird is crowned a king bird which values as much as a young buffalo.

Duoye is performed in the night. In the Dong language, duo means "singing and dancing", and ye means "group singing". According to the custom, duoye is performed in antiphonal style between a female team and a male team. Usually female singers sing first and male singers sing in reply. Each part sings three folk songs in all. The female singers, forming a ring, hand in hand, sing each verse twice in chorus, and then sing in duet while dancing. The male singers stand in a circle, one's hands on another's shoulders; all dancing, their leading singer sings a verse and the other singers repeat the last three words of the verse. The male singers' verses must be answers to, and rhyme with the female singers' verses. Therefore, the leading singer must be quick-witted and able to improvise verses up to the requirements, or he would get stuck.

The Fireworks Festival, a great attraction, surely brings about a big trade fair, which is a superb collection of commodities such as local embroidery, arts and crafts, and farm produce.

Bringing merry to holiday makers and prosperity to the local e-
conomy, the festival is loved by all the Dong people. That's why
the festival is getting livelier and livelier each year.

42.打铁节

打铁节是云南省基诺族人民的传统节日,基诺语称为"特毛且",即过年,寓意为大家打铁,准备生产工具。节日的时间在基诺历的一月,选择其中最吉利的一天开始过年,节期三天。但因基诺族各村寨选择的吉日不尽相同,所以打铁节不在同一天开始。

基诺族人民把过新年称为打铁节,那是源于一段远古时期的传说。据说在很久很久以前,有位基诺族的妇女已经怀胎九年零九个月了,孩子还生不下来,她很着急,到处求巫师施法术,访问行人找原因,都无济于事。一天,她感到腋下肋骨巨痛难忍,浑身汗如雨下,躺在床上昏了过去。过了一会儿,肚里的孩子咬断了她的七根肋骨,从腋下跳了出来。这孩子生下来时一手握着火钳,一手拿着铁锤,会打铁制造各种器具。从此基诺人进入了铁器时代,开始使用铁制工具。促进了生产发展。基诺人为了不忘铁制生产工具的出现和使用,就把那个孩子出生的日子定为节日,取其意称为"打铁节"。

在打铁节前夕,当寨父寨母家敲响牛皮鼓时,全村寨的人都集中到寨父寨母家开会。其主要内容是摊派各家出钱买牛,以及安排剽牛仪式和指定剽牛人。节日的准备工作还有:每家出一人持弓箭或火药枪,一同上山猎黄嘴老鼠两对,献给寨父寨母,作为儿女孝敬父母的过年礼物。同时还要捉一对竹鼠送给打铁匠,作为新年备耕砍树仪式的礼物,以及使用铁器的纪念品。另外每户人家都要自备材料,请铁匠打一件铁制农具。然后各家各户都酿酒、杀猪、宰牛,备办丰盛的食品。并在节日到来时邀请附近村寨的亲戚朋友们前来一同欢度新年。

过节期间男女都要盛装打扮。女子一般绾发结髻于头顶上,戴白色厚麻布后披翅尖帽,上身穿白色或杂色镶边绣花的无领对襟小褂,内衬薄布紧身衣,下系棉麻布红白镶边蓝黑色的前开合短裙,绑裹腿,戴耳环或坠子。男子一般上身穿白色镶边无领对襟麻布或棉布褂,下身穿蓝色或白色裤子,用黑布或蓝布帕缠头,绑裹腿,赤脚。

过节的第一天,全寨人都到长老家去祝贺,每人带去一斤米。长老家要倾其所有招待好他们,让大家吃饱喝足,尽兴而归。这一天还要举行剽牛仪式,其程序是首先把牛的四肢捆住,接着由一名年轻人用刀砍牛的后脚,然后在牛未死之前割下牛屁股上的一块鲜肉作为祭祀用,最后把牛肉分给村寨里的各家。

过节的第二天,家长们集中去打铁房,举行简单的象征性的备耕打铁仪式:首先由铁匠杀两只鸡祭祀,把鸡血洒在风箱上,再拔几根鸡毛沾在风箱上。仪式结束后,铁匠开始给每户人家打刀。

过节的第三天,白天由长老带领大家去巡视、修整道路、标示村寨界线。晚上举行备耕仪式:先在门坎外铺三层最好的芭蕉叶,每层上依次放着鲜鱼、猪肉和米饭等食品,然后祭祀鬼神。这时人们准备好了长刀、火把,等长老吹响号角,人们就一手举火把，一手挥长刀，在道路两侧东砍一下，西砍一下，以此象征砍树标界，表示本村寨的地盘外村寨不得侵犯。这天，寨父寨母要杀一条狗，宰两只鸡为客人们送行。宴席开始时，全体宾客要举杯向牛皮鼓敬酒，并将几滴酒洒在牛皮鼓上，然后将杯中酒一饮而尽。客人们吃饱喝足，携带着主人赠送的礼物，辞别主人，离寨而归。

过节时除了进行上述活动外，还要举行各种娱乐活动，其中敲牛皮鼓是一项最隆重的活动。牛皮鼓长约一米，直径约半米，用一截原木挖空而成，两端外侧各有二十个木柄环绕鼓身，呈放射形，鼓面是带毛的黄牛皮。牛皮鼓是基诺族人民最神圣的吉祥物。它的神圣源自一段民间传说：据说在远古时候洪水泛滥，人们为了逃生，有一户人家把一个儿子和一个女儿装进牛皮鼓里，并告诉他们每天击鼓三次，当鼓声清脆时洪水就退了，才可以用刀割开牛皮出来。他们兄妹二人在牛皮鼓里随波逐流，漂泊了七天七夜，一直漂到了攸乐山附近的节苴地方，洪水才退了，只剩下他们兄妹二人，他们就在节苴定居下来。他们的子孙就是基诺人，所以后世基诺人认为是牛皮鼓救了他们的祖先，于是就视牛皮鼓为神器，十分崇拜，平时挂在寨父寨母家里，不准敲击。过新年敲鼓时必须先祭鼓，给牛皮鼓插上五颜六色的鲜花。敲牛皮鼓时男子抬着，女鼓手用木槌击打，牛皮鼓发出浑厚的响声，在村寨四周回荡。击牛皮鼓时由口含槟榔的老翁仰头打钹和头戴大尖顶帽的老妪低头鸣锣伴奏。若女鼓手累了，可由另一名女鼓手替换，男性不能充当鼓手。敲牛皮鼓时其余的青年男女们围成一个圆圈跳舞，他们的头上插着鲜花，手里也拿着鲜花，边歌边舞。从远处望去，宛如五彩缤纷的花簇在随风翩然，灿烂美丽。

在节日里，每个基诺人都是歌手。晚上村寨里的男女老少都聚集在篝火旁，由长老和最善长唱歌的人坐在正中领唱，其他人围在四周合唱。在他们唱的传统歌曲中有一种叫做"巴什"的情歌，其内容是反映由氏族内的血缘家庭和血缘婚姻过渡到氏族外婚姻，被认为是原始情歌的一件瑰宝，也是研究血缘家庭史的珍贵资料。基诺族人民为了使节日更加热烈愉快，歌手们有时还要邀请其他村寨的歌手来对歌，而且去请歌手的人要用歌声邀请对方，被邀请的人也要用歌声来回答。若客方歌手对歌时输了，要留下一条包头帕，等第二年的打铁节再去对歌时取回来。

跳笙则是一项歌舞同演的活动。跳笙时由两三人弹着三弦琴，男女老少手拉手围成一圈，由一名歌手即兴组词领唱，大家跟着齐声附和，边唱边舞，十分热闹快活。

青年男女都喜欢的活动是翻竹竿比赛。比赛开始时，一位姑娘双手握住竹竿的上部，下部插在地上。翻竹竿的那位小伙子双手握住竹竿的下部，面向上背朝下，双脚着地，挺起胸腹部，围绕竹竿旋转，旋转次数多的为获胜者。参加活动的小伙子必须力气大，技艺娴熟；姑娘也必须密切配合。许多未婚的青年男女通过翻竹竿比赛的紧密配合，开始互相认识，互相了解，互相合作，产生感情，最后成为终身伴侣。因此翻竹竿比赛的活动被誉为"体育恋爱"，很受未婚青年男女们欢迎。

除此而外，还要根据不同年龄与性别开展各项文娱体育活动。儿童喜欢玩陀螺；妇女们喜欢荡秋千和玩毛毛球；小伙子们则喜欢掷标枪、踢球和踩高跷。

打铁节的庆祝活动丰富多彩，节日里的基诺人也极其欢乐愉快。

42. Forging-Iron Festival

The Forging-Iron Festival is observed as the New Year by the Jinuo people in Yunnan Province. It is called Temaoqie in the Jinuo language, which means celebrating the New Year and implies that all join to forge iron to make farm tools. The festival lasts three days from a supposedly auspicious day in the first Jinuo calendar month. It actually begins on different days of the month because villagers in different villages may think different days auspicious.

Why the Jinuos call their New Year the Forging-Iron Festival has a legend from ancient times. Long long ago, the legend goes, a Jinuo woman had conceived a child for nine years and nine months without bearing it. The anxious woman resorted to sorcerers' magic arts for solution and consulted many passers-by for advice, but nothing worked. One day she felt an unbearable pain in her ribs under one of her armpits. Sweating all over, she had to lie on bed and finally fell into a coma. After a while the child broke seven of her ribs and forced out from under the armpit, a tongs in one hand and a hammer in the other. Strange enough, he was able to forge iron to make different tools at such young age. His birth was thought to be the beginning of the Jinuos' Iron Age, in which they began to use iron tools for promoting production development. In memory of the event, the Tinuos set the day the child came out the Forging-Iron Festival.

The pre-festival activities are: A village's Chief Parents would beat an oxhide-headed drum to call all villagers to meet at their house, mainly to apportion each household the share of money for buying an ox to be slaughtered at the ox-slaughtering ceremony held on the first day of the festival, arrange the ox-slaughtering ceremony, and appoint ox slaughters; hunters, one from each family, bringing along shotguns or bows and arrows, go to the mountains to bag four susliks as New Year gifts for the Chief Parents, and two bamboo rats as gifts to be presented to the village's blacksmith at the ceremony of felling trees for spring ploughing, and also as a commemoration of the birth of iron tools; the blacksmith, on request, produces an iron farm tool for each household with the iron given by the latter; every household brews wine, slaughters hogs and cattle, and prepares many other foods, which are to be shared by relatives and friends from neighboring villages at a dinner during the festival.

All the Jinuos are dressed in their holiday best during the festival. The women of them wear topknots, top-pointed hats with white gunny hangings at back, jackets which are white or variegated, collarless and laced, and embroidered, tight-fitting shirts, and gunny skirts which are laced, have their legs wrapped with puttees, and adorn themselves with earrings or ear lobes; the men of them, barefooted, wear gunny or cotton-cloth jackets which are white, collarless and laced, trousers which are blue or white, and turbans which are black or blue, and have their legs wrapped with puttees.

On the first day of the festival, all of a village pay a New Year call to the village's Elder, each presenting him a catty of polished rice, while the Elder entertains the guests to so nice a meal that the latter eat and drink their fill. This day also sees the ox-slaughtering ceremony. At the ceremony some of the slaughters first bind an ox's four limbs, then a young man chops off the animal's rear legs, cuts from its bottom a piece of beef as sacrificial offering, and finally distributes all the beef to the villagers, each household a share.

On the second day all the families' heads attend a ceremony of symbolically forging iron to make farm tools for spring ploughing, held in a special room. At the ceremony, the blacksmith first kills two chickens, then worships gods with them as sacrificial offerings, and still then sprinkles some of their blood over a bellows and pastes some of their feathers on it. After the close of the ceremony the blacksmith begins to forge hacks for all households.

In the daytime of the third day the villagers, led by the elder, repair roads and demarcate supposed boundary lines of the village. That night sees a ceremony of preparing spring ploughing. At the ceremony they first place three banana leaves on the ground outside a threshold, one on another, with fresh fish, pork and steamed rice on each; then they worship spirits and gods; still then they each hold a torch in one hand and a long hack in another and begin to hack, on bugle horn calls from the elder, at plants on either side of a road to demarcate a supposed boundary line of the village territory, which is not to be intruded by outsiders. On this day, the Chief Parents kill a dog and two chickens for a farewell dinner for the guests they invite from other villages. At the beginning of the dinner, every guest sprinkles some wine over an oxhide-headed drum and drinks the wine in one gulp as a sacrificial toast to the drum. Then the guests eat and drink their fill and, bringing along the gifts given by the Chief Parents, bid farewell for home in great satisfaction.

The festival, in addition, is marked with various entertainments, of which the Oxhide-Headed Drum Beating is the major one. The drum consists of a hollow cylinder from log, about one meter long and half a meter in diameter, with 20 short wood handles fixed around both oxhide-headed ends. It is seen as a holy mascot by the Jinuos, which hangs a legend. In ancient times, the legend goes, a serious flood took place. Two children, a boy and a girl, were placed in a drum by their parents to keep them safe and they were told to beat the drum thrice every day, and not to cut its oxhide open trying to come out until the flood receded. They floated to Jieju near the Youle Mountain after the flood of seven days and nights had gone down. There they came out of the drum to find that they were alone. Later they settled down at the place and became the ancestors of the present Jinuo people. Thinking that the drum saved their ancestors, the Jinuos see it a holy object and have it preserved in the Chief Parents' house in normal times. When it is to be beaten for New Year celebration, it should first be offered a sacrifice and adorned with multicolored flowers, then the drum carried by young men is beaten by a girl, with deep sounds reverberating in the air. At the same time, an old man, chewing a betel nut and raising up his head, strikes a pair of cymbals and an old woman, wearing a top-pointed hat, strikes a gong. The girl drum beater may be replaced by another girl, but not a man, if she is tired. To the accompaniment of the instruments, other young people in a circle dance and sing, with flowers held in their hands and fixed on their heads. Viewed from afar, the merry-makers are like a cluster of beautiful flowers moving in the wind.

During the festival nearly all of a village are singers. At night they sit around a bonfire, with the elder and better singers in the center and others around them. Those in the center lead singing and the others respondently sing in chorus. They are especially fond of the love songs locally known as "bashi", which reflect the evolution of the Jinuos' marriage from between consanguine families tobetween non-consanguine families. The songs are seen as gems of primitive love songs and rare materials for insight into the past marriage between consanguine families as well. To make the festival more joyful, singers from one village often invite singers from other villages to do antiphonal singing. Both the invitation and the reply to it are to be conveyed by singing. The invited singers, if they lose the singing contest, are to leave a turban to the invitees till it is retrieved at a similar singing contest next year.

Tiaosheng, an item of singing accompanied by dancing, is performed during the festival. In this performance villagers, hand in hand and standing in a ring, sing and sway to the accompaniment of the sanxian (a three-stringed plucked instrument), one leading the singing and others singing respondently in chorus. The scene is very exciting and lively.

The Bamboo Pole Game, given during the festival, is most favored by young Jinuos. In playing it, a girl holds a bamboo pole's upper part with both hands and forces the pole upright on the ground, then a young fellow holds its lower part with both hands and, throwing out his chest upward, walks round the pole. The one who moves round the pole the most times is the winner of the game, so the young fellow should be skilled and physically strong while the girl should skillfully cooperate with the young man. Many unmarried young people, through the game, get to know each other and become husbands and wives later. Hence the game is also named "a dating sport".

Some other entertainments and sports offered during the festival are loved by particular groups of Jinuos. For example, children like to whip tops, women are fond of playing on swings and playing down-covered balls, and young men love to throw javelins, play football and walk on stilts.

The Festival is marked with so varied and colorful festivities that its celebrators feel happier than on any other occasions.

43. 畲族新年

　　新年是福建省福安市和毗邻地区畲族人民的传统节日,在每年的正月初一至十五这段时间内举行,与汉族的春节基本一致,但活动内容不尽相同。

　　畲族人民非常重视过新年。他们从农历十月开始做准备,用糯米酿制过年酒,用灰碱水浸沧粳米做年糕,临近年末时各家各户都要宰鸡鸭杀肥猪,备办各种美食佳肴。

　　到除夕这天,各家各户的火塘热灰里都煨着一截着火的硬质干木柴,一直缓慢燃烧到次日,畲族人称为"隔夜火种"。这天晚上要守岁,人们通宵不眠。前半夜的主要活动是人们相互走访祝福,后半夜各家都点燃香烛、鸣放鞭炮辞旧迎新,然后全家人团聚吃新年饭。

　　有些地区的畲族在除夕要做麻糍,当晚吃一部分,把剩余的放在谷仓里,待到元宵过后再取出来吃,寓意"有吃有余。"

　　初一凌晨,畲族有一种奇特的习俗:男人起床后赤身裸体地走出门外,手里握住竹响板,围绕住房边跑边敲,使房前屋后响彻着"呱呱呱……"的响声,他们认为这样可以除病消灾,全家平安。天亮后孩子们跑到竹林里去,用手摇撼毛竹,以期盼自己像竹笋那样快速成长,早日成才,兴家立业。早餐时有的人家要在饭里掺入少许番薯丝,表示过年时节也不忘节俭。

从初二开始,畲族村寨里的猎手们要集体上山打猎。过去,猎手们出发前要举行祭狩猎神的仪式,仪式结束后再一同上山打猎。如果猎手们捕获到野猪、山羊、鹿等大型野兽,抬回去后要首先祭祀"射猎师公"。祭祀时首先点燃香和蜡烛,然后鸣猎枪,最后大家一起礼拜,感谢"射猎师公"的恩赐。祭祀完毕后,由开第一枪击中猎物的猎手割下猎物的头归己,开第二枪的猎手割去猎物的颈。剩下的由其余猎手们平分,那些出猎的猎狗们也可分得一份。若狩猎的人多,猎物又太小,那就把猎物肉煮熟,让全村寨的男女老少都分食一点,名曰"散野神"。

节日期间的娱乐活动主要有对歌、打尺寸、登山、打秋千等。畲族是个善唱山歌的民族,有关畲族历史传说的山歌家喻户晓,人人会唱。畲族山歌的内容广泛,歌词生动活泼,易记易唱;曲调有低平快速、高亢中速、高亢拉长音等三种唱法。唱歌时男女歌手都用假声,其形式有独唱、对唱和二重唱。但过新年时只有某些家里来了客人时才对歌,那时夜间就热闹起来。如来的是青年男客人,要由女歌手盘歌对唱;若来的是青年女客人,则要由男歌手盘歌对唱;若来的是青年孕妇或抱着婴儿的妇女,那就不准找她对歌。唱歌时必须首先由主人开始,其歌词内容是表达一些欢迎的话。如果客人是位好歌手,那就很快开始对唱起来,气氛立即变得很快活,如果客人不善长对歌,主人有时要唱一两个小时之后客人才能开始对唱。但不论客人怎么拖延,最终必须开口对唱,否则是过不了关的。有时候会遇上双方都是好歌手,从天黑唱到天亮也分不出胜负,那就要接着连续唱两三个夜晚,而且要求歌词内容不重复,以便互相"比肚才"。如对唱结果主人输了,要好好招待客人吃一顿点心，若是客人输了，有可能会受到主人的教训。有些地区的畲族在对完歌之后，主人要给客人发红包，包里的钱数多少要视客人对歌的多少和内容好坏而定。

"打尺寸"是一种传统的游戏活动。参加人数至少两人，多则五六人；使用的器具为木棍和竹条。比赛前在场地上划一个直径数米的圆圈。比赛开始时一人站在圆圈内，一手握木棍，一手握竹条，用木棍把竹条击打向远处，站在圆圈外前场上的其他人则奔跑着去接竹条，接住者可得到规定的尺寸；脱手或落地的竹条，可以捡起来再投向圆圈。对于投向圆圈的竹条，持木棍者可用手接住或用木棍击回去，若系接住了，可得到一定的尺寸；如果投者将竹条投入圆圈而未被持棍者接住或击中，则双方交换场地。他们就这样通过对竹条的击打、跑接、回投、接击等动作展开比赛。比赛要规定时间和尺寸数，到时所得尺寸最多者获胜。

登山比赛不限地域，不分男女，任何愿意的畲族人都可以参加。比赛那天，人们天不亮就来到预定的出发地点。待太阳刚升起来的时候，随着一声枪响，参加比赛的人群就如潮水一般向高山上蜂拥而去。首先到达终点的优胜者，一般可获得一面锦旗，有些畲族村寨在人们都登上终点后还要举行打猎、会餐和唱山歌等活动。

畲族的秋千非常特别，完全不同于其他民族的秋千。他们是把一根碗口粗细的毛竹砍来，将顶上的枝条编成一个竹圈，大小可供一人坐上，然后再将毛竹竖在活动场上。打秋千的人坐在竹圈里，柔韧而又富有弹性的毛竹，因人身体重心的不固定而在空中不断变换方向，并忽升忽降地摆动，人坐在上面也就随其上下左右不停地转悠飘荡，轻松自如。其状别具一格,胜似其他任何一种形式的秋千,使其场面异常生动、活泼,热烈,不时博得观众的欢呼声和鼓掌声。

正月初八,是畲族人民祭祀祖先盘瓠的隆重祭日,传说盘瓠十分英俊骁勇,曾因帮助皇帝平息外患而娶了公主。婚后迁居深山,生了三子一女,长子名盘,次子名兰,三子名雷,女婿名钟,由他们四姓繁衍成畲族。后世世代子子孙孙为了缅怀祖先,在过年节的正月初八这一天,同祖同姓家族的男女老少,都分别汇集到各村寨本姓氏的祠堂,举行隆重的祭祖活动。首先在祖先的图像前设一神案,案上摆着香炉、蜡烛、祖杖和牛、羊、猪、鸡及其他饭菜等食物。祭祖仪式由本姓中辈份高、年龄大的老人主持、领唱祭祖歌,讲述畲族历史渊源和祖先盘瓠的传说故事。仪式结束后,人们一起到祭房家里去吃"太公饭"。祭房家要设宴烫酒,热情招待同祖同姓客人。妇女和姑娘们在席间为客人们斟酒上菜,热情款待,人们都不分彼此,融洽相处,谈笑风声,同欢共饮,洋溢着诚挚友善的亲情。

43. The She People's New Year

The She people, who live in Fuan City and its contiguous areas, Fujian Province, celebrate their New Year from the first to the 15th of the first lunar month. The festival celebrations are a bit different from those of the Han's Spring Festival, though both cover the same period of time.

The Shes attach much importance to their New Year celebration. They usually begin preparations for the festival in the 10th lunar month, brewing glutinous rice wine, soaking nonglutinous rice to make New Year cakes, and so on. Near the end of the old year, all households are busy killing chickens, ducks and hogs for various appetizing foods.

On the eve of the festival, every household has an ember buried in the ashes of its fire pit until next day, and the resultant tinder is locally called "an overnight tinder". The festive celebrators stay up all New Year's Eve, usually calling on neighbors or relatives during the first half of the night, and burning sacrificial joss sticks and kindles, letting off firecrackers and eating the New Year family reunion meal during the second half.

The Shes living in some areas make glutinous rice cakes surfaced with some sesame on the eve of the festival. They eat some of them the same night, and keep in barns the rest to be eaten after the Lantern Festival, which is on the 15th of the first lunar month, to express a wish for surplus grain in the year to come.

They practice an odd custom at daybreak next day, which goes that men of a family run around their house, stark naked, while clapping two bamboo clappers. They believe this wards off diseases and disasters. After the dawn, children go to a bamboo forest to shake bamboo plants, wishing that they could grow as fast as bamboo shoots so as to build up their own families and start their own careers earlier. Some of the She families, for breakfast, have some sliced sweet potatoes mixed in steamed rice, suggesting that they should remember frugality even in the New Year.

On the second of the month, She hunters of a village go into a mountain, in a group, to shoot wild game. They used to hold a service to worship the hunting god at their departure, but the custom fell into disuse now. If they catch big beasts like a wild boar, goat, deer, etc., they first carry them back home and hold a service to worship their "hunting master", and then share the bag. At the service they burn joss sticks and kindles, fire gunshots and kowtow, to express their thanks to the "hunting master" for his favor. As regards the division of bag, the one who fires the first shot and hits the animal gets its head, the one who fires the second shot and hits it gets its neck, and the other hunters equally share the rest, even the hunting dogs having their shares. If the hunting party is big and the hunted animal is small, they just cook it for all villagers to eat. This practice is locally known as "shared by all gods".

The main entertainments, offered during the festival, include doing antiphonal singing, hitting a short bamboo piece, mountain-climbing contest, playing on swings, and the like. Being good singers, almost all the Shes can sing folk songs, especially those on the legend of their history, which are wide in content, vivid in words and easy to remember. They sing some of them in a low-pitched and speedy tone, some in a high-pitched and medium-speeded tone, and some in a high-pitched and slow-speeded tone; they sing them in forms of solo, antiphonal singing or duet, all in falsettos. However, they do antiphonal singing merely between hosts and guests who are on a New Year visit. The custom has it that a female from the host side starts singing in challenge if guests are male, and vice versa; pregnant guests and children guests won't be challenged. Usually a host or hostess starts the singing by singing some polite words. If the guest is a good singer, the singing immediately goes into a hot contest; if not, the challenger should sing alone for hours until the guest sings in reply. No matter how bad a singer, the guest must sing something to tide over the awkward moment. If both are good singers, they might sing songs of different words for a night, even days and nights, before the better composer is decided; if the host or hostess is the loser, he or she should entertain the guest to nice pastry and, if the guest is the loser, he or she would be mildly criticized by the host or hostess. Towards the end of the antiphonal singing in some places, the host would offer to the guest money wrapped in a red envelope, whose sum depends on how long the singing lasts and how exciting the songs are.

The Short-Bamboo-Piece Hitting is one of their traditional games, with players of two to six. Before the game begins, a player stands inside a circle with several meters in diameter, a wood stick in one hand and a short bamboo piece in the other. When the game begins, the player hits, with the wood stick, the bamboo piece far away while the other player or players outside the circle rushes forward trying to catch the flying bamboo piece. If he catches it, he is the winner and is to be given the set points to his credit; if he fails to catch it, he may pick up the piece and throw it back to the player inside the circle, and the latter may try either to catch it or hit it away. If the latter catches or hits it, he also gets the set points; if he fails to catch or hit it, both sides change positions. The final winner is the one who gets the most points.

The mountain-climbing contest is open to all who enjoy it. The participants and spectators come to the starting point even before daybreak. When a gunshot signals the start at sunrise, all competitors rush to the set mountain peak like surging water. The one who first reaches the peak is usually rewarded a pennant as a memento. The contest is followed, in some villages, by hunting, picnics, folk-song singing and other entertainments.

The She people's swing is quite different from other swings. It is a very thick, tough and tensile bamboo pole, freshly felled and erectly fixed in the ground, with a crate woven from its slender twigs at its upper part and able to accommodate one player. The player in the crate may swing up, down, left or right as he changes the center of gravity of his body, feeling comfortable and at ease as if floating in the air. This item often arouses cheers and applause from excited audience, bringing about a hilarious scene.

On the 8th of the month, the She people offer a grand sacrifice to their ancestor named Panhu. According to legend, he was handsome and brave. Because he helped to put down a foreign invasion Panhu won the king's favor and married one of the king's daughters. After marriage, he and his wife settled down in a high mountain. His wife gave birth to three sons and one daughter, the eldest son named Pan, the second named Lan, the third named Lei and the son-in-law named Zhong. These people are supposed to be the second-generation ancestors of the present She people. So on the 8th of the month, all the Shes in a village, usually belonging to the same clan, attend a grand memorial ceremony held at their ancestral temple to worship Panhu. On a sacrificial desk before the figure of Panhu are burning joss sticks, burning kindles, a walking-stick for the worshipped, beef, mutton, pork, chicken and other foods. The most prestigious elder of the clan chairs the ceremony, first leading the worshipper in singing their ancestral song and then telling legendary stories about Panhu and the history of the She People. After the ceremony, they all go to the ceremony chairer's house to have a dinner, locally known as a "taigong meal". The host family offers nice food and wine to the guests. At the dinner, women and girls from the host family hospitably serve food and wine, while the guests talk and laugh over food, presenting a very cordial and harmonious atmosphere.

44. 端　节

　　端节,水族人称为"借端",意为过年,是贵州省水族人民最隆重的节日。

　　水族历法将一年分为十二个月,每月三十天,以子、丑、寅、卯、辰、巳、午、未、申、酉、戌、亥记日,并规定从一月的初亥日起各地区的村寨轮流过端节,直到三月上旬才能过完。这段时间相当于中国农历的九月至十月上旬。节期各地均为一天。

　　关于端节的来历,在水族人民中有多种传说,其中流传较广的说法是:在很久很久以前,水族居住的地区发生水灾,有兄弟三人漂流到了三都地区。水灾过后,兄弟三人于次年水历一月初亥分别,各自去他乡开荒种地,自谋生计。一年过后,兄弟三人都带着丰收的喜悦心情团聚,庆贺丰收。从此他们决定将分别的日子一月初亥定为丰收节(即现在的端节),年年庆贺。后世水族人民为了表达对祖先的怀念和庆祝丰收,就按三兄弟年龄的大小和所居住地区之不同,分别于初亥、双亥和三亥依次轮流过端节。其中老大居住的三洞地区在初亥过端节,老二和老三居住的水龙和恒丰等地区则分别在双亥和三亥过端节。

　　水族人民非常重视过端节。在端节前夕,水族的各家各户都要宰鸡鸭杀肥猪，舂新糯米。端节前一天的晚上，各个村寨都要把专供喜庆和节日用的一面或十几面大铜鼓悬挂在房梁上或庭院里的鼓架上，以皮鼓指挥和伴奏，尽兴击打，彻夜不停，表示辞旧迎新。

在端节的早晨，男女老少都穿上新衣服，用丰盛的美食佳肴祭祀祖先。祭祖是端节的重要活动内容。他们在堂屋里的餐桌上摆满用糯米做的新米饭和各种好酒好菜，其中必不可少的是"鱼包韭菜"，这种菜制做精细，味美可口，用于祭祀祖先最富有传统意义。其原因是据说水族人民的祖先生活在南方的水乡泽国，鱼是他们的主要食品之一。北迁后居住地区水源不多，很难吃到鱼，只有到过节时才能吃到一点鲜鱼。所以他们就把珍贵的鲜鱼进行精细加工，做成美味食品祭祀祖先，以表示继承祖先的传统生活习惯。

水族人民在端节的早餐吃素，但可以吃鱼，午后才开荤。早餐过后人们相互走访，即使有些并不相识的人也会受到热情接待。在有些水族的村寨里，人们早起祭祖，仪式完毕后就敲响铜鼓，听到铜鼓声的父老兄弟们就陆陆续续汇集到一个事先约定的家庭。人们见面时互相祝贺新年愉快，人寿年丰。主人要用当年收割的糯米煮成新米饭，用大活鱼煮成鲜鱼羹，热情招待前来祝贺的客人们。让客人们入座后大家一同用餐，在欢呼声中依次干杯。随后众人又起身跟在铜鼓队后面再去挨家挨户拜年，吃庆贺端节的年酒。许多孩子们也跟着长辈一同去分享赠品。他们每到一家，主人就要把糖块、水果、干鱼等食品分发给孩子们。水族人认为，获得赠品最多的孩子最能干，在新的一年里将得到幸福，身体健康。

拜完年后举行各种娱乐活动，其中主要有极富民族风格的铜鼓舞和场面盛大的赛马活动。参加铜鼓舞的水族姑娘们身着蓝色大襟无领半长衣,下穿青布长裤和青色围腰,佩戴耳环、项圈和手镯等银质饰物;小伙子们则身穿大襟长短衫,用青布包头。他们汇集到举行端节活动的"端坡",一起参加有皮鼓伴奏的铜鼓舞。铜鼓的直径大约50厘米,重量在30千克以上;最大的直径有1米,重量约200千克。皮鼓是把一段长约75厘米的泡桐树木材挖空,在两端绷上牛皮做成的。敲铜鼓时,两名鼓手用左手握住硬木条侧击铜鼓的边沿,右手握着带红绸穗的鼓槌正击铜鼓中心;一名皮鼓手则在铜鼓手的左边,随着铜鼓的节奏击打皮鼓。在铜鼓和皮鼓同时敲响后,铜鼓手后面的一个抱着水桶的水桶手随着鼓点向前或向后起舞,同时,舞场上的青年男女们也都踩着"咚咚当!咚咚当!咚咚当咚当咚当!……"的鼓点尽情欢跳。鼓点的节奏一般是由缓慢到快速,鼓声则是由轻快到激昂。姑娘小伙子们的舞姿十分优美,气魄极为雄壮,既表现出了水族人民的美好文化,又表现出了他们英勇豪迈的气概。

赛马时各村寨的水族和邻近各族人民都云集于赛马场观看赛马表演。参加赛马的骑手中既有年近七旬的老人,也有六、七岁的儿童,还有妇女。那些因年迈不能参赛的老人们,也要骑着骏马在场上走几圈,以表示参加了赛马活动。在赛马前要请一位德高望众的人骑着马绕场一周,然后各路骑手们正式开始比赛。那些优秀骑手们的飞马夺标十分精彩,常常受到观众们的大声欢呼喝彩,赛场上不断爆发出震天撼地的欢呼声和掌声。

在节日期间,除了跳铜鼓舞和赛马外,在端坡上还要举行拔河、斗牛、唱花灯、唱民歌和跳斗角舞等活动,供人们尽兴娱乐。

晚上各家各户都举行丰盛的家宴，全家人都围坐在火塘边吃佳肴、喝米酒，他们手拉着手，一边吃喝一边喊"干杯！干杯……"。在过端节的水族村寨里，节日的欢歌笑语不绝于耳。人们在幸福欢快的气氛中度过良宵。

44 . Duan Festival

The Duan Festival is the most important festival observed by the Shui people who live in Guizhou Province. It is also named Jieduan in the Shui language, meaning the New Year.

According to the Shui calendar, a year consists of 12 months and each month consists of 30 days, which are designated by the twelve Earthly Branches-zi, chou, yin, mao, chen, si, wu, wei, shen, you, xu and hai. The calendar also stipulates that villagers in an area take turns, village by village, to celebrate their own one-day Duan Festival, starting from the first hai day of the first Shui calendar month. Usually the whole festival period of an area lasts until the first ten-day period of the third month by the Shui calendar, which coincides with the period from the 9th month to the first ten-period of the 10th month by the lunar calendar.

The origin of the festival hangs different versions of legend. Long long ago, according to the most popular one, a serious flood occurred in a Shui-inhabited area, and three Shui brothers floated to what is today's Sandu County of Guizhou. On the first hai day of the first Shui calendar month the next year, the three brothers parted with each other and reclaimed wasteland to make a living in different areas. One year later, they had a reunion, at which they joyously congratulated each other on bumper harvests, and decided to make the day they had first parted a time for yearly reunion and congratulation on good crops in the future. This is the birth of the Duan Festival. To commemorate the three brothers and congratulate on good crops, the later Shui people in the three areas of Guizhou, where the three brothers are said to have lived, successively celebrate their own Duan Festivals on three different hai days, starting from the first hai day of the first Shui calendar month, in the order of the seniority of the three brothers. Concretely speaking, those in the Sandong area where the elder brother lived, celebrate it on the first hal day, those in the Shuilong area where the second brother lived do it on the second hai day and those in the Hengfeng area where the youngest brother lived do it on the third hai day which is to be in the second Shui calendar month.

The Shui people attach great importance to the observance of the Duan Festival. Towards it, all households kill chickens, ducks and hogs, and pound glutinous rice in a mortar, all for festive dinners. On the night just before the festival, villagers in every village beat one or a dozen big bronze drums hung from house beams or special supports in a courtyard, which is accompanied by the beats of some oxhide-headed drums. They beat to their heart's content throughout the night, meaning to bid farewell to the old year and usher in the new year.

Early on the morning of the festival all members of a family, in new clothes, attend a service offering nice foods as sacrifices to their ancestors, which is one of the major activities they conduct in celebration. The custom has it that they have a table, in the main hall, loaded with steamed glutinous rice and other nice foods as sacrifices, the indispensable one of which is the chives-stuffed fish. Well-cooked and appetizing, the fish is linked to a story. According to the story, the Shui people's ancestors had often eaten fish when they had lived in a south region rich in water, but things so changed that they ate fish only on festive occasions after they moved to a north region short of water. Hence the present Shui people usually offer well-cooked and appetizing fish as a sacrifice to their ancestors, to mean that they carry forward the living habit of their ancestors.

The Shuis abstain from eating meat, but fish, for breakfast at the festival. After breakfast they pay each other festive calls, and even strangers are hospitably received as guests on the day. After a sacrificial service held for ancestors early on the day's morning, people in some villages, according to custom, gather at an appointed villager's house as New Year callers at the sound of the bronze drum. Meeting each other, they exchange words wishing each other a happy New Year, healthy and bumper harvests in the year to come. The host entertains the guests to glutinous rice cooked with fresh rice, and thick fresh fish soup. While eating, they toast each other amides cheers. After the meal, they go to pay New Year calls and drink New Year wine from door to door, in a procession headed by a group of drummers beating bronze drums. Following them are children who are to be offered sweets, fruit, dried fish and the like, by each household they reach. The children who get more offerings are seen to be able ones who would be happy and healthy in the new year. Varied entertainments follow the New Year calls. The majors of them are the Bronze Drum Dance with distinctive Shui flavor and the spectacular horse race. The girls dancers wear blue collarless blouses, black trousers, black aprons, silver earrings, silver necklaces and silver bracelets; the young men dancers have on collarless jackets and black turbans. They gather and dance on a lot locally known as "duanpo", to the accompaniment of the oxhide-headed drum. The bronze drum is usually 50 centimeters in diameter and over 30 kilograms in weight, but the biggest one may be one meter in diameter and about 200 kilograms in weight. The oxhide-headed drum is a 75-centimeter-long hollowed cylinder of paulownia with a membrane of oxhide tightly stretched over either end. When the dance begins, two drummers each beat the bronze drum's edge with a hard wood slip in the left hand and beat its center with a drumstick hung with red silk tassels, and another drummer to their left beats the oxhide-headed drum; then a man, behind the drummers and carrying a wood bucket, and all other young people begin to joyously dance, bending forwards and backwards to the accompaniment of the drumbeats, which usually go from slowness to quickness and from liveliness to loudness. The young dancers dance in movements graceful and vigorous, an embodiment of Shui people's fine culture and, their bold and uninhibited character.

Their horse race often draws large crowds of spectators to the arena. The competitive riders include men aged about 7 to 70, and women. Those who cannot take part in the race for advanced age go on horseback round the arena several times, to mean a symbolic participation. A prestigious man goes on horseback round the arena once before the race begins. When the race really begins, riders gallop ahead at full speed for championship, arousing thunderous cheers and applause from audience.

Other festive items for merry making are the tug of war, bullfight, huadeng opera (a local opera) singing, folk song singing, imaginary horn-locking dance, and the like. All are very joyful.

On the night of the festival, all members of a family sit around a fire pit, enjoying a sumptuous feast. They eat nice foods and drink rice wine, which is sometimes interrupted by the shouting: "A toast! A toast!" All holidaymakers have a happy, joyous and harmonious night.

45. 会街节

　　会街是云南省德宏地区的陇川、盈江、梁河等地阿昌族人民的传统节日。"会街"是汉语的叫法，阿昌族语称为"熬露"。会街于每年农历九月中旬举行，节期五天。

　　阿昌族人民庆祝会街节来源于一个菩萨取经的传说故事：据说阿昌族人民居住的那片美丽的地区，过去曾经遭受恶魔奇力卡的侵扰，它用干旱枯死地里的庄稼，用洪水冲毁房屋。菩萨为了护佑阿昌族人民，就去找如来佛祖取经学法。他在途中历经了千山万水，克服了许许多多困难，终于取到了经书，学会了降魔伏怪的法术，预定九月十五日归来。阿昌族人民听说菩萨要归来，就赶着白象去迎接他。菩萨降伏了恶魔奇力卡，阿昌族人民从此安居乐业，过上了幸福的生活。从此他们于每年的农历九月十日到十四日的五天中耍白象，供斋饭，开展各种歌舞活动，以示铭记菩萨取经学法之艰辛，感谢救民于水火之恩情。阿昌族人民根据这一传说故事开展的祭祀活动，在传承过程中逐步演变成为传统的民族节日。

　　为了庆祝每年一次的会街节，阿昌族各村寨都要提前十多天做好准备，大家出钱做白象和扎青龙。白象和青龙由村寨里的艺人们用竹子和木材精心制做。白象一般用竹子和木材做成骨架，糊上白纸和各色彩纸做象皮。用布做鼻子。青龙则用竹子做成龙骨,糊以彩纸。

参加会街活动的人们都要穿上节日的民族盛装。男子一般身穿蓝色、黑色或白色对襟上衣、黑裤子,缠在头上的包头布必须留一段约一尺长吊在脑后;已婚妇女穿袖子长而窄的对襟衣,裙子的长度必须超过膝盖,裹绑腿,头缠蓝布或白布包头;未婚姑娘则将一根长辫子盘在头顶上,用约二寸宽的布条围在辫子下,胸前并排四个银纽扣,每个银纽扣上各挂一根长长的银链,头戴银泡,还戴耳环和项圈等首饰。人人都穿戴打扮得非常漂亮。

会街期间的主要活动内容除耍白象外,还有玩青龙、跳舞和对歌等。节日的第一天上午,各村寨的男女老少都簇拥着白象和青龙绕村寨一周,然后一同去村寨的会街场。小伙子们敲着象脚鼓和铜锣,打着彩旗,放着鞭炮,走在白象和青龙之后,最后是手执树枝的其他人。等到各村寨的人都到齐后,就举行会街庆祝仪式。首先是仪式主持人致词,对应邀前来参加会街的各族来宾表示欢迎;接着是来宾代表赠送彩礼,并致贺词,表示向阿昌族人民祝贺节日快乐;最后给白象和青龙系上红绸,仪式即告结束,开始各种娱乐活动。

耍白象和舞青龙同时进行,历来都是会街活动的主要节目。各村寨的男女老少分别围着各自的白象和青龙。其中有的敲锣,有的打鼓,而耍象者和舞龙者则在人圈中和着鼓乐声跳着各种舞蹈动作。例如,坐在白象肚子里的人双手不停地拉扯连着象鼻和滑轮的绳子,白象的大鼻子便随之上下左右甩动,栩栩如生;同时,舞青龙者手举青龙做出各种翻腾动作。舞到高潮时,观众中有些人也两两相伴(其中一人打镲)和着鼓乐声跳起象脚鼓舞来。象脚鼓舞兼融音乐、舞蹈、体育于一体,主要舞步为跨、退、蹲,舞姿潇洒刚健。另外一些观众手执树枝,同声欢呼"哦——会——会!哦——会——会!"使欢庆的声势达到高潮。

"蹬窝罗"是另一个传统表演项目,其中"蹬"意为"边歌边舞","窝罗"意为"堂屋边的欢乐"。它实际是融歌舞为一体的娱乐节目,因唱词开头的衬词为"窝罗"而得名,"蹬窝罗"中的歌有固定的曲词,但也可酌情依曲变词。表演时,由一位能歌善舞者领歌领舞,其他表演者双手叉腰,跟随其后,一步一趋,边唱边舞。观众也常常高歌应和,使会街场上高潮迭起。

在会街节日期间还有对唱山歌的活动。阿昌族的山歌曲调优美,内容含蓄多样,如邀约、结交、辞别、送路等。随着对歌内容的变化,歌场上也随着表现出不同的欢乐气氛,从而给人们留下难以忘怀的快乐感觉。热爱生活而又能歌善舞的阿昌族人民,就这样欢度自己的传统节日。

45 . Huijie Festival

The Huijie Festival is a traditional festival observed by the Achang people inhabiting Longchuan, Yingjiang and Lianghe counties in the Dehong Dai and Jingpo Autonomous Prefecture, Yunnan Province. The festival, known as Aolu in the Achang language, lasts five days somewhere in the first ten-day period of the 9th lunar month.

The origin of the festival has behind a legend, which tells how a Bodhisattva acquired scriptures to help the Achang people. The Achang-inhabited area, the legend goes, used to suffer from frequent droughts and floods, with crops parched and houses destroyed, because a demon named Qilika often exercised evil influences over the place. To protect the Achangs from the calamities, a Bodhisattva went to acquire scriptures from Tathagata. Having traversed numerous rivers and mountains, and experienced untold hardships, he got the scripture book and, through the book, he mastered magic arts to subdue demons at last. Then he decided to go back to render help to the Achangs on the 15th of the 9th lunar month. At the news, the Achangs went to greet him, with a white elephant going together. At last, the Bodhisattva put the demon under control, which brought a safe and happy life to the Achang people. Later the Achangs began to dance the White Elephant Dance, offer sacrificial steamed rice to the Bodhisattva and perform various entertainments from the 10th to the 14th of the 9th lunar month, to commemorate and thank the Bodhisattva who had saved the Achangs from untold miseries through magic arts. These commemorative activities gradually evolved into the Huijie Festival.

The celebrators usually begin to make preparations for the festival over 10 days before it arrives: Craftsmen of each village make an image of a white elephant and an image of green dragon with the money pooled by all villagers of the village. The white elephant image has a trunk made of cloth and a skeleton which is made of bamboo and wood, and pasted with white or colored paper; the green dragon image has a bamboo skeleton pasted with colored paper.

The men celebrators usually have on blue, black or white collarless jackets, black trousers and turbans, which are so wrapped around their heads that each has its ending piece, about 30 centimeters long, hanging down the back; the married women celebrators usually wear blouses with long and close-fitting sleeves, skirts extending to knees, puttees and blue or white headscarves; unmarried girl celebrators have on the same blouses, but each with four silver buttons neatly lining at the front and each button hanging a long silver chain, have on topknots with silver trinkets, and wear earrings and necklaces. All look attractive.

The recreational items on the festive programme are the White Elephant Dance, the Green Dragon Dance, antiphonal singing and what not. On the first day of the festival, all of a village walk in a procession first around their village once and then towards the Huijie Ground shared by the villages in an area. At the head of the procession are an image of a white elephant and an image of a green dragon respectively carried by men; then come young fellows holding up colored flags, beating elephant-leg-like drums, striking bronze gongs or letting off firecrackers; and finally come other celebrators holding twigs with leaves. After all the villages' celebrators arrive, a ceremony of celebration is held. At it, first the chairman delivers a speech welcoming the guests from other nationalities, then a representative of the guests presents congratulatory gifts and extends their congratulations, and finally they tie red silk ribbons on the white elephant image and the green dragon image. The ceremony is followed by entertainments.

The White Elephant Dance and the Green Dragon Dance, performed simultaneously, are two important items on the festive programme. In performing them, all of a village stand in a ring around their white elephant image and green dragon image. Some of them strike gongs, some beat drums and some play other musical instruments, while the performer of the White Elephant Dance and the performers of the Green Dragon Dance dance in varied movements to the musical sounds. For instance, the performer, sitting in the big belly of the white elephant image, keeps so pulling a rope connected to the elephant's trunk and a pulley that the drunk keeps moving up, down, left or right; at the same time the performers of the Green Dragon Dance make the dragon image in their hands to turn over in different ways. At the climax of dancing, many of the spectators pair off, one of each pair striking small cymbals, and begin to dance to the accompaniment of the beats of the elephant-leg-like drums, and the sound of other musical instruments. Combining together singing, dancing and sporting, the dances are performed in varied movements such as forward ones, backward ones and squat ones, all very natural and unrestrained. When all the performers are busy, the spectators keep shouting "O—Hui—Hui", bringing the excitement to a climax.

Dengwoluo is another item on the festive programme; in the Achang language, deng means singing companied by dancing, and woluo means making merry beside the main hall of a house. Actually it is a song-and-dance item, which gets its name because each verse of the song begins with woluo. The song sung in the item is based on the set tune and words, but the words may be changed on the spur of the moment. In performing, one performer, who is usually a good singer and dancer, leads singing and dancing while other performers, with arms akimbo, follow suit after the leading performer. And spectators sometimes sing loud to accompany the performance, arousing one climax after another.

Antiphonal singing is also favored by the Achangs. The folk songs sung in their antiphonal singing are sweet in tunes, connotative and varied in content. Mostly they are about inviting guests, making friends, bidding farewell, and what not. The atmosphere on the Huijie Ground changes with the changes of the song's content, leaving an unforgettable impression on spectators.

The Achang people, who love life, singing and dancing, always offer exciting items at the Huijie Festival.

图书在版编目(CIP)数据

中国传统节日及传说/靳海林编译.—重庆:重庆出版社,
2001.11
ISBN 7-5366-5557-6

Ⅰ.中... Ⅱ.靳... Ⅲ.节日—风俗习惯—中国—
对照读物—汉、英 Ⅳ.K892.1

中国版本图书馆 CIP 数据核字(2001)第 052544 号

中国传统节日及传说
ZHONGGUO CHUANTONG JIERI JI CHUANSHUO
靳海林 编著

出 版 人:罗小卫
责任编辑:陈世勇 杨 帆
封面设计:吴庆渝
技术设计:聂丹英

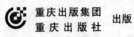 重庆出版集团
重 庆 出 版 社 出版

重庆长江二路 205 号 邮政编码:400016 http://www.cqph.com
自贡新华印刷厂印刷
重庆出版集团图书发行有限公司发行
E-MAIL:fxchu@cqph.com 邮购电话:023-68809452
全国新华书店经销

开本:787mm×1 092mm 1/32 印张:10 字数:215 千字 插页 4
2001 年 11 月第 1 版 2007 年 1 月第 2 版第 2 次印刷
印数:5001-8000
定价:16.00 元

如有印装质量问题,请向本集团图书发行有限公司调换:02368809955 转 8005